Economic Policymaking in a Conflict Society

*Written under the auspices
of the Center for International Affairs,
Harvard University*

CAMBALACHE
(Popular Argentine Tango)

Siglo veinte, cambalache, problemático y febril . . .
El que no llora no mama y él que no afana es un gil!
Dále nomás! Dále que va!
Que allá en el horno nos vamos a encontrar!
No pienses más, sentáte a un la'o,
Que a nadie importa si naciste honra'o!
Es lo mismo él que labora noche y día como un buey,
Que él que mata, que él que cura o está fuera de la ley!

THE PAWNSHOP

The Twentieth Century: hectic pawnshop of problems . . .
Who doesn't beg doesn't drink, and who doesn't steal is a fink!
Right on! For best you be knowing
That to hell we're all going!
Don't give it a thought, swim with the stream,
For no one cares how honest you've been.
Why work like an ox if 'tis all the same
To kill, to cure or cheat at the game.

Economic Policymaking in a Conflict Society: The Argentine Case

Richard D. Mallon
in collaboration with Juan V. Sourrouille

Harvard University Press
Cambridge, Massachusetts
and London, England
1975

Library of Congress Catalog Card Number 74-21227
ISBN 0-674-22930-4
Printed in the United States of America

To my three women

R.D.M.

Preface

The need to write this book developed while we were working with the Argentine National Development Council in 1963-1966. From this vantage point we were able to observe first hand the difficulties of policymakers in coping with the familiar stabilization versus growth dilemma. What most impressed us was that government technicians, both those in development planning organizations like the Council and in current policy bodies such as the Central Bank, were not of much help in clarifying the tradeoffs—short and long term, economic and political—that decision-makers were obliged to take into account in formulating their policies. Indeed, the conventional framework of economic analysis seemed ill-suited for policymaking in a pluralistic "conflict society," in which the feasibility of economic measures is largely determined by the need of regimes to mobilize and retain shifting coalition support. Economists instead seem more at home under strong, stable governments, the kind that in Argentina has required rule by military dictatorship.

This book therefore represents the search for a policy approach appropriate for constitutional democratic governments in pluralistic conflict societies. The analysis deals only with Argentina, but we are persuaded that our approach is also relevant to other semi-industrialized countries whose socioeconomic development has not been paralleled by institutional modernization. The work is focused on balance of payments and anti-inflationary stabilization policies, although the range of issues considered is much broader and is not confined to the disciplinary boundaries of economics. No analytical tools outside the field of economics have been used, however, and no formal model is presented as an alternative to those employed in conventional economic analysis. We are not completely satisfied with the results, but feel that the important problem addressed has received too little attention in the literature, and that our approach, although fundamentally pragmatic, is generalizable and useful for technical advisers to policymakers.

This book is being published in two slightly different editions. The Spanish edition, aside from deletions of explanatory material unnecessary for Argentine and other Latin American readers, has a more complete statistical appendix than could be accommodated in the English edition. The latter, on the other hand, contains some more recent revisions, mainly of form rather than substance, that it was not possible to include in the Spanish version.

During the years of research that have gone into this book we have incurred so large an intellectual and logistical debt that it would be materially impossible to acknowledge all creditors. Without the generous, protracted support of the Harvard University Development Advisory Service this book would not have been possible. Support from the Social Science Research Council was also indispensable for making this work a truly international collaborative effort. The Center for Economic Research of the Instituto Torcuato Di Tella provided generous logistical support in Buenos Aires, and several Argentine government organizations, especially the Statistical Institute of the Economics Ministry, were helpful in supplying information.

The list of professional colleagues to whom we are intellectually indebted would, if we attempted a complete enumeration, resemble a roster of Argentine Economics Ministers, Central Bank presidents, and National Planning Directors over the last twenty years; of the Argentine Political Economy Association; and of the economic development faculty of Harvard University. From the first group, however, we would like to express our special appreciation to Alfredo Gomez Morales, Antonio Cafiero, Aldo Ferrer, and Roque Carranza for their cooperation. Alberto Fracchia, Marcelo Diamand, and Mario Brodersolm gave us especially valuable intellectual encouragement and stimulus. At Harvard, Walter Falcon, Simon Kuznets, Edward Mason, Gustav Papanek, Daniel Schydlowsky, and Raymond Vernon were particularly generous in commenting on earlier drafts. Neither these colleagues nor the many others who gave of their time to help our enterprise should of course be held responsible for the final results, with at least some of which they may well disagree.

Finally, we would like to thank our research assistant, John Miranowsky, for his dedicated help with the computer; Nancy Hall for bibliographical aid; Sr. Raul Sourrouille for his invaluable linguistic assistance with the Spanish edition; and a long sequence of secretaries who performed the thankless task of typing and collating, among whom Dodi Mitchell and Peg Weiner were the pioneers. The greatest debt of all we owe to our families, who tolerated (unusually silently) our absences and ill humor over more years than we led them to believe would be necessary.

R.D.M.
J.V.S.

Contents

Figures

Tables

Economic Policymaking in a Conflict Society

Introduction

Professional economists are inclined to view their role in practical policymaking as advocates of economically "optimal" decisions. If politicians turn a deaf ear, they are commonly considered to be ignorant, weak, or demagogic. Quite a different view is taken in this book: policymaking is the art of reconciling trade-offs between equally legitimate political and economic objectives which, especially in the shorter run, are often conflicting. The economic adviser is therefore frequently obliged to assist decision-makers to strike a viable balance between these two kinds of objectives. This task is referred to as an art because generally accepted models, techniques, or criteria do not yet exist for this purpose. It should be mentioned at the outset, however, that no attempt is made in this book to formulate rigorous criteria for policy advising similar to those that exist for policy advocacy.

Macroeconomic policymaking will be the main subject of analysis, especially the problem of reconciling the maintenance of economic stability with the promotion of full employment and growth. This is a subject that has received insufficient attention in the economic development literature, because less developed countries have traditionally been assumed to live in a non-Keynesian world where growth is limited by inadequate supply rather than a deficient demand. There is clearly an element of truth in this assumption, but the scope for more autonomous monetary and fiscal policy is expanding as less developed economies become more monetized, tax bases broaden, domestic production substitutes for imports, and the public sector assumes greater responsibilities. It is indeed only natural that governments interested in forcing the pace of development should try to maintain or expand domestic income and employment more independently of fluctuations in primary exports. Reconciliation of more rapid growth with internal and external equilibrium has, however, proved even more difficult in semi-industrial than in advanced economies.

One reason for this difficulty is that economic diversification does not necessarily reduce a developing country's dependence on the foreign sector. Taxes on foreign trade often continue to be the main source of fiscal revenue, and a substantial proportion of new economic activity is frequently accounted for by local branches of foreign firms which are able to short circuit the policies of national monetary authorities through their independent access to outside financing. Important as these and other direct linkages between the domestic economy and the foreign sector may be, however, an even more binding form of external dependence can be found in countries that have long followed a policy of import substitution behind high protective barriers. Ironically, the result of this policy has been to make most nonprimary domestic output and a large share of imports highly noncompetitive and thus to reduce the responsiveness of exports and imports to changes in relative prices. The independence of domestic policy has thereby been severely limited by obliging governments to rely largely on adjustments in the overall level of economic activity and employment to resolve short-term balance of payments problems.

A second reason for the special difficulties encountered by developing countries in the management of macroeconomic policy is the prevalence of sociopolitical conflict. Conflict is of course universal in human experience, but in most advanced societies institutions have evolved to mediate or repress its most disruptive manifestations. Relatively strong and respected agencies like central banks and treasuries have been set up to coordinate economic affairs according to some generally accepted rules. This is less true in developing countries not under strong totalitarian or single party rule: more typically the coalitions forged at an earlier stage in support of certain politico-economic rules of the game have been subjected to attack, if not completely disrupted, by the emergence of new, increasingly well organized, competing interest groups spawned in the process commonly referred to as "modernization." Not only do these new forces find it extremely difficult to agree on new rules of the game, but by disrupting the preexisting coalition they have frequently helped revive traditional regional, ethnic, and other divergencies previously integrated into national life or suppressed by the old regime. One of the consequences has been that macroeconomic policy management has been very poorly institutionalized and has also become one of the main targets of conflict.

If open conflict were only a trauma of the early stages of building a nation-state, one might reasonably expect the orderly institutionalization of policy management to develop apace with the need to use it. This expectation does not, however, seem to be warranted by experience: the institutional development of many semi-industrial countries has lagged far behind their economic progress. One explanation is that these countries did not have to rely much on their own sociopolitical and economic institutions to become suppliers of foodstuffs and raw materials in the foreign trade and investment boom of the nineteenth and early twentieth centuries. During this period of rapid economic growth they were usually governed by elites closely associated with foreign interests, and their financial, commercial, and transportation systems were largely under foreign control. When the international boom ended in the late 1920s, they were consequently ill-prepared to redirect their economies in ways that depended to a greater extent on the capacity of their own unevenly developed institutions and to cope with post-Keynesian welfare state concerns that have shaken institutions in even the most advanced countries.

This book analyzes these structural and institutional problems of policymaking, using the experience of a country that in many respects already appears quite advanced: Argentina, like a number of other Latin American and Mediterranean nations at a similar level of development, has a fully monetized economy, a domestic manufacturing sector that occupies a large share of the active labor force and fabricates a broad range of both producer and consumer goods, a relatively high level of literacy, and many other attributes such as automobile traffic congestion that remind one more of Europe than of the developing world. On the other hand, Argentines have found it much more difficult to develop the institutions of a modern nationstate. Efforts to incorporate into a national polity the very mobile and largely immigrant population, and to domesticate the nation's foreign-dominated commercial and financial institutions, public utilities, and ruling class mores, have met with limited success. To judge by this experience, nation-building is an exceptionally difficult enterprise when leaders must deal, on the one hand, with a highly literate but alienated proletariat demanding greater participation, and on the other with an entrepreneurial class accustomed to the laissez-faire system under which the country previously prospered. In no other respect have these stresses and strains of frustrated institutionalization had greater repercussions than in the conduct of macroeconomic policy.

It is the central hypothesis of this book that the factors complicating successful macroeconomic policy management must be sought mainly in the institutional environment in which policies are made in semideveloped countries. Insofar as policy conflicts are symptoms of the difficulty of agreeing on new rules of the game, and truly pluralistic institutions are preferred to absolutist systems, *policymaking and conflict mediation must form integral parts of the same decision process.* Advocates of policy behavior in accordance with some "ideal" norm, be it Pareto optimality or the organization of an ideal society, do not therefore contribute to the integration of this process. Instead they tend to reinforce the ideological polarization of decision-making and to promote either impasse or government by coup d'etat. The resulting situation is often the worst of all worlds: the economy is caught up in a crisis syndrome that destroys any semblance of policy continuity, and in the absence of overall direction, policymaking tends to fall under the de facto control of subordinate functionaries in protected enclaves such as central banks, which manipulate the few policy tools under their control in pursuit of the parochial objectives of their particular institutions.

This is not to say that normative advocates do not have a legitimate role to play in such societies; they certainly do, but it should be recognized that in societies lacking strong mediative institutions this role is more likely to be revolutionary. Those Hegelians who view open conflict and policy impasse as only a brief interlude between collapse of the traditional status quo and emergence of a new popular synthesis will of course insist that nothing can be done that is not purely cosmetic or intended to postpone the coming millennium. History appears to indicate, however, that conflict societies can continue in turmoil for extended periods of time and that a new synthesis is not likely to emerge until effective mediators or dictators win control. Since most dictators must also usually cope with constituencies of divergent factions and interest groups, mediative policy analysis is likely to have an important role to play even in undemocratic societies.

Decision-makers in Argentina have quite consistently attempted to adopt policy positions that seemed designed to tear society apart rather than to forge new coalitions, or positions that at least required a degree of political power and duration of commitment that far exceeded practical limits. In this masochistic pursuit they have been reinforced quite effectively by international organizations and the economics profession in general. Does this mean that no mediative policy alternatives exist? This is the central question to which this book is addressed. Argentine balance of payments and stabilization policies will be the main subjects of analysis, but especially in the final chapter an attempt will be made to reach some conclusions about macroeconomic policymaking that may also be relevant for other semi-industrial conflict societies.

1 Argentine Policymaking: Background and Experience, 1948-1970

Major economic policy disagreements in modern Argentine history have their main roots in the conflict between two divergent streams of thought: liberalism of the British Manchester School variety and what can be called national populism. Although policy positions have differed between factions within each stream and have also changed over time, in general the liberals have stood for the virtues of a society open to international opportunities and influences, whereas the national populists have emphasized indigenous, autonomous development.

After the last of the traditional *caudillos* was overthrown in the middle of the nineteenth century, the educated elite assumed power in Argentina to consolidate the nation under a strong federal government and promote its development along liberal lines. At the time, Argentina was a sparsely populated country of less than two million inhabitants with a rudimentary economy and much of its territory (including a large part of the rich pampas) still under Indian control. A major effort, therefore, was made to develop public education under the influence of the ideas of Horace Mann, to promote massive immigration from Europe, to attract foreign investment, and to drive the Indians off land that could be employed in the rapid expansion of agricultural production for export to Europe, made possible by the recent revolution in transport technology.

The famous "generation of the 1880s," as the dynamic notables of the period were called, showed little concern, on the other hand, for the development of a new polity with broader participation on the part of the indigenous and immigrant populations. Political power continued to be held very closely and paternalistically, despite sometimes violent opposition from an organization named the Civic Union (founded in the late nineteenth century to fight for universal suffrage), until liberal President Saenz Pena was finally persuaded to permit free elections at the beginning of World War I. Liberals were never again able to gain access to political power except through the direct action of pressure groups or by electoral frauds or coups d'état carried out with military help. In fact, they never even bothered to organize themselves politically on a national scale.

With some important exceptions, however, military leaders could be counted on to sympathize with the liberal point of view, although their constituency has become increasingly pluralistic over the years.

5

The military-supported regimes of the 1930s were thus capable of adopting antipopular measures, such as the Roca-Runciman Treaty granting special trade privileges to Great Britain to protect Argentine agricultural interests, while at the same time they introduced exchange controls, increased import duties, generalized bilateral trade agreements, and adopted an income tax. The policy approach of military governments during the post-Peron period, particularly those of Generals Aramburu, Levingston, and Lanusse, has also been distinctly eclectic.

National populist ideas initially found their chief political expression through the Radical party, successor to the Civic Union. Under the leadership of Hipólito Yrigoyen the Radicals won three successive presidential elections in 1916, 1922, and 1928, but aside from their rhetoric there was little that could be considered antiliberal. The party represented a polyglot array of largely middle class interest groups without a clearly defined policy approach except for their strong commitment to constitutional electoral democracy. Other political movements were therefore encouraged to rise up and, particularly after the overthrow of the Yrigoyen government in 1930, to fight for the role of standard-bearer of national populism. None of these movements, however, was able to win a broad popular following, either the conventionally organized communist and socialist parties or the large number of ad hoc intellectual groups that helped keep the political environment in constant ferment.

In June 1943 a group of nationalistic army officers belonging to an organization known as the GOU (Group of United Officers) participated in a coup d'état that finally brought to power the charismatic architect of a new political coalition. Colonel Juan Domingo Perón quickly advanced from junior member and labor adviser in the new government to the post of secretary of labor, was appointed minister of war in February 1944 and vice president in July of the same year, and was elected president in 1946 in one of the fairest elections conducted in Argentine history. During this brief period he amassed a popular following that no other Argentine political leader except perhaps Yrigoyen has ever come close to achieving by amalgamating nationalist and populist elements whose strength had been growing rapidly but who did not feel represented either in the government or by any major political movement.

Nationalistic ideas have deep roots in the Argentine past, but as long as foreign capital was financing one third to one half of total fixed investment (as it did between 1880 and 1914) and the growth of foreign trade was leading an expanding economy, popular misgiv-

ings were kept in check. With the breakdown of world trade and finance that accompanied the Great Depression and continued into
World War II, however, these misgivings rapidly rose to the surface.
The government's decision not to default on payment of the foreign
debt despite the increase in such payments to over 30 percent of the
reduced value of exports by 1933, the humiliating Roca-Runciman
Treaty, successful refusal of foreign meatpacking houses to cooper-
ate with a congressional investigating committee, alleged graft in the
extension of a foreign-owned electric power concession in 1935, and
a series of similar incidents were at the same time symptoms and additional causes of xenophobic antagonism toward the very visible
control that foreigners held over vital segments of the national
economy. The decision of Perón to retire the foreign debt, national-
ize most foreign-owned public utilities, and take a generally hard
line toward external capital thus served to pull together political
support from widely divergent nationalist elements on both the right
and the left.

Argentine populism has tended to be as concerned with popular
participation in the conduct of the nation's political and economic
life as with the distribution of income and wealth. This concern with
participation constituted the main appeal of the Radical party and
may have contributed to the weakness of elitist political movements
on the left, but it did not lead to the formation of strong participa-
tory institutions. From its very inception the Argentine labor movement was seriously divided ideologically, mainly by disputes among
anarchists, syndicalists, and socialists over tactics and organization,
so that it was never able to attract a total membership of more than
half a million, which at the beginning of the 1940s represented only
about 8 percent of the total labor force. This poor showing was highly anachronistic in a country with a very literate population, over 20
percent of its labor force engaged in industry for two decades, and a
per capita income comparable to that of southern Europe.

Conditions were therefore ripe for Perón to build a mass worker
movement, and this he proceeded to do by engineering one of the
most sweeping labor reforms ever experienced by a country in the
brief span of two years. Industry-wide bargaining was instituted;
labor courts were set up to enforce the rather progressive laws already on the books as well as new laws; social security coverage was
greatly expanded; increased minimum wages were decreed not only
for urban employees but also for rural workers through the famous
Statute of the Peón in 1944; the system of *aguinaldo* was introduced
(one month's extra pay at Christmas time); and a controversial Law

of Professional Associations was adopted in 1945, which provided
for obligatory withholding of union dues by employers, recognition
of only one union per branch of activity, and direct union participation in political action under supervision of the state. As a result,
total union membership tripled or quadrupled and for the first time
included large numbers of *cabecitas negras* (the so-called "black-
haired ones," or migrants from the interior of the country) and *des-
camisados* (the "shirtless ones" or marginal laborers), who of course
gave unswerving loyalty to their leaders.

This new national populist coalition was brought together in 1946
under a semisyndicalist form of government with greatly enlarged
powers. The National Labor Confederation (CGT) was represented
directly in the executive branch and through the Peronist party in
Congress, and a new industrial employer's federation (CGE) was
created to represent the interests of management in place of the liberal Industrial Union (the old established employers' organization).
Agreements with the military, the church, and some professional
and student associations gave the necessary breadth to Perón's political base.

Aside from nationalization of foreign-owned public utilities, the
chief new extensions of state power were in the areas of commerce
and finance. An Argentine Trade Promotion Institute (IAPI) was set
up in 1946 to regulate commercialization of agricultural products
and imports of essential goods; quantitative import controls were
progressively intensified; the system of price controls was strength-
ened; rents were frozen; and (during brief periods) limitations were
also placed on profit margins. All bank deposits were nationalized in
the Central Bank, mortgage financing was monopolized by the
National Mortgage Bank, insurance was brought under government
control, and stock market regulations were intensified.

It should be noted, however, that Perón did not choose to extend
the sphere of the state into the production of goods, except for nationalization of thirty German firms at the end of the war and some
expansion in the operations of the previously established Office of
Military Factories, particularly in naval construction. Nor did he
ever attempt to carry out a land reform or to introduce greater workers' participation in the management of enterprise. In fact, even
IAPI did not interfere to any significant extent in the organization of
the traditional export marketing system, which continued to be controlled mainly by large private firms such as Bunge Born and Drey-
fus; and the "nationalization" of bank deposits merely replaced
minimum reserve requirements by a system of Central Bank redis-

counts, leaving management of most traditional lending functions to private banks. Thus, although in some ways the advent of Perón resembled a leftist revolution, unlike such a revolution it hardly touched legal proprietary rights. This was perhaps the new movement's greatest contradiction: its leaders did not have a clear understanding of the limits to income redistribution imposed by the existing distribution of wealth and by the need to provide incentives for its efficient employment.

Perón's "period of assault" came to an end in 1948, a year that marks a watershed in Argentine economic history. During the following quarter century the economy became trapped in a persistent stop-go cycle produced by severe balance of payments and domestic inflationary problems accompanied by great political instability. As a result, the growth of real per capita gross domestic product averaged only 0.5 percent per year between 1950 and 1963 (see table 1-1). During the last seven years of the decade the average rate of growth of per capita product increased to 4 percent, but this period also contained years of economic stagnation (1965-1967) and terminated in another economic slowdown and two successive coups d'état. The underlying economic problem can be observed clearly in table 1-1: most of the growth was concentrated in industry and supporting infrastructure, whereas agriculture expanded very slowly and erratically. The reasons why policymakers were unable to cope with this and related problems, and the interrelationship between economic and political instability, are the subjects of the remainder of this chapter.

From Period of Assault to Period of Consolidation, 1948-1955

Implementation of Perón's national populist program was facilitated by the strong balance of payments position of Argentina at the end of World War II and by rapid postwar growth of the economy. Between 1945 and 1948 the volume of merchandise imports increased fourfold and real gross domestic product (GDP) rose by 28 percent. The availability of goods and services—total domestic production plus imports minus exports—increased during the same three-year period by an even more impressive 45 percent, aided by the marked improvement in the external terms of trade and the reduction in service payments on foreign loans and investments in Argentina. This boom permitted the national government to raise its total expenditure from about 16 percent of GDP in 1945 to almost 29 percent in 1948, and at the same time to expand bank credit to

Table 1-1   Real gross domestic product, 1950–1970. (at factor prices of 1960)

Year	(billions of pesos)				(thousands of pesos)
	Agriculture	Industry and infra-structure	Services	Total GDP	Per capita GDP
1950	124	294	271	689	412
1951	133	303	280	715	420
1952	114	293	272	679	392
1953	149	294	273	716	407
1954	148	312	285	745	414
1955	154	342	302	798	436
1956	147	358	315	820	441
1957	146	387	329	862	456
1958	153	421	343	916	477
1959	151	379	326	857	437
1960	154	420	352	925	465
1961	153	461	377	991	490
1962	159	440	375	974	475
1963	162	425	365	951	457
1964	173	491	386	1050	495
1965	184	549	413	1146	533
1966	177	558	420	1154	529
1967	184	572	427	1183	533
1968	177	616	445	1238	550
1969	184	676	476	1336	583
1970	187	717	487	1391	600

Source: Banco Central de la República Argentina, *Origen del producto y distribución del ingreso, 1950–1969*, supplement to the *Boletín Estadístico*, no. 1 (January 1971); the figure for 1970 is from a more recent number of the regular *Boletín.*

The three-sector aggregation of GDP is composed as follows: Agriculture: agriculture, hunting, and fishing. Industry and infrastructure: manufacturing, mining, construction, electricity, gas, water, transportation and communications. Services: commerce, finance, government, and other services.

the private sector by more than 250 percent, without generating serious immediate inflationary repercussions. It became apparent by 1948, however, that this very expansionary policy had been based on extraordinary short-term conditions that could not be expected to continue.

The first serious occurence to force a change in policy appeared in the form of a gap in the balance of payments, when at the end of 1948 gold reserves fell below $150 million (equal to less than two months of imports from the dollar area), payments arrears amounted to about $200 million, and import licenses outstanding stood at $1.5 billion. At the same time inventories of export products, which were held off the market by IAPI to support highly favorable export prices and to maintain the differential between them and much lower prices paid to domestic farmers, reached alarming proportions as foreign demand receded from the extraordinary levels produced by critical international agricultural shortages immediately following the war.[1] Both imports and exports declined in 1949 by about one third and remained depressed during the next three or four years. Such a large cut in trade compelled the government to consider ways of reducing total claims, generated by its socioeconomic policies, on available resources, but the transition from "period of assault" to "period of consolidation," as Perón's policy shift has been somewhat inaccurately described, appeared initially to be much easier to announce than to implement.

Strong statements were made by the president and other officials indicating that the new economic team, now headed by Economics Minister Gomez Morales, was aware of the seriousness of the situation and intended to change the direction of policy. Nevertheless, the policies actually followed (which will be analyzed in greater detail in later chapters) fell far short of what was needed to cope with the rapidly deteriorating trade situation and the pressures of excess internal demand. Instead, production for export declined steadily and domestic expenditures shifted increasingly from fixed investment in machinery and equipment to personal consumption and construction, the former competing with exports for declining availabilities of beef and other agricultural products, and the latter contributing little to the expansion of productive capacity.

Thus, between 1948 and 1952 the domestic availability of goods and services fell by approximately 6 percent, which, combined with still expansionary monetary and fiscal policies and a continued rise in wage rates, helped set off an inflationary spiral that reached its peak in 1951 with increases of 37 percent in the cost of living index and 48 percent in wholesale prices. These developments, combined with a disastrous drought in 1951-1952, finally convinced Perón in February 1952 to adopt a program of tightened economic austerity. The spirit of this new program was explained in typical style in a speech he delivered to worker delegates of the Committee for Latin American Union Solidarity: "The *justicialista* economy asserts that the production of the country should first satisfy the needs of its inhabitants and only export the surplus; the surplus, nothing more. With this theory the boys here, of course, eat more each day and consume more, so that each day the surplus is smaller. But these poor guys have been submerged for fifty years; for this reason I have let them spend and eat and waste everything they wanted to for five years . . . but now we undoubtedly must begin to reorder things so as not to waste any more."[2]

Redirection of policy required skillful manipulation of the political coalition that had originally been brought together in support of a very different national populist program. Perón encountered no major obstacle in obtaining cooperation from his labor constituency, which had been the main intended beneficiary of his original policies and formed the backbone of his political party. A National Commission for Prices and Wages was set up, a system of two-year wage contracts was introduced, and further wage increases were substantially scaled down, with the result that the annual rate of inflation was reduced to about 4 percent by 1954 (see table 1-2). It should be pointed out, however, that stabilization of official price indices did not signify elimination of underlying inflationary pressures: price controls were used vigorously, as well as official subsidies to domestic consumers of meat, bread, other agricultural products, and public services. The cost of these subsidies increased steadily from less than 20 percent of total government current expenditure in 1952 to about 30 percent in 1955.

The subsidies at the same time enabled the government to protect farmers (who were understandably among the strongest opponents of the regime) from the post-Korean War decline in international commodity prices. This represented quite a change in official policy and succeeded in halting the downward trend in crop area and output. But after the dramatic recovery of agricultural production in 1953, a year of very favorable weather, the new policy did not induce any further significant expansion in export availabilities, and neither farmers nor any other liberal segments of the business and financial communities were won over to support the regime.

Perón's balance of power therefore rested critically on continued support from nationalist elements in the military. The long-depressed level of fixed investment in machinery and equipment and the lack of introduction of new technology, however, had created serious bottlenecks in the production of key goods and services and impeded industrial modernization. Constrained by a capacity to import that could at best take care only of the rising

Table 1-2 Annual increases in prices, 1949–1970. (percentages)

Year	(1) Cost of living index	(2) Wholesale price index	(3) GDP price deflator
1949	32.7	22.2	–
1950	24.6	20.0	–
1951	37.2	48.8	35.9
1952	38.1	30.9	24.0
1953	4.3	12.0	9.0
1954	3.5	3.3	7.7
1955	12.5	8.6	10.4
1956	13.1	26.1	25.4
1957	25.0	23.7	21.0
1958	31.4	31.2	36.7
1959	113.9	133.5	102.2
1960	27.1	15.7	18.6
1961	13.7	8.3	9.6
1962	26.2	30.3	28.7
1963	25.9	28.8	27.9
1964	22.1	26.1	27.3
1965	28.6	23.9	27.8
1966	31.9	20.0	22.9
1967	29.2	25.6	24.5
1968	16.2	9.6	10.7
1969	7.6	6.1	7.6
1970	13.6	14.1	–

Source: Col. (1). Instituto Nacional de Estadística y Censos, *Costo del nivel de vida en la Capital Federal*, 3d. ed. (March 1968), for the period 1948–1962; and *Boletín mensual de estadística*, various numbers, for the period 1963–1970. Col. (2). Banco Central de la República Argentina, *Boletín Estadístico* (September 1962), for the period 1948–1956; Instituto Nacional de Estadística y Censos for later years. Col. (3). Banco Central, *Origen del producto*, table 50, p. 43.

imports for current production needs, and by the government's inability to increase capital expenditure substantially without generating larger inflationary fiscal deficits, Perón decided to call upon the assistance of foreign capital. A new foreign investment law was adopted in 1953 that increased permissible profits remittances abroad, a special deal was made with several foreign companies to set up a tractor industry in Argentina, Mercedes Benz and Kaiser Motors were encouraged to initiate the production of automotive vehicles, negotiations were begun with the United States Export-Import Bank to finance construction of the San Nicolás steel mill, and a number of other important foreign loans and investments were either agreed upon or under consideration by 1955. The most controversial was the proposed concession agreement with the California Petroleum Company.[3]

Since the establishment of YPF (the government petroleum monopoly) in the 1920s, reservation of natural resources for domestic exploitation had been one of the principal rallying cries of Argentine nationalism. The proposed reversal of this policy, combined with a drastic shift in the official attitude toward foreign capital in general, was bound to alienate nationalist support for the regime. Perhaps this alienation would not have had serious political repercussions, however, had not Perón at the time irritated the military by his extremely personalistic style and offended their *machismo* by selecting his wife Evita to be his vice presidential running mate in the election of 1952 (a decision later vetoed by the military). Still more threatening was Perón's diversionary tactic of stirring up the militancy of his popular following by organizing violent attacks against new and old alleged opponents of the regime: the Jockey Club and the Buenos Aires Cathedral were burned; relations with the Catholic church were broken off and the Papal representative was expelled from Argentina; and violent measures (including torture) were used to repress the escalation of terrorist reaction against the regime. By 1955 little remained of Perón's original coalition except for the CGT and military comrades with close ties of personal loyalty.

The breakdown of Perón's national populist coalition did not by any means signify that Peronism itself was dying. On the contrary, during the next fifteen years, despite factional disputes and struggles over leadership of the movement, Peronism continued to be one of the strongest political forces in the country. Many subsequent national leaders, however, viewed it as a temporary aberration in the political history of Argentina, an aberration that could be purged and left behind as a bad memory while the nation went about its business of picking up the threads of its previous life. Few leaders understood that Peronism was a durable interest group that had to be either incorporated into a new political coalition or repressed by force to maintain any future government in power.

The Provisional Government, 1955-1958

In September 1955 Perón was overthrown in a military uprising led by General Lonardi, a nationalist whose main immediate objection to the deposed leader was his break with the Catholic church. After a brief struggle for power among the victors, Lonardi was in turn deposed by General Aramburu, who quickly emerged as undisputed head of a provisional government committed to the difficult task of dismantling Perón's administrative apparatus and political power base while preparing the country for a return to constitutional democracy. These two conflicting objectives proved very difficult to reconcile in practice, particularly after the hard line taken in the early months of the regime to punish former members of the Perón government and to reduce labor union power.

The CGT was "intervened" in November 1955 (that is, a military officer was placed in charge), the Law of Professional Associations was annulled, the right to strike was restricted, and police action was taken on numerous occasions to break up union demonstrations. These and other measures had the intended effect of weakening the unity of the labor movement so meticulously built up by Perón: the CGT subdivided into various factions, the most important of which were the sixty-two Peronist organizations, the thirty-two democratic unions, and the communist Movimiento de Unidad y Coordinacion Sindical (MUCS). Peronists nevertheless continued to be the most influential force in the labor movement and tenaciously resisted further efforts to alter the powers and privileges won during the previous regime.

Labor and Peronist participation in the procedure adopted by Aramburu to develop a new national policy consensus was thus effectively precluded, although most other interest groups and shades of political opinion were represented. First, a series of studies were prepared by a select group of Argentine experts headed by Raul Prebisch, recalled temporarily from his post as executive director of the United Nations Economic Commission for Latin America to become chief economic adviser of the government. Recommendations based on these studies were then submitted to representatives of the major political parties for criticism and suggestions. As might have been expected, the weight of opinion tended more in the direction of moderate national populism than of liberalism, but quite broad support was given to the general objectives of opening up the economy, reducing government controls, and trying to eliminate the more serious economic distortions and bottlenecks.

The less controversial parts of the recommended program were soon adopted: the peso was devalued from 8.8 to 22.0 per dollar (average implicit exchange rates in 1954 and 1955); bilateral trade agreements with most West European countries were annulled when Argentina joined the European Payments Union as an associate member under the so-called Paris Club arrangement; the country became a member of the International Monetary Fund and World Bank; domestic bank deposits were denationalized; and IAPI was liquidated along with a few other minor state entities. It proved much more difficult, however, for the two strongest factions in the Aramburu government to agree on more controversial policy issues.

The first economic team, led by Eugenio Blanco of the Radical party, was particularly concerned with the objective of guiding the country back to constitutional democracy and thus with following a policy strategy that could win national populist support. After he resigned in 1957 in a dispute over the handling of a foreign public utility concession, Blanco was succeeded by Krieger Vasena, a pragmatic liberal mainly concerned with rapid stabilization of the economy before the government was turned over to elected officials. Neither faction seemed to perceive clearly the difficulties of guiding the country back from a system of pervasive state intervention to a freer market economy, and neither appreciated the severity of the balance of payments and the domestic constraints under which policy had to be made.

Balance of payments policies were designed under the apparent impression that the supply and demand for foreign exchange could soon be brought into equilibrium with a rising level of economic activity if increasing reliance were placed on the price mechanism. On the supply side, policymakers overestimated the speed with which agricultural production would respond to more favorable price incentives, and they underestimated the declining trend in international commodity prices, made worse for Argentina by a domestic price policy that induced farmers to shift land from cattle to grains and dump beef onto the already saturated British market. Despite a significantly larger volume of exports, their dollar value thus increased by a mere 7 percent between 1955 and 1958. Foreign capital receipts were also of minor quantitative importance after the special assistance received in 1956 in view of the cautious policy adopted toward private equity investment (epitomized by the cancellation of negotiations with the California Petroleum Company) and the length of time it took to negotiate new foreign loans.

On the other hand, the authorities seriously underrated the pressure of the long pent-up demand for foreign exchange that would become effective if decontrol of imports were accompanied by still expansionary domestic policies. The most dramatic example was the increase in automotive imports which were permitted to enter at the free exchange rate after payment of a variable surcharge. Although for automobiles this amounted to the equivalent of $8,000 to $9,000 per vehicle, between 1955 and 1957 and the volume of automobile imports doubled, automotive spare parts more than tripled, and chassis for trucks and buses rose eight times. A valiant effort was made to hold back the deluge of imports without resorting to renewed quantitative restrictions by shifting different categories of goods to higher exchange rates and by adopting a system of prior import deposits; but the trade balance continued to deteriorate until quantitative restrictions were finally reimposed in 1958 (see table 1-3).

This unhappy experience was matched on the domestic side when efforts to promote economic expansion with stability broke down in the struggle over distributive income shares. In his reports to the provisional government, Prebisch had estimated that the initial impact of devaluation would increase the domestic price level by only 10 percent, after which price stability could be restored. A general wage adjustment in this amount was therefore granted at the end of 1955, but within the next several months it became clear that numerous businessmen considered that their own prices and profit margins, held down during many years of controls, also required readjustment. When price increases exceeded the initial 10 percent wage award, labor difficulties began to multiply until the economy became partially paralyzed by strikes beginning in September 1956. Another general wage adjustment was finally granted averaging 40 percent above the level of March 1954 and retroactive to March 1956, thus restoring in effect Perón's system of bi-yearly wage rounds every other March.

At the same time the other dimension of Perón's incomes policy—effective pressure and control on prices—was progressively relaxed, so that by 1957 the rate of increase in the cost of living index accelerated to 25 percent. When the Krieger Vasena team took over at the beginning of 1957, a one-year wage freeze was decreed, the government ran a fiscal surplus for the first time in many years, and monetary policy became somewhat more restrictive. These measures helped to slow down the rate of inflation markedly by the end of the year, but not in time to prevent a further absolute reduction in total real wage income, which fell from almost 47 percent of gross national income in 1955 to only a little over 42 percent in 1957.

This redistribution of income, had it contributed to a substantial increase in savings and investment, could perhaps have been justified by the argument that sacrifice was necessary to rebuild the

Table 1-3 Balance of payments, 1948–1970. (millions of dollars)

Year	Merchandise Exports	Merchandise Imports	Services (net)	Balance on current account	Capital[a]	Change in reserves[b]
1948	1,409	1,491	−52	−30	−	−
1949	934	1,073	33	−106	44	−150
1950	1,168	1,045	6	129	−38	167
1951	1,169	1,480	−13	−324	−10	−334
1952	688	1,179	−46	−445	272	−173
1953	1,125	795	6	336	−143	193
1954	1,027	979	12	60	−54	−6
1955	929	1,173	5	−239	−13	−252
1956	944	1,128	−55	−129	147	18
1957	975	1,310	34	−301	161	−140
1958	994	1,233	−17	−256	42	−214
1959	1,009	993	−2	14	115	119
1960	1,072	1,249	−20	−197	371	174
1961	964	1,460	−76	−572	410	−162
1962	1,216	1,357	−127	−268	−28	−296
1963	1,365	981	−150	234	−116	118
1964	1,411	1,077	−298	36	−59	−23
1965	1,488	1,195	−98	195	−104	91
1966	1,593	1,124	−213	256	−224	32
1967	1,465	1,096	−192	177	261	438
1968	1,368	1,164	−204	−15	155	140
1969	1,612	1,576	−255	−219	138	−81
1970	1,773	1,685	−223	−135	394	259

Source: 1948–1950, Banco Central, *Boletín Estadístico*, no. 1 (January 1950). 1951–1958, Banco Central, *Balance de pagos de la República Argentina, 1951–58*, supplement to *Boletín Estadístico*, no. 1 (January 1960). 1959–1970, Banco Central, *Memorias*.

[a]Difference between balance on current account and change in reserves.

[b]Includes compensatory changes in Central Bank and National Treasury liabilities as well as in gold and foreign exchange assets (see table 1-4). For a fuller explanation of Argentine balance of payments concepts and methods, and for more details on capital account and compensatory transactions, see Appendix E.

economy. Only 16 percent of the increase in gross national income between 1955 and 1957 is estimated to have been saved, however, and the share of gross domestic investment in GDP declined slightly. A strong presumption therefore existed that the main result of income redistribution was to reduce consumption of wage earners in favor of that of the more well-to-do.

It is difficult to believe that this was the policy objective of the provisional government; and if it was not, it demonstrates how sanguine policymakers were about the possibility of shifting from one set of rules of the game to another without at least introducing stronger incentives and disincentives to induce private behavior in desired directions. Such incentives were made even more necessary by the decision of the government to balance the fiscal budget, not so much by increasing taxes as by curtailing increases in both current and capital expenditures, thereby reinforcing a declining trend in public investment from almost 5 percent of GDP in 1953 to 3.4 percent in 1957. Official policy not only failed, therefore, to promote healthy growth with stability, but it contributed to alienating political support for the regime instead of helping to build a new moderate coalition that might have had a chance to win the presidential election of 1958.

The Attempt to Build a New Liberal-National Populist Coalition, 1958-1962

Arturo Frondizi, an astute politician who broke away from the traditional wing of the Radical party in the mid-1950s to form a new Intransigent Radical movement, knew where to find the votes he needed to win the 1958 election. After the Peronists were prevented from running their own candidate, anyone who could gain broad support from the alienated wage earning classes was bound to be the victor. His campaign was therefore conducted with strong national populist fervor and rhetoric, and after he was elected president he proceeded to revoke the anti-CGT decrees adopted at the beginning of the Aramburu regime. He also went considerably farther and ordered a general wage increase of 60 percent over the level of February 1956, so loosening up monetary and fiscal policies that money supply rose by 46 percent in 1958 and the national government budget deficit reached almost 5 percent of GDP. A major inflationary and balance of payments crisis naturally ensued.

It is difficult to resist the impression that Frondizi's extravagant initial policies were motivated not only by a desire to fulfill campaign promises but also by the need to produce an economic crisis of sufficient proportions to justify a clean break with past policies so that he could introduce his own "developmentalist" strategy.[4] This strategy, associated closely with the thinking of his chief economic adviser Rogelio Frigerio, embraced an ingenious combination of ideas designed to appeal to both liberal and national populist interest groups:

(1) Development of an integrated industrial complex in Argentina with emphasis on the so-called basic industries (steel, chemicals, pulp and paper, machinery and equipment), full exploitation of the nation's natural resources, and strengthening of regional development to assure complete integration of the national economy.

(2) Rejection of the concept of the international division of labor, which was a pretext used by advanced countries to maintain less developed nations in the role of cheap suppliers of foodstuffs and raw materials through a steady deterioration of their international terms of trade. It was also asserted that Argentina had been earmarked by the United States to continue as a basically agrarian economy, whereas its main rival, Brazil, had been chosen for development into a secondary industrial power.

(3) Agricultural development would follow the same path as industrial expansion: rapid mechanization and technological improvement. The redistribution of land was a retrograde step, since modern technology required larger, more efficient producing units, not small peasant farms.

(4) The resources necessary to carry out a developmentalist strategy could never be mobilized without a massive inflow of foreign capital, and if Argentina observed the rules of the game of the international financial community, the supply of external resources was virtually unlimited. Utilization of foreign capital posed no threat to national autonomy: the source of savings was immaterial so long as they were used to develop a modern, economically powerful, and independent nation.

The broad appeal of developmentalism to most important national interest groups was clear: entrepreneurs need not fear foreign competition, although in other respects the economy would remain open; agricultural proprietary rights would not be tampered with; the military could have their domestic production of strategic materials and strong regional economies resistant to infiltration from envious neighboring countries; nationalists could find succor in the strongly anti-imperialist rationale of the strategy once they overcame their prejudice toward foreign capital; and wage earners would soon find that the most effective way to improve their real incomes was through rapid growth in overall output and employment.

For the economist the most intriguing aspect of the developmentalist doctrine was that it assumed away the capital constraint in the allocation of resources. All desirable investment programs could be financed rapidly and simultaneously with a massive inflow of foreign investment, which would also take care of the balance of payments constraint. Once the rate of capital inflow began to subside because of a shortage of new investment opportunities, import substitution from past investments would suffice to assure external equilibrium, except possibly for full payment of external obligations; but if foreign creditors were unwilling to roll over Argentina's debts, what could they do once the country became economically independent and no longer needed external capital? This was an "all or nothing" strategy that for success required maintaining a critical forward momentum: if any signals of distress appeared along the way, confidence in the economy could be shaken, causing a slowdown in new foreign capital receipts that could quickly escalate into disaster.

Frondizi's first task in pursuit of his developmentalist strategy was to win the confidence of domestic investors and the international financial community. He appointed Alvaro Alsogaray, a strong free enterprise liberal, as his new Economics Minister (Alsogaray's brother Julio was also an influential army general), and in December 1958 he entered into a stiff standby agreement with the International Monetary Fund. Marginal bank reserve requirements were raised to 60 percent, government mortgage financing for residential construction was terminated, central bank financing of the fiscal deficit was rapidly cut back, most price controls were immediately lifted, quantitative trade restrictions were eliminated, and the exchange rate was freed to find its own level. Very liberal income tax deductions ranging up to 100 percent for machinery and transport equipment were granted on new investment, and duties and surcharges on imports of capital goods were drastically reduced or eliminated altogether. Wage increases were held substantially below the more than 100 percent rise in prices during 1959 and were then frozen (theoretically) in two-year contracts without the cost of living escalator clauses.

Frondizi had already taken his first and most controversial step toward attracting foreign capital during the furor over his strong national populist policies in 1958. Beginning in July of that year ten petroleum concession agreements were made with foreign companies, five of which were in areas, already explored by YPF, where deposits had been found; and three more foreign firms were contracted to drill wells for YPF. In December a new law was passed granting foreign investors the rights enjoyed by domestic investors and permitting completely free remittance of profits abroad. Certain pending disputes with international investors were settled, such as with the CADE electric power company which was converted into a mixed enterprise (SEGBA) eligible for foreign loans; and over $200 million in balance of payments credits and program loans were obtained to guarantee the foreign exchange liquidity of the country.

The medium-term effects of these new policies were impressive. After a sharp but brief recession began to subside and the rate of inflation to decelerate in the second half of 1959, the exchange rate was fixed at 83 pesos to the dollar, and foreign capital began to pour into the country along with large repatriations of private Argentine funds held abroad. Despite swelling imports and continued stagnation of exports, net gold and foreign exchange reserves rose by $550 million between December 1958 and the end of 1960 (see table 1-4). Total fixed investment, which in previous years had fluctuated around 17 or 18 percent of GDP, increased progressively to over 24 percent by 1961, and the composition of investment shifted strongly from construction to the acquisition of new machinery and equipment. During the three years 1960-1962 such acquisitions almost equalled in constant prices the total for the whole six-year period 1953-1958. By 1962 Argentina had also become almost self-sufficient in the supply of petroleum products; in fact, it became necessary to export small quantities of crude for lack of domestic storage and refining capacity.

The difficulty of synchronizing such a free-wheeling set of policies, however, soon began to open cracks on both the economic and political fronts. The sudden freeing of the economy from controls at the beginning of 1959 not only led initially to a rapid increase in the general price level but also caused some violent changes in relative prices. One of the most important was the 250 percent increase in the price of beef, which had been held under rather stringent control up to this time. Since the price of grains increased by substantially less, farmers were induced to shift land rapidly from crops to pasture and retain animals to build up their herds, a process that in the medium term led to a reduction in total output of both beef and grains for export.

On the labor front, the increase in employment that Frondizi had counted on to offset the initial decline in real wage rates caused by his stabilization policies did not materialize; between 1958 and 1961 total employment is estimated to have remained practically constant and the labor force participation rate to have declined from 40.3 to 38.3 percent of the population. The main explanation seems to be that expansion in new capacity and output was very intensive in the

Table 1-4   International reserves and foreign exchange rate, 1948-1970.

| Year | International reserves (millions of dollars) | | | Exchange rate (pesos per dollar) |
	Gold and foreign exchange	Other (net)	Total	
1948	674	–	674	4.23
1949	524	–	524	4.85
1950	691	–	691	6.56
1951	449	-92	357	7.50
1952	281	-97	184	7.50
1953	474	-97	377	7.50
1954	458	-87	371	7.50
1955	196	-77	119	10.12
1956	412	-275	137	18.00
1957	324	-327	-3	18.00
1958	133	-350	-217	18.00
1959	380	-478	-98	80.63
1960	697	-621	76	82.80
1961	496	-582	-86	83.13
1962	192	-574	-382	115.98
1963	322	-586	-264	138.61
1964	192	-479	-287	141.00
1965	265	-461	-196	171.62
1966	251	-415	-164	209.35
1967	736	-462	274	333.50
1968	696	-281	414	350.00
1969	442	-110	333	350.00
1970	555	37	592	379.17

Source: International reserves at end of year from Banco Central, *Memorias*, 1958-1970. Included are the net position of Argentina with the IMF and other liabilities of the Central Bank, and since 1961 liabilities of the National Treasury.

Exchange rate is the annual average selling rate from Techint, *Boletín informativo*, no. 183 (1971) and is calculated from monthly quotations of the Banco de la Nación Argentina.

use of capital and imports, and that production of more labor-intensive traditional consumer goods actually declined during the period due to the drop in effective demand and in total real wage income, which even by 1961 still remained more than 5 percent below the level of 1958.

These unexpected difficulties came to a head in 1961 when they were dramatized by poor weather and wage contract renegotiations.

The developmentalist strategy did not of course rely on strong export growth to maintain balance of payments viability; but when continued export stagnation was reinforced by a smaller harvest in 1961, the Central Bank became a net seller of foreign exchange in April for the first time in two years and continued losing reserves thereafter. Foreign lenders at first reacted with caution, but by November when arrival of the new crop at market still did not enable the bank to start rebuilding its reserves, it became clear that confidence had been lost in the stability of the peso. Even though the balance of payments was extremely vulnerable to loss of confidence because of the large amount of short-term financial obligations abroad—two thirds of noncompensatory capital receipts during 1959-1961 are estimated to have corresponded to deferred payment imports, short-term commercial credits, and so-called "liquid capital"—Frondizi decided not to reimpose exchange controls or change the rate of 83 pesos per dollar, policies which he considered cornerstones of his developmentalist program.

Loss of confidence in the economy was also reinforced by a prolonged struggle with labor unions over wage readjustments and rationalization of public sector employment, notably in the state-owned railways. Under pressure because of lagging real wage rates and rising unemployment since 1958, Frondizi did not feel able to follow a hard line on wages and featherbedding in government employment, particularly in view of the coming provincial elections in March 1962. The concessions he made to labor demands caused the resignation of two consecutive Economics Ministers and were generally considered to have breached official incomes policy. Liberal support for the regime sagged further when Argentina was declared in violation of the IMF standby agreement because of excess government borrowing, and military support began to crumble when Frondizi, in a further attempt to cultivate electoral popularity, assumed a "third position" in the inter-American dispute over Castroism and permitted Peronists to run their own candidates in the provincial elections.

Frondizi thus became a prisoner of a rigid set of policies that he was unwilling to change even after results demonstrated they were not working as expected. Like Perón, who had neglected to try to forge a new coalition after he changed the direction of policy, Frondizi then proceeded to improvise ad hoc measures designed to stir up popular support in the vain hope that this would offset the alienation of important members of his political coalition. Instead, they became even more convinced that the rules of the game they had agreed upon when they entered the coalition had been violated without their consent. The overthrow of the Frondizi government after Peronists won some important victories in the provincial elections of March 1962 again underlined the impossibility of following policies that did not maintain the support of a broad enough coalition.

Reconstruction of a National Populist Government under the Traditional Radical Party, 1963-1966

The period between the overthrow of Frondizi and the election of a new president in 1963 was symptomatic of that kind of crisis syndrome, mentioned earlier, in which policymaking tends to fall under the de facto control of subordinate functionaries in protected enclaves such as central banks. Overall direction and continuity of policy was made impossible by an open struggle between military factions: the so-called "blues," led by General Ongania, and the "reds," a term having nothing to do with communism but referring to a group that in general favored formation of a nationalistic military government. The blues, who eventually won, advocated early election of a civilian government, but again without participation of Peronist candidates.

In the otherwise fair election that ensued, the popular vote was widely split among eligible candidates and blank ballots, with Arturo Illia of the traditional wing of the Radical party (now named the Popular Radicals) picking up a narrow plurality of less than 30 percent. This outcome was generally greeted with a feeling of relief over termination of the period of semianarchy, a feeling that helped the new government put together a voting majority in the newly elected Congress. Other than this, the Popular Radicals were unwilling to take any further initiatives, either at this time or later, to build a stronger coalition of interest groups, since the main plank in their platform was, in the tradition of Yrigoyen, restoration of strict legal constitutionality. The fact that the most powerfully organized interest groups—Peronist labor, the military, and liberal business and financial interests—were grossly under-represented or even unrepresented in the legislature and were given few if any posts in the executive branch led to increasing isolation of the government from the sources of ultimate political power.

Ironically, the fact that the Popular Radical party itself was virtually a microcosm of Argentine economic interests and ideological opinions, from labor leaders to businessmen and from moderate liberals to strong national populists, impeded its effective conduct of government. Just as no strong interest group or ideology felt that it had enough influence in the party to identify with it politically, so its leadership was under constant pressure to accommodate to the lowest common denominator of a most diverse internal party constituency. Appointments to key positions in the central government administration, semiautonomous agencies, and state enterprises reflected this diversity and made close coordination of policy formulation and implementation extremely difficult, thereby complicating the task of the unified economic team appointed to take charge of overall economic policies.

The initial strategy of the new government can only be understood against the background of the very severe recession of 1962-1963. After the fall of Frondizi an extremely restrictive monetary policy was adopted, the exchange rate was again freed to find its own level, and other measures were taken to purge the economy of "excess demand" and restrain the massive outflow of capital. Real per capita GDP and personal consumption fell to their lowest levels in a decade; utilization of installed manufacturing capacity, greatly augmented during the previous investment boom, is estimated to have declined below 55 percent; and in 1963 open unemployment reached an estimated 9 percent of the active population in Greater Buenos Aires, and even larger figures in the interior of the country (see table 1-5). This last development was not unrelated to the fact that unions and employers, left to their own devices without an official incomes policy, preferred to raise wage rates roughly *pari passu* with the increase in the cost of living and to eliminate labor made redundant by the fall in demand.

Eugenio Blanco, reappointed Economics Minister by President Illia, considered that his first responsibility was to reactivate the depressed economy with expansionary monetary, fiscal, and wage policies. As a result real GDP grew at a rate of about 8 percent in both 1964 and 1965, led by an almost 15 percent per year growth in manufacturing, and unemployment was cut in half. It was initially feared, however, that rapid economic recovery and service of the heavy public and private foreign debt, which at the end of 1963 was projected to require payments of about one billion dollars during the next two years, would again produce a crisis in the balance of payments. Exchange controls were consequently reimposed on capital and invisible transactions (although commodity trade was left mostly free); and special measures were taken, such as selective credit controls and an increase in the legally required share of domestic components in local automobile manufacture, to hold down the import content of production. Even though debt refinancing was kept to a minimum, there was in fact little net

Table 1-5 Unemployment rates, 1963–1970. (percent of economically active population)

Metropolitan areas	1963	1964			1965			1966			1967		
	July	April	July	Oct.	April	July	Oct.	April	July	Oct.	April	July	Oct.
Buenos Aires	8.8	7.5	7.4	5.7	5.5	6.1	4.4	6.4	5.2	5.0	6.2	6.8	6.2
Córdoba	—	—	—	9.5	8.6	—	6.3	7.3	—	6.6	8.9	—	7.3
Rosario	—	—	—	7.6	8.9	—	5.5	7.2	—	5.8	6.5	—	6.1
Tucumán	—	—	—	9.2	5.5	—	6.4	9.5	—	7.4	10.3	—	10.2
Mendoza	—	—	—	9.2	6.0	—	4.7	3.8	—	2.7	2.4	—	2.6

Metropolitan areas	1968			1969			1970			Total population, 1970 census
	April	July	Oct.	April	July	Oct.	April	July	Oct.	
Buenos Aires	5.4	4.7	4.7	4.0	4.8	4.0	4.8	4.7	5.0	8,352,900
Córdoba	7.3	—	4.3	6.1	—	3.2	4.2	—	4.7	798,663
Rosario	4.7	—	5.9	5.5	—	5.5	5.5	—	4.9	798,292
Tucumán	10.8	—	12.7	12.4	—	11.4	10.9	—	10.4	326,208
Mendoza	2.5	—	2.4	2.5	—	2.7	3.8	—	3.3	480,841

Source: Instituto Nacional de Estadística y Censos.

change in Central Bank reserves during 1964-1965, but the explanation for this apparently successful management of balance of payments policy lay as much on the foreign exchange supply as on the demand side.

Exports kept rising continuously from less than one billion dollars in 1961 to almost $1.6 billion in 1966. Part of this phenomenal rise can be attributed to exceptionally good weather and the improvement in international commodity prices, but during the following years it became increasingly clear that it was also the result of a long awaited increase in total agricultural output and productivity in response to generally favorable foreign exchange rate and other policies. The Illia government, even though it reintroduced exchange controls, avoided any drastic reversal of these policies by adopting a "crawling peg" exchange rate so as to prevent export prices from getting far out of line with rising domestic costs. Technological progress in agriculture was also promoted by a permanent pasture improvement program and by other measures designed by an Agricultural Secretariat headed by the former chief of the government agricultural research and extension service (INTA). The increasing influence of competent technical staffs on the design of macroeconomic policies was also notable, particularly in the National Development Council (CONADE) and in the preparation of annual financial programs under the supervision of the Central Bank.

These achievements of the Popular Radical regime were nevertheless insufficient to win even tacit acceptance from the three important nonparticipating constituencies. The liberal business and financial communities were shocked at the very beginning of the new government when President Illia decided to cancel foreign petroleum company contracts and to adopt a rather hostile attitude toward the international financial community, as manifested by the abrupt termination of the IMF standby agreement and the controversy with the World Bank over their intervention in the management and rate policy of SEGBA, the Buenos Aires electric power company. Liberal opinion was equally distressed by the reimposition of exchange controls and by what was referred to as a revival of excessive statism, an opinion based not only on the government's efforts to enforce certain irritating regulations but also on the reduced influence of private pressure groups on government decision-makers. Policy was instead being formulated by government technocrats without "adequate" private sector participation.

The events that most dramatically polarized opposition against the government, however, were increasing labor difficulties and the inability of the authorities to coordinate effectively the policies of decentralized agencies and state enterprises. Labor featherbedding and excessive wage concessions were alleged to be the main causes of burgeoning deficits in these entities, the most notable of which was the state railway deficit that by 1965 accounted for almost 20 percent of total central government expenditures. Wage increases throughout the economy also far exceeded guidelines laid down by the economic team after economic recovery was well under way and it was decided to put on the brakes. It was announced that wage adjustments should be limited to increases in labor productivity plus what employers were willing to transfer from profits, but the inability of the government to hold the line on wages of public employees and the reluctance of President Illia to call out the troops to prevent occupation of factories, sabotage, and other acts of labor violence convinced employers that it would be more prudent to follow a line of less resistance. The wage-price spiral therefore accelerated and the cost of living index rose by about 38 percent between December 1964 and the end of 1965. When the economic team decided not to validate wage and price increases by holding to their more restrictive monetary and fiscal targets durng 1965 and the first half of 1966, businessmen naturally objected energetically instead of supporting the team's firm stand.

At the same time, military pressure to give the army greater responsibility for imposing labor discipline and to accept the formation of a de facto coalition government was rebuffed by President Illia as a violation of constitutional legality. Discussions between the regime and its opponents and among the latter were quite fully reported in the press, so that the coup d'état of June 1966 caused little surprise and created only minor visible adverse reaction. General Ongania was brought out of retirement to head a new military government, with the declaration that the political party system had been given another chance but failed and that it was therefore time to try a different approach.

Reimposition of Liberal Policies through Military Authority, 1966-1970

Although by 1966 the military had mended most of the schisms that had led to the brief civil war of 1962, there still did not exist any consensus with respect to the economic policies the new government should follow. General Julio Alsogaray, who had personally led the coup d'état, was therefore unable to take over power himself or to obtain the appointment of his liberal free enterprise brother, Alvaro, to the post of Economics Minister. General Ongania, on the other hand, was a prestigious military figure completely disassociated from any political philosophy and therefore an ideal compromise choice for president. His search for an acceptable economic team and new policy directions during the following eight months consequently created a period of drift, during which the difficulties that plagued the Illia regime (except for labor strife) became even more accentuated.

In March 1967 General Ongania, after listening to the long stream of lobbyists who paraded through the Casa Rosada (government house), finally decided to call Krieger Vasena back as Economics Minister to implement the first "economic stage" of his proclaimed three-stage program (the other two were the social and the political stages). The basic strategy of Krieger was to eliminate inflation in rapid steps by means of an incomes policy that froze distributive income shares at approximately their average real levels of 1966. The chief measures were as follows:

(1) In a compensated devaluation the exchange rate was raised from about 280 pesos per dollar and pegged at 350, while taxes on traditional exports were increased and import duties reduced so as to ameliorate the effect of devaluation on the domestic price level and at the same time provide an incentive for expansion of nontraditional exports.

(2) Wage rates of different unions were adjusted in stages to restore their average real purchasing power of 1966 and were thereafter frozen until December 1967.

(3) Business firms were obliged to enter into "voluntary" agreements with the government to limit price increases in return for more liberal access to bank credit and preferential treatment in sales to official agencies.

(4) The government undertook to reduce the fiscal deficit by improving tax collections, raising public utility rates, reducing the number of civil servants, and cutting the losses of state enterprises.

(5) Investor confidence in the economy was to be restored by expectations of greater stability, the elimination of exchange controls, renewal of foreign petroleum company contracts, a new standby agreement with the IMF, and in general by an improvement in relations with the international financial community.

This program differed significantly in both design and results from any previous stabilization effort. Effective restraints were imposed simultaneously on both wages and prices, so that the fall in real wage rates was not very large; and the fiscal deficit was reduced by raising taxes as well as by curtailing increases in current expenditures, with the result that the public sector was able to play a major role in rapidly expanding total fixed investment almost back to the boom level of 1960-1961, this time mostly financed from domestic savings. A much larger share of this investment went into new construction, stimulated by an expansion of bank credit to the private sector *pari passu* with the reduction in Central Bank lending to government, which reduced interest rates and revitalized the long-stagnant mortgage market. The construction boom that followed not only took up most of the slack created by a slowdown in the rest of the economy, but because construction is relatively labor-intensive, it also quickly reabsorbed the temporary increase in unemployment.

By the end of 1968 Krieger Vasena could show that the annual rate of inflation had been reduced to less than 10 percent, net foreign exchange reserves had risen by almost $600 million, a serious economic recession had been avoided, there had been no increase in unemployment, and the economy was beginning to expand again at an increasing pace. Unfortunately, however, an imposed two-year truce is very different from a free association of interest groups, sufficiently strong to keep a government in power and committed to a set of policies they think will minimize their losses if not maximize their gains. An imposed truce tends to be a time for regrouping forces, for staking out new positions in anticipation of the negotiations that will inevitably follow. A judgment of how appropriately policies were made during a truce must therefore necessarily be based on the extent to which they subsequently facilitated a negotiated settlement.

In this sense Krieger Vasena's policies do not rate so highly as might otherwise appear. His stabilization program was geared to a fixed set of real income and price targets—for example, real wage levels of 1966 and an exchange rate of 350 pesos per dollar—that left little room for maneuver. The pinch on wages was somewhat alleviated by financing a small salary increase from a reduction in social security contributions, which produced a deficit in the social security system without completely preventing a decline in real wages; and maintenance of the exchange rate at 350 involved some worsening of relative agricultural prices. After initial adjustments, it in fact became increasingly difficult to permit any revision of prices, regardless of how far they got out of line, for fear that the stabilization boat would be rocked.

Perhaps the best illustration of this dilemma is Krieger's exchange rate policy. Limited flexibility was given to the exchange rate through subsequent reductions in export taxes on agricultural exports and increased subsidies for nontraditional exports, but in both cases compensation was incomplete. Before the end of 1968 the "real" exchange rate—that is, the nominal exchange rate deflated by the increase in domestic prices over the rise in world prices—had already fallen below the pre-March 1967 devaluation level. By this time export taxes on wheat, corn, wool, and some other important traditional export products had already been reduced from an initial 25 percent to 8 percent or less, so that the authorities quite logically reasoned that any further reduction would jeopardize confidence in the pegged rate. It is difficult to explain otherwise how they could have permitted the prices of wheat, corn, and linseed to have declined absolutely during the first half of 1970, thereby helping to reinforce another cattle cycle that led to a doubling of steer prices during the course of the year and placed the whole stabilization program in greater jeopardy.[5]

Preparation for a negotiated settlement was helped even less by the heavy-handed manner in which the Ongania regime "intervened" the universities, repressed dissent, invoked censorship of the press, and perhaps most important of all, virtually eliminated any semblance of provincial autonomy. In a country that had shed much blood in the struggle over establishment of a federal system of government, the unilateral decision of the national authorities to impose a de facto unitary system, and even worse to appoint unpopular governors who often carried out policies supported by the most reactionary forces in the provinces, was interpreted as a blatant violation of the political rules of the game. Unrest gradually built up, starting in Tucumán and spreading to Rosario, Cordoba, and other provincial cities, until open riots led by students and workers broke out in May 1969. The riots were soon brought under control by the violent intervention of the armed forces and declaration of martial law throughout the country. But these events also produced schisms within the regime that obliged Ongania to ask for the resignation of his entire cabinet. Krieger Vasena was replaced as Economics Minister by José María Dagnino Pastore, a technocrat who had previously held the same post in the Buenos Aires provincial government and was then serving as director of CONADE (the National Development Council).

The change in leadership of the economic team did not represent much of an alteration in policy, but Dagnino Pastore's influence in the cabinet was considerably less than that of his predecessor. This was a considerable handicap as problems began to escalate, first as continued economic expansion and doubts about stability of the peso set off an import boom that began to drain away foreign exchange reserves, reinforced for a while by panic buying after the resignation of Krieger; and then when continued protest and violence, such as the assassinations of the collaborationist labor leader Vandor and ex-President Aramburu, led to increasing military unrest over the managerial capability and personal ambitions of Ongania himself. By July 1970 the stage was set for another coup d'état that replaced Ongania by General Levingston, who was equally uncommitted to any particular political philosophy or economic policy position and was furthermore presumed to lack the personal prestige and charisma to turn himself into a personalistic dictator.

The new president was faced by most of the same economic issues that had confronted his predecessors when they took office. The acceleration in the rate of inflation to over 20 percent in 1970 generated irresistible pressure for wage adjustments, so that an emergency general increase of 7 percent was granted in September and a further "selective" increase of 6 percent was authorized early in 1971. The fiscal authorities were at the same time struggling to readjust lagging prices of public services and to prevent inflationary erosion of the tax base, whereas the tighter monetary policy (started in 1969) was beginning to affect the level of economic activity, particularly that of the construction industry, thereby posing again the old question of rising unemployment. The balance of payments was not yet in serious difficulty, but the exchange rate, which was devalued from 350 to 400 pesos per dollar during the brief tenure of Levingston's first Economics Minister, Moyano Llerena, again rapidly deteriorated to the "real" predevaluation level by the end of 1970, by which time a menacing external payments gap had reappeared. The government's position with respect to such perennial issues of dispute as foreign investment and incomes policies, the agricultural terms of trade, and industrialization strategy also remained undefined, except that import duties were again raised, thus reversing Krieger's previous policy.

With the passage of time it became increasingly apparent that President Levingston, even though he was able to recruit some talented technocrats for his economic team, was not succeeding in mobilizing the necessary political support for a coherent line of policy action. Consequently in March 1971 he was deposed in another bloodless coup and replaced by General Lanusse, a much more prominent and forceful military leader. After assuming power President Lanusse devoted most of his energy to negotiating a new political settlement with the country's major interest groups, including the Peronists. He apparently assumed that no longer-term economic program could be adopted until a political accord had been reached, because during the remainder of his tenure in office economic policy was conducted basically as a holding operation.

Conclusion

The Argentine experience teaches valuable lessons with regard to the integration of policymaking and conflict mediation into a single, coherent decision process. Given Argentina's weak mediative institutions, a constitutional settlement like that which brought Illia into power is unlikely to work if it relegates labor, liberal businessmen, and the military to the role of nonparticipating constituencies. Their voluntary participation in a coalition government, on the other hand, can only be obtained if the rules of the game are negotiable: they will not join simply to implement policies adopted by a previous military regime wedded to the idea that economic and sociopolitical problems can be dealt with separately, as Aramburu and Ongania seemed to think. On the contrary, it is probably easier to form a coalition government when the economy is in crisis and interest groups fear they have more to lose by not helping to reach a political settlement than by participating in it. The efforts of Frondizi and Illia to gain initial support for their policies were undoubtedly assisted by the crises of 1958-1959 and 1962-1963; the first may in fact have been consciously worsened by Frondizi with this purpose in mind.

Winning initial participation of diverse interest groups in support of an economic program during a crisis is an easier task than holding a coalition together once the crisis has passed. The initial motive for participating in a coalition—that is, to head off disaster—must soon be replaced by the expectation of receiving adequate rewards for continued cooperation. This requires reconciliation of conflicting claims on income increments and raises a familiar dilemma: the more rapid is economic expansion the easier it is to satisfy the claims of coalition participants, but at the same time the more difficult is preservation of internal and external economic equilibrium. The life of a coalition government therefore depends on how adroitly it can walk the razor's edge between unsatisfactorily slow growth and a new economic crisis. It is therefore advisable that an initial policy agreement not be based on fulfillment of an inflexible set of targets. Frondizi virtually guaranteed his own failure by locking his policy to a fixed exchange rate and an economic program that generated less employment than he had anticipated; Krieger Vasena likewise based the success of his whole program on maintenance of an exchange rate fixed at the beginning of his tenure in office as well as on constant real wage rates. If based on greater policy flexibility, coalitions may not have to be renegotiated with such frequency as they have been in recent Argentine history, and greater policy continuity may thus be attainable.

The best that can be expected from political leaders and their technocrats, therefore, is that whenever possible they avoid using rigid shock therapy tactics that may bring temporary relief from economic crises but which in conflict societies with weak mediative institutions tend to tear society apart. Their conduct should instead be based on a recognition of the essentially contingent nature and seriality of policymaking, and of the inescapable fact that policy design and conflict mediation constitute integral parts of the same decision-making process in pluralistic societies.

2 Agriculture and Export Expansion

Argentine agriculture is not only the principal supplier of foreign exchange but also the provider of almost all the nation's food supply and of an important share of its industrial raw materials. All Argentine policymakers have thus been obliged to make assumptions either explicitly or implicitly about the supply response of this important sector when designing their economic programs. Perhaps for this very reason the sector has been one of the main victims as well as the chief intended beneficiary of many of the most controversial measures taken by government in the income distribution and political power struggle of recent decades.

At the time the Argentine pampas was opened up to the world trade boom in the latter part of the last century, agricultural property was so concentrated that a relatively small elite was able to appropriate most of the benefits of agricultural expansion. The cattle barons and the so-called *agro-exportador* oligarchy, who virtually monopolized political power up to World War I and continued to exercise considerable influence in later years, were closely identified with foreign trading and financial interests and with antiprotectionist, antinationalist and antipopular policies. After national populism came to power under the leadership of Perón in 1943, the pendulum of policy swung violently in the opposite direction and never again returned to its initial position. Many of the farmers most adversely affected by the new rules of the game steadfastly refused to accept anything short of a complete reversal of these rules.

In this highly charged emotional environment it was exceedingly difficult to straighten out what was actually happening to Argentine agriculture. The passage of time and the systematic, quantitative research on the subject initiated in the 1960s have, however, made it possible in recent years to clarify a number of facts and relationships that are extremely important for policymaking. Those chosen for special analysis in this chapter are trends in land use and output, institutional reforms and changes in land tenure, technological advances and improvements in productivity, and the response of farmers to changes in relative prices.

Land Use and Output Trends

At the outset it is useful to distinguish broadly between the agriculture of the pampas and that in the rest of the country. The pampas is a flat, alluvial plain in the eastern bulge of Argentina with an extension of about 56 million hectares of arable land, representing some 20 percent of the total area of the country and embracing the provinces of Buenos Aires, La Pampa, most of Córdoba, and parts of San Luis, Santa Fé, and Entre Rios. It is equal in size to the states of Iowa, Kansas, and Nebraska combined. With a deep topsoil almost devoid of stones, an average annual rainfall of 700 to 800 millimeters (somewhat more in the eastern humid zone of 35 million hectares, somewhat less in the western semiarid zone), and a temperate climate which permits cattle grazing and cultivation throughout the year, the pampas is generally considered one of the richest agricultural regions in the world. Over 80 percent of the total cropped area of the country is located here and it has traditionally produced 80 percent or more of Argentina's export revenue.

The value of agricultural output in the pampas is divided about equally between cattle and crops. Although sheep, horses, and hogs are of some significance, beef (and to a minor extent, dairy) cattle account for the major part of the value of animal production. The principal crops are grains (especially wheat and maize) and oilseeds (notably linseed), which are cultivated on 15 to 20 million hectares often in combination (and traditionally in rotation) with pasture for livestock. The methods of production are those of extensive dry farming employing relatively little labor: in 1956 it was estimated that an average of only 4.7 man-days per hectare per year were used in contrast with 45 man-days per hectare employed in agriculture outside of the pampas.

As can be surmised from this last figure, methods of crop production in the rest of the country are typically much more intensive, not only in terms of labor but also with respect to land, a significant part of which is irrigated. Each geographical region outside of the pampas tends to be specialized in a particular crop: sugar cane in the northwest, yerba mate in the northeast, vineyards in Mendoza, fruit orchards in the Rio Negro valley in the south, and so forth. Thus, although the nonpampean zone possesses only 20 percent of the country's cropped area, it produces 40 percent of the value of crop output. Cattle raising is also important outside the pampas in terms of the area devoted to pasture, but in contrast to crops, livestock is produced on an extremely extensive basis and generally under very backward conditions. With some important exceptions (chiefly Patagonian wool, yerba mate, and fruit), agricultural production of the nonpampean region is much more for domestic use than for export. Partly for this reason, and partly because each region and special crop has its own particular problems, most of the analysis in this chapter will deal with pampean agriculture.

The rapid growth of total Argentine farm output began in the latter part of the nineteenth century and leveled off after the 1920s. In the pampas this slowdown or stagnation in the rate of growth was associated both with difficulties in export markets during the Great Depression and with the disappearance of new arable land to bring under cultivation. Neither of these factors, however, had as much effect on agriculture in the rest of the country, with the result that production outside of the pampas continued to expand quite rapidly, in fact four times as fast as Pampean output between the 1920s and the mid-1950s. This development gave an increasing antiexport bias to Argentine agriculture, a bias that was greatly reinforced by rising domestic demand for the stagnant or declining output of products produced mainly in the pampas (see table 2-1).

It would be difficult to argue that weak foreign demand continued to depress exports after World War II. On the contrary, it is clear from table 2-2 that Argentina did not take full advantage of the postwar revival in world trade: its share of trade in most major agricultural commodities declined drastically between the 1930s and the early 1950s. The main explanations for the export-led decline in Argentine agriculture during this period must, therefore, be looked for on the supply side. As will be seen below, abundant reasons exist

Table 2-1 End use of total agricultural production. (in percentages)

	Crops		Cattle	
Years	For export	For domestic use	Export	Domestic
1935–1939	47	53	37	63
1945–1949	23	77	35	65
1950–1954	22	78	21	79

Source: United Nations, ECLA, *El desarrollo económico de la Argentina*, Part II, table 7, p. 12.

Table 2-2   Share of Argentine exports in world trade. (in percentages)

Product	1934–1938	1950–1954
Maize	64	20
Wheat	19	9
Linseed and oil	68	44
Wool	12	10
Meat	40	19

Source: United Nations, ECLA, *El desarrollo económico*, Statistical Appendix table IV, p. 48.

to explain the lack of improvements in agricultural output and productivity during the postwar period; indeed, these reasons have been iterated and reiterated so frequently and convincingly in Argentina that many observers appear to believe that they have been stifling agricultural development ever since. This impression has persisted largely because of the lack of convincing evidence until very recent years of renewed agricultural expansion, again led primarily by production for export.

After recovering from the disastrous drought of 1952, rural production leveled off until 1961, after which it made another spurt to a new plateau in 1965. Each of these plateaus represented a substantial increase over the average level of production in the previous period, but even more significantly the output of principal export products, after remaining stagnant or declining since the 1930s, rose more rapidly than the general agricultural production index (see figure 2-1). The increase in the output of corn and of

Figure 2-1. Agricultural production indices, 1935–1967 (1960=100).

Table 2-3   Output of selected export crops, 1950–1970. (thousands of
metric tons)

5-year averages	Wheat	Corn	Sorghum	Sunflower	Peanuts
1950/51– 1954/55	5,884	5,051	29	554	148
1955/56– 1959–60	6,143	4,083	429	665	255
1960/61– 1964–65	7,117	4,984	1,144	625	386
1965/66– 1969/70	6,481	7,666	2,856	972	300

Source: For the period 1950/51 to 1964/65, U.S. Department of Agriculture,
Economic Research Service, *Argentine Agriculture: Trends in Production and
World Competition*, ERS-Foreign 216 (Washington, D.C., July 1968); for the
period 1965/66 to 1969/70, Ministerio de Economía y Trabajo, *Informe económico*, fourth quarter of 1970, Buenos Aires.

some of the newer agricultural export crops was especially rapid (see
table 2-3). Still, the average rate of growth in total agricultural
production in the Argentine pampas between the early 1950s and the
end of the 1960s was only about 2 percent per year, a rate that made
it difficult to prevent rising domestic demand from reducing export
availabilities. Longer term comparisons make this problem even
clearer: total crop production in the pampas at the end of the 1960s
was still only slightly above the pre-World War II level. Livestock
production scored more impressive gains since prewar, especially
during earlier years when crop output was declining; but since the
early 1950s its rate of growth has been less than that of crop
production (see table 2-4). Thus, although postwar rural stagnation
has long been overcome, renewed expansion has not been fast
enough to reconcile competing domestic and export demands for
agricultural products if the country is to sustain a more rapid rate of
overall growth.

Land Tenure and Institutional Reform

The area which now comprises Argentina was unattractive for
settlement and sparsely inhabited during the Spanish colonial era,
so that the hacienda system did not have much influence on the
initial distribution of agricultural property. It was not in fact until
the 1870s that the Indians were driven completely out of the pampas
and the entire area became available for commercial use. Except for

Table 2-4 Argentina: agricultural production indexes in the Pampean region, 1935-1970. (1935-1939 = 100)

Period	Crops	Livestock	Total agriculture
1940–44	102.1	128.6	108.4
1945–49	75.2	135.8	94.9
1950–54	65.8	133.5	89.3
1955–59	80.4	144.3	102.2
1960–64	95.0	154.0	114.2
1965–67	101.8	171.8	124.0
1968–70[a]	102.5	186.0	127.0

Source: Darrell F. Fienup, *The Agricultural Development of Argentina* (New York, 1969), table 21, p. 62.

[a]Estimated from indices of the physical volume of production given in the *Boletín Estadístico* of the Central Bank.

a few districts in the northern part of the pampas, the new land was not colonized with farm families according to United States practice during the nineteenth century. Instead, beginning in the 1820s state land was leased and finally sold to private landholders under a system called *enfiteusis* to raise revenue for military expenses; and following the "campaign of the desert" which liberated the pampas from the Indians, large tracts were awarded to those who had participated in the campaign. In both cases land tended eventually to fall into the hands of those with influence or the highest bidders with few if any effective restrictions on the size of individual holdings. The degree of concentration of landed property which emerged is illustrated by the 1928 land tax directory (*guía de contribuyentes*) of Buenos Aires province, which listed about one third of the total area of the province as belonging to a little more than one thousand families, including fifty families owning over 4.6 million hectares in individual parcels of 30,000 hectares or more.[1]

The preferred activity of medium and large-scale pampean landholders was cattle raising; crop raising in fact tended to be looked down on as a socially inferior occupation. The predominant system of farm organization was one in which a portion of each property was left in pasture and operated by direct-hire labor, and the rest was let out in small plots to tenants for crop raising. The rental contracts were typically of a few years' duration, at the termination of which the tenant was obliged to sow alfalfa on his plot and move on to another location, usually one which had previously been used for pasture. Although this system had obvious advantages in providing for rotation between crops and pasture to prevent soil depletion, its social consequences were open to severe criticism. The tenant lived a precarious existence more akin to a migrant laborer than a permanent farmer. At each move he had to tear down his shack and uproot his family, with the result that it was extremely difficult for him to improve his living conditions, provide a steady education for his children and establish permanent community ties.

The landowner-tenant-worker relationship consequently became an increasing concern of Argentina's popular nationalists, whose influence was growing rapidly during the 1930s. Soon after Colonel Perón was appointed secretary of labor by the military government that took power in the coup of 1943, a farm worker statute (Law No. 28,169 of 1944, better known as the Estatuto del Peón) was adopted which authorized the ministry of labor to review and adjust periodically minimum salary scales of permanent rural laborers, benefits which were extended in 1946 to dairy workers and in 1947 to seasonal labor. The following year, after Perón had been elevated to the presidency, a land rental law (No. 13,246 of 1948) was promulgated which froze rural rents and prohibited landowners from moving or ejecting tenants from their property. These sweeping modifications of the rural labor and farm tenant systems did not undergo any major revisions until after Perón was overthrown in 1955.[2]

The new tenancy and rural wage regulations, combined with the government's agricultural price policy (see below), had a profound impact on income distribution in the rural sector. Real agricultural wages improved very substantially though erratically, but their improvement was particularly impressive in relation to the prices of principal crops: between 1948 and 1954 wage rates almost doubled in relation to the prices of linseed and sunflower and rose by about 74 and 22 percent respectively relative to the prices of wheat and maize.[3]   The real rental income of landowners, on the other hand, is estimated to have declined by 1955 to only 10 percent of the prewar level.[4]   These changes in relative factor remunerations—together with increased uncertainty created by the spread of labor disputes at harvest time and frequent squabbles over the number of hired workers required for different tasks and over the use of farm family labor—undermined traditional producer incentives and provided strong inducements for changing prevailing methods of farm organization and production.

The first adjustment which landowners tried to bring about,

insofar as they were able, was a shift to less labor-intensive activities. One obvious way to make such a shift was to take land out of crop production and devote it to pasture, and indeed available statistics on land use show a drop from about 21 million hectares sown to grains and oilseeds prior to World War II to about 19 million during the war and 16 million in the late 1940s and early 1950s (the low point was 14.4 million hectares in the drought year 1951-1952). The index of pampean livestock production, on the other hand, rose by about 35 percent during the same period (see again table 2-4). Significant differences also existed in the amount of labor required in the production of different crops, the most notable of which was that more than two times as many man-hours per hectare were needed for maize than the other major grains and oilseeds.[5] It is not surprising, therefore, that the area sown to maize declined by one-half between prewar and the early 1950s, the largest reduction for any major crop except linseed, even though the relative price of maize fell proportionately less than that of most other crops.

Landowners also had a strong incentive to try to rescind land rental contracts, although this must have been quite difficult and expensive under existing regulations of the time. Nevertheless, between the censuses of 1947 and 1960 the number of agricultural units working rented land in Argentina declined from 120,000 to 50,000 and their total area fell from 21 million hectares to only 9 million. During the same period the economically active population in the pampean region declined by no less than 37 percent. Thus, contrary to the probable intent of the framers of the rural wage and land rental reforms of the 1940s, two of their chief longer run effects were to accelerate the migration of labor out of agriculture and to reduce the amount of land available for rental.

Finally, the sharp increase in rural wage rates and the accelerated migration of labor out of agriculture was naturally associated with greater efforts toward mechanization. There were, however, serious impediments to overcome. Import restrictions adopted to correct the deteriorating balance of payments after 1948 fell particularly heavily on purchases of capital equipment, although an effort was made to give preference to imports of agricultural machinery and to start domestic production. The government's more liberal licensing policy and the preferential exchange rate accorded such imports resulted in a substantial increase in the acquisition of new tractors, but purchase of other types of agricultural equipment did not respond until import controls were liberalized and finally abandoned in the late 1950s.[6]

Another impediment to mechanization was the deterioration in the agricultural terms of trade and presumably in the savings rate of farmers, combined with increased uncertainty about the purpose and direction of government policy. Available statistical evidence indicates a reduction in the rate of fixed investment in agriculture up to the mid-1950s, if not an absolute decline in the sector's total capital stock; but the change in government price, import, and land rental policies at this time appears to have brought about a complete reversal of the trend. The resulting acceleration in the rate of mechanization and investment in agriculture will be described in the next section.

As with many far-reaching social reforms, the effects of the land rental and rural wage laws of the 1940s proved difficult to modify at first but eventually resulted in conditions probably worse than the ones they were originally intended to correct. Substantial increases in land rents were permitted beginning in 1957, but regulations restricting the ejection of tenants were renewed year after year while various inducements were provided to encourage the sale of rented land to tenants. Systems of quasi-tenancy consequently proliferated in the pampas—arrangements such as contracts for a single harvest and short-term grazing rights—which did not fall under existing regulations and provided even less stability for tenants than the old system. The decline in rural wage rates relative to major crop prices was slight up to 1958, but thereafter the decline accelerated so that by 1959-1963 they had fallen back to the prewar level or below.[7]

The modification of Peronist policies did not, however, reverse long-term trends in land tenure patterns. Between the censuses of 1914 and 1960 the proportion of holdings with more than 5,000 hectares fell by one half to less than 15 percent of agricultural land in Buenos Aires Province, whereas holdings of between 100 and 1,000 hectares (the range that includes the minimum viable farm size under pampean conditions) rose from 34 to almost 44 percent. Another way to evaluate the relative size of holdings is according to the number of workers required to operate different kinds of farms. In the land tenure study previously cited the two middle classifications—family-sized farms and medium multifamily units occupying between two and twelve workers—were estimated in 1960 to account for over three quarters of the area devoted to agriculture in the pampas. At the same time only 20 percent of the area was still exploited exclusively under some form of rental or sharecropping arrangement.[8]

Although the trend toward a reduction in the average size of holdings and in the use of rental and sharecropping contracts appears to be fairly well substantiated, it is difficult to reach any conclusion about the significance of the remaining degree of concentration of landed property in the pampas. Compared with other countries in Latin America which are currently engaged in carrying out agrarian reforms, the distribution of pampean land seems relatively equitable, as can be observed from table 2-5, which is based on similar land tenure studies carried out for the period between 1950 and 1960 in the countries listed.

It would be difficult to conclude from such figures, however, that the system of land tenure no longer impedes the more efficient use of agricultural resources in Argentina. The CIDA study already cited found the value of output per hectare inversely correlated with farm size in the pampas. On the other hand, this fact tells us very little about the effect of tenure on the supply responsiveness of agriculture in the absence of information by size of holding on differences in land quality and in land use, in the cost of inputs per unit of output, and in other factors which might also help to explain the variance in output per unit of land. The only conclusion that seems warranted by existing information is that sociopolitical attitudes toward the agricultural sector in Argentina will continue to be influenced by the fact that one out of every five hectares in one of the richest farming regions in the world is still held in properties of 2,500 hectares or more and produces profits for the relatively few.

Table 2-5 Percentage of total farm area by size of holdings.

Holding	Argentine Pampas	Colombia	Chile	Peru
Subfamily (fewer than 2 workers)	3.2	4.9	0.2	7.4
Family-size (2–4 workers)	40.7	2.3	7.1	4.5
Medium multifamily (4–12 workers)	36.0	23.3	11.4	5.7
Large multifamily (over 12 workers)	20.1	69.5	81.3	82.4

Source: Solon L. Barraclough, "Agricultural Policy and Land Reform," Part II, Journal of Political Economy, 78 (July/August 1970). The Argentine figures are from Pan American Union, CIDA, Tenencia de la tierra, table 13, p. 32.

Technology, Investment, and Productivity

The general impression has long existed that Argentine agriculture is appallingly backward technologically and that many proven techniques are available today that, if adopted, could greatly increase productivity. This impression is undoubtedly correct in the sense that output per unit of land is far below that achieved in Europe and in other countries with scarce land resources, and that the degree of mechanization and use of manufactured inputs is much lower than in the United States and in other countries with relatively high labor costs and/or a protected agriculture. It is much more difficult, however, to evaluate the distance of Argentine agriculture behind the production possibility frontier determined by techniques that have actually proven profitable under pampean conditions. This distance depends on domestic research and extension efforts to adapt the impressive technological break-throughs of recent decades to local conditions, and on the degree to which relative prices have provided the correct signals for a "rational" allocation of resources. A priori reasoning with respect to these issues can lead to very mistaken policy conclusions.

Conditions in Argentina have in general been quite favorable for the adoption of modern commercial techniques of agricultural production since the pampas was opened up as the bread and beef basket of Europe. The organization of agriculture in rather large production units, the scarcity of indigenous labor and level terrain, the largely literate population, have all been conducive to mechanization and technical innovation. Argentina is said to be the first country in the world to have used the corn gatherer (*juntadora de maíz*) in 1903; it was in the vanguard of countries employing the airplane to fight locust plagues; and within twelve years after the United States combine was introduced in Argentina in 1918 over 30,000 units were in operation. At least until World War II Argentine agriculture did not appear to be lagging far behind the most advanced countries in the application of modern methods then available. Average per hectare yields of wheat, corn, linseed, and a number of other major crops in the 1930s were in fact higher in Argentina than they were in the United States.

Up to this time total farm output in Argentina appears to have expanded with approximately constant returns to scale and in fixed proportions between land, labor, and capital. From 1905-1909 to 1935-1939 total output and individual factor input indices approximately doubled, although there is some evidence of a decline in "total factor productivity" up to World War I and a recovery thereafter, according to estimates made by Carlos Diaz Alejandro.[9] Since the 1930s, however, land inputs have remained relatively constant, inputs of labor have fallen abruptly, and capital inputs, after remaining almost constant during the 1940s (the increase in cattle stocks offsetting a decline in machinery and equipment), began to increase rapidly in the 1950s. The net result of these trends in factor inputs and in total agricultural output was to raise the "total factor productivity" index in 1955-1959 to 132 (1935-1939 = 100), although changes in the composition of output and in factor proportions appear to have been so substantial since World War II as to cast serious doubt on the significance of this index.[10]

It is generally agreed that agricultural investment rose very substantially beginning in the 1950s,[11] but its effect on total factor productivity of the sector is hotly disputed. Some observers claim that this investment went almost entirely into replacing men and horses with mechanical motive power, leaving other production methods about the same as they were in the 1940s. The increase in the tractor pool was truly dramatic during this period and represented a large share of statistically measurable investment: from less than 30,000 in 1947 the number of tractors in use rose to approximately 120,000 in the mid-1960s.[12] This in itself must have had a significant impact on the value of output per hectare: the drop in the number of horses from over 6 million in 1937 to only 3 million in 1960 released land for cattle grazing or cropping, and greater use of the tractor must have permitted deeper plowing, more rapid and timely sowing and harvesting, and utilization of heavier, more modern equipment than could be drawn by horse.

What can be said, however, about technological improvements other than mechanization? Technical progress through greater use of current inputs such as improved seeds, fertilizer, pesticides, and better practices is more difficult to quantify than investment in machinery; but in 1965 a questionaire was circulated by a Ford Foundation-sponsored research team among commercial agricultural specialists in Argentina to ascertain prevailing technical levels in the production of different crops. The results shown in table 2-6 reveal extremely diverse levels of technological progress.

Use of improved seeds appears to be related to the period of time they have been commercially available in Argentina and to the rate of expansion in the area devoted to each particular crop. Improved varieties developed for use under Argentine conditions have been available for wheat, linseed, and barley since the 1930s, but

Table 2-6   Percent of crop area incorporating certain techniques.

Technique	Wheat	Corn	Linseed	Barley	Sun-flower	Sor-ghum
Improved seed	100	70	85	80	55	50
Fertilizer	1	0	0	0	0	0
Insecticides	5	1	85	0	90	5
Herbicides	10	90	40	2	0	25
Improved cultural practices	55	55	40	7	60	75

Source: Fienup, *Agricultural Development*, table 44, p. 123.

improved corn seed was only introduced in 1950. Sunflower and sorghum, on the other hand, are relatively newer crops, the former becoming an important user of land in the 1940s and the latter only in the 1950s and early 1960s; in these cases the supply of improved seed has not kept up with demand.[13] The use of improved cultural practices is related to similar factors: the newer the crop (sunflower and sorghum) or the more rapidly older crops have been expanding in recent years (corn and wheat), the more prevalent appears to be the employment of such practices.

The minimal use of fertilizer on pampean crops must be shocking to agronomists from other temperate climate agricultural countries. In some writings on the subject the lack of fertilizer application is attributed largely to the pride of farmers in the inexhaustable fertility of the pampean soil, but note the following comments on the result of fertilizer experiments in Argentina: "Fertilizer research has been carried out on corn since 1960, but there are still no definite recommendations on fertilizer application to this crop"; "INTA [the government agricultural research institute] has not made fertilizer recommendations for linseed, and response data are not available"; "there are no fertilizer recommendations for barley, and no research is currently being carried out by INTA to develop fertilizer recommendations"; "up to the present time INTA trials have shown little or no response to fertilizer on sunflower"; and "fertilizer research on sorghum has just recently been initiated and there are still no data available."[14]

Wheat, being by far the most important grain sown in the pampas and with the longest history of applied agronomical research, is the only major crop for which fertilizer experiments produced positive results by the mid-1960s. Even in this case, however, results have not been spectacular. In the previously cited report it is stated that if "wheat follows directly after corn, sunflower or sorghum on low fertility soils," a 50 percent rate of return could be realized from the use of fertilizer; but in another study citing results of over 200 fertilizer experiments carried out on wheat in 1962 and 1963 at the Pergamino and Balcarce stations of INTA, it was reported that increased yields paid for the cost of fertilizers in only 26 percent of the cases using nitrogen and in only 12 percent of the cases using P_2O_5, either alone or in combination with nitrogen.[15] These results are rather discouraging in view of the considered opinion of experts that increased yields of at least 50 percent or preferably 100 percent are necessary if rapid adoption of improved technology is to be achieved.

Evidence with respect to the use of improved seeds, fertilizer, insecticides (such as on linseed and sunflower), and herbicides (on corn in particular) and of improved cultural practices thus indicates that modern technology has been or is progressively being adopted in cases where such use has clearly proved profitable to farmers. If more rapid adoption is desired, greater efforts will have to be made in agricultural research and extension, and relative input/output prices will have to be altered to enhance the profitability of using new inputs. With regard to the first policy, it should be pointed out that INTA was only established in 1956 and that by the mid-1960s there was still only about one extension agent per 4,600 farm families in Argentina. The organization's recent growth indicates, however, that the technological frontier will probably be pushed back at an accelerating pace in the future and that the main constraint on the rate of technical progress may very likely be the availability of qualified agronomists and extension agents to help put it to use.

The problem of relative input/output prices will be dealt with in the next section, but a word should be said here about the prices of certain key inputs. Although domestic prices and exchange rates have fluctuated wildly during the period under analysis, it is probably accurate to say that fertilizers have in general been significantly more expensive than in the United States, but that the picture is more mixed with respect to insecticides, herbicides, and agricultural equipment. For example, benzene hexachloride, the most widely used insecticide in Argentina, was actually considerably cheaper than in the United States in 1964, and the domestic prices of windmills in general and of spreaders in 1955-1956 and automotive harvesters and high powered sprayers in 1961 also appeared to be competitive with international prices. Many other examples could of course be given of the opposite situation in view of the 20 to 300 percent import duties charged on agricultural inputs and the expansion of protected domestic production. What has clearly been lacking is a coherent agricultural input price policy.[16] Despite the lack of such a policy and spotty technological progress, however, Argentine agricultural productivity does not in general compare unfavorably with that in other countries employing mostly extensive techniques (see table 2-7).

Again we are confronted with the paradox of tremendous variability in performance. The change in Argentine yields since the 1930s ranges from plus 68 percent for wheat to minus 26 percent for sunflower, and although yields of wheat and linseed are higher in Argentina than in both Australia and Canada (and in the last mentioned crop even superior to average United States yields), corn does not appear to have responded at all to the introduction of hybrid seed and other improved practices. Even more perplexing, there seems to be little if any correlation between the rankings in tables 2-6 and 2-7. More detailed analysis of trends in wheat and corn cultivation, to take two of the extreme examples, may be of help in clarifying this paradox.

Improvement in Argentine wheat yields was particularly marked between prewar and the 1950s when sown area declined sharply, but further improvement was more modest when the area became stabilized at around 5 to 6 million hectares. Because there is a

Table 2-7   Yields of major crops in Argentina and in other countries using extensive methods of cultivation.

Crop	Average 1961/62 to 1963/64 in bushels per acre			Percent increase in yields 1935–40 to 1962–64
	Australia	Canada	Argentina	Argentina
Wheat	18.4	19.6	20.6	68
Corn	33.9	71.4	28.7	-4
Linseed	9.5	10.2	10.4	7
Barley	20.3	29.2	21.7	35
Sunflower	20.4	28.7	20.7	-26
Rye	6.6	16.7	11.2	25
Oats	24.2	44.7	33.9	41

Source: Fienup, Agricultural Production, table 34, p. 86.

spread of more than two to one between average yields in major producing regions of the country, the rapid increase in yields up to the 1950s is believed to be attributable in no small degree to a reduction of sowings on less suitable land. The area devoted to corn, on the other hand, fell by an even larger proportion than wheat between prewar and the 1950s, but as was observed in the previous section, corn was particularly hard hit by the shortage and higher cost of labor following the reforms of the 1940s. The consequent reduction in crop rotation (uncompensated by greater fertilization) also appears to have had especially serious repercussions on soil fertility in corn-growing areas. Following the introduction of hybrid seed in 1950 and rapid mechanization in recent years, however, corn yields have experienced an impressive recovery.[16]

Lucio Reca has attempted to estimate the contribution of technical change to the increase in output of individual crops by fitting the following Cobb-Douglas type function to the data in log form:

$$\text{Output} = \text{Area}^a + \text{Weather}^b + \text{Time}^c$$

where the exponent c is assumed to measure the yearly growth in production attributable to technical improvements. Estimated c values for wheat and corn during the period 1945-1965 were .0249 and .0311 respectively in Buenos Aires province and were significant at the 1 percent level. Significant technical change was also found in the provinces of Córdoba and Entre Rios for wheat and in Córdoba for corn. Rates of technical improvement of 2.5 to 3 percent per year are clearly encouraging if not spectacular.[18]

The most convincing indication of overall technological progress in the pampas is the simultaneous increase in total crop output and cattle herds on the same quantity of land. By 1935 some 92 percent of pampean cattle were "modern" breeds (that is, bred from imported stock), three quarters of which were of the fatty Shorthorn variety. The change in tastes toward leaner beef, particularly in markets other than the United Kingdom that became progressively more important for Argentine exports, led to the rapid multiplication of breeds such as the Aberdeen Angus to replace the Shorthorn, which by 1960 represented only about one third of total cattle numbers. This development is certainly indicative of a response of producers to market incentives and available technology, as was the increase in the area devoted to seeded pasture (as against natural grasses) from less than 7 million hectares before

Table 2-8 Comparison of beef cattle stock estimate. (millions of head)

Year	Official figures, June 30	Jarvis estimates June 30	Jarvis estimates Annual "availability"[a]	Reca estimates, June 30
	(1)	(2)	(3)	(4)
1948	41.0	41.1	47.7	–
1949	–	41.1	47.8	–
1950	–	40.9	47.6	–
1951	–	40.2	46.7	–
1952	45.7[b]	40.6	47.2	–
1953	41.2	40.4	47.0	–
1954	43.6	42.9	49.9	–
1955	43.8	45.8	53.3	–
1956	46.9	48.0	55.8	–
1957	44.0	48.6	56.5	–
1958	41.3	47.5	55.2	–
1959	41.2	46.0	53.4	–
1960	43.5[c]	45.9	53.4	45.4
1961	43.2	47.3	55.0	47.4
1962	43.2	48.6	56.2	48.6
1963	41.2	47.4	55.3	48.4
1964	–	46.5	54.0	46.9
1965	46.7	47.3	55.0	48.8
1966	–	49.8	57.9	51.5
1967	51.3[c]	51.8	60.2	52.8
1968	51.5[c]	–	–	52.9
1969	48.3[c]	–	–	52.9
1970	–	–	–	51.8

Source: Cols. (1)–(3), Lovell S. Jarvis, "Supply Response in the Cattle Industry," Ph.D. diss., MIT, 1969, table 4.1, p. 203; Col. (4), Lucio G. Reca, "El aumento de existencias de ganado vacuno en 1971," *Estudios sobre la economía argentina*, 11, (January 1972).

[a]Total number of animals available during the year equals number in herd at beginning of year plus total calves born during year. The official census date of June 30 falls just prior to the calving season.
[b]This figure, which corresponds to November 11, is generally considered to have a strong upward bias (see Jarvis, "Supply Response," p. 204).
[c]Junta Nacional de Carnes; figures for 1960 and 1969 are from agricultural censuses carried out on September 30.

World War II to about 13 million in the late 1950s and early 1960s.[19] More specific quantitative measurements of the productivity of cattle raising in Argentina are, however, exceedingly shaky.

The most serious statistical deficiency has been the lack of reliable data on the size of cattle herds. Improved and enlarged sampling techniques, together with the check now provided by the nearly 100 percent use of inoculations against hoof and mouth disease, have enabled new estimates to be made that inspire greater confidence. One of the best of these is by Jarvis, who has calculated that total cattle numbers rose from around 40 million at the beginning of the 1950s to almost 52 million in 1967, an increase of approximately 29 percent (see table 2-8). Even after adjusting pasture land for the decline in horses during this period, it does not appear that the area available for beef cattle increased by anything approximating this percentage. It seems reasonable to conclude, therefore, that there has been some improvement in the carrying capacity of pampean grasslands.[20]

Equally pertinent for measuring the productivity of meat production are figures on stock-flow relationships. The quantity of beef produced per head of stock of course fluctuates according to the phase of the cattle cycle, which has been especially violent in Argentina. In table 2-9, however, years are compared when stocks were relatively stable, although it has been particularly hard to find such periods in recent years. It nevertheless seems justified to conclude that the volume of meat produced per head has increased since the early 1950s.

Comparison of these figures with stock-flow relationships in other countries is an even more slippery business because of fundamental differences in methods of cattle raising. In Argentina, animals are bred and fattened on open range, whereas in the United States the use of feed lots for finishing has become dominant. Thus, output of beef per head of stock in Argentina today is similar to what it was in the United States before large scale adoption of the feed lot system prior to World War II; the current U.S. relationship is closer to 80

Table 2-9 Kilos of beef produced per head of cattle stock.

Period	Range of variation in cattle stock (millions of head)	Average annual production per head
1936/37–1939/40	35.6–36.2	47.7
1949/50–1952/53	40.2–40.9	47.5
1955/56–1957/58	47.5–48.6	49.0
1962/63–1964/65	46.5–47.4	50.0

Source: Cattle stocks from table 2–8; annual production is from official figures supplied by the National Meat Board (Junta Nacional de Carnes).

kilos of beef per head. In Canada, which also uses feed lots to a considerable extent, the rate is somewhat less—about 65 kilos per head in 1962/63-1964/65 according to the FAO *Production Yearbook*—and in Australia, where production methods are more similar to those in Argentina, the average during the same period was a little over 50 kilos per head, or about the same as in Argentina. It would appear, therefore, that although there is ample scope for increasing the carrying capacity of pasture in the pampas, for improving animal nutrition, for reducing mortality rates, and for adopting other technical improvements, further important physical productivity gains are likely to come mainly through a change in the organization of production, the economic advantage of which again depends largely on relative factor and product prices and their stability.

Relative Prices

The extent and rapidity of farmer response to changes in relative agricultural prices is a controversial topic in Argentina which can only be understood in the context of the acrimonious struggle between rural and nonrural interests since the rise of Perón to power. Before Perón the state had already begun to intervene widely in agricultural marketing by establishing support prices and a Grain Regulating Board in 1933, by introducing foreign exchange controls, by buying and burning grain surpluses during World War II, and by other measures that were about as interventionalist as Perón's later policies except that they were intended largely to protect agricultural interests, not to attack them. Under Perón the Grain Regulating Board was replaced by the Argentine Trade Promotion Institute (IAPI) which was used along with exchange regulations to capture for the government most of the windfall from high export commodity prices after the war. Even when domestic inflation accelerated and world market prices declined, IAPI continued its policy of buying cheap and selling dear, with the result that the domestic terms of trade turned sharply against agriculture.

Beginning with Perón's new economic policy introduced in 1952 and continuing in subsequent years in response to the series of exchange rate devaluations and decontrols, relative agricultural prices began to improve and by the early 1960s regained approximately their prewar level (see table 2-10). Year to year fluctuations, however, were extremely violent: between 1952 and 1964 the average annual rate of improvement in the ratio of

Table 2-10 Indices of the "real" exchange rate and relative agricultural prices in Argentina. (indices 1935-1939 = 100)

Years	(A) Real average exchange rate for exports	(B) Ratio of rural/nonrural wholesale prices	(C) Ratio of rural/nonrural implicit GDP prices
1953–55	50	68	85
1956–58	104	78	93
1959–61	109	85	96
1962–64	94	93	103
1965–67	89	78	97
1968–69	105	75	95

Source: Diaz Alejandro, *Essays*, tables 2.12, 2.13, and 2.15, pp. 88–92. The figures in column A represent the average annual exchange rate for merchandise exports (in pesos per dollar) divided by the ratio of the Argentine to United States wholesale price indices. Figures for 1965–67 and 1968–69 were estimated by the authors from official statistics.

wholesale prices of rural to nonrural goods was about 3.7 percent, but the standard deviation of this ratio was 7.6 percent, or over twice as great (using half-yearly data). Such instability certainly must have had an effect on the way relative price signals were interpreted for purposes of resource allocation.

It is very difficult to say anything meaningful about the "adequacy" of the current overall level of relative agricultural prices. To draw any firm conclusion from relative price data one must assume that the commodity terms of trade accurately reflect movements in the factoral terms of trade, that is, in income accruing to factors of production instead of increases in the cost of material inputs per unit of output. We have seen that there has probably been some improvement in total factoral productivity in agriculture since prewar, but it is quite impossible on the basis of existing information to compare long-term changes in the productivity of factors in competing uses. If, however, the presumption is made that manufacturing has become relatively less "efficient" over time because of rising protective barriers, it is conceivable that restoration of the prewar terms of trade may have enabled agriculture to bid away factors of production from industry. This is even more likely in view of the fact that the incidence of domestic taxation has since the mid-1950s fallen much more heavily on industry than on agriculture.

Trends in the overall agricultural commodity terms of trade in other countries that are major exporters of temperate agriculture commodities are compared with those in Argentina in figure 2-2. Their improvement in Argentina during the 1950s was opposite to the trend in other countries, but relative wholesale prices of agricultural goods still remained lower in Argentina even by the 1960s. This is not true, however, with respect to agricultural parity price indices, that is, the ratio of prices received to prices paid by farmers.[21] This discrepancy, however, may be due largely to changes in intrasectoral agricultural prices and the resulting shifts in the composition of output, which have been so pronounced that base year weights tend to give a downward bias to the wholesale agricultural price index.[22]

More relevant than intersectoral relative price trends in the analysis of export production incentives is the extent to which intrasectoral price changes reflect international market signals. It is quite conceivable that the favorable allocation effects of an improvement in the overall relative agricultural price level could be largely offset by increasing distortions in the structure of individual commodity prices. Such distortions were undoubtedly introduced by

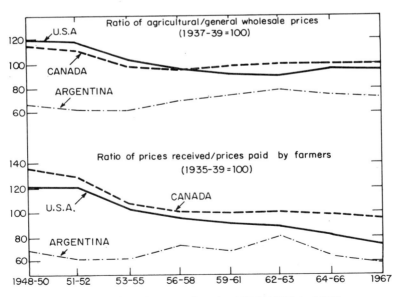

Figure 2-2. Agricultural terms of trade, 1948–1950 to 1967.

government policy in Argentina during the period between prewar and the early 1950s and may have continued to have been generated by erratic year-to-year fluctuations in exchange rates, differential export taxes, and the wild cattle cycle during much of the subsequent period.[23] Recent longer term trends in relative intrasectoral prices in Argentina, however, do not appear to deviate substantially from those in the United States, Canada, and Australia, as can be seen in figure 2-3.

The relative price of wheat, which has been taken as the numeraire for other comparisons in figure 2-3, declined in a similar fashion in both Argentina and the United States, and the very sharp rise in the beef/wheat price ratio since prewar has been common in all countries compared. The behavior of relative maize and linseed prices in Argentina also does not appear to be far out of line with trends in other producing countries. As will be seen below, relative prices and factor productivities (what might be called "revealed" comparative advantage) as of the late 1960s strongly favored expansion of beef and maize production at the expense of wheat and other crops. According to the FAO, this is in line with future foreign trade expectations: in a recent study meat and coarse grains were singled out with forest products as the commodities developing countries would be most wise to promote, whereas "import requirements of wheat will tend to decline."[24]

Getting price signals "right" would of course be irrelevant for policy if farmers do not respond to changes in relative prices, a possibility that is still hotly debated in Argentina. One of the reasons for skepticism is that the increase in total production following improvement in the rural terms of trade was rather slow and irregular, and no reversal in production trends was noticeable as a result of the moderate decline in relative agricultural prices after 1964. Considerable significance has also been given to the mixed results produced by regression studies of the price-elasticity of total output. Diaz-Alejandro was not very successful with data for the period 1929-1965 and neither was Colomé for the periods 1941-1959 and 1945-1959, although for the years 1945-1960 he finally found a relative price elasticity of about 0.4 that was statistically significant at the 5 percent level. Perhaps the most serious attempt in Argentina to specify and estimate a total supply response model has been made by Lucio Reca for the period 1935-1967.[25]

Reca's justification for the specification of his model is, in brief: "When the supply of one or more factors of production is limited—in the sense that the producer cannot use the quantity of a

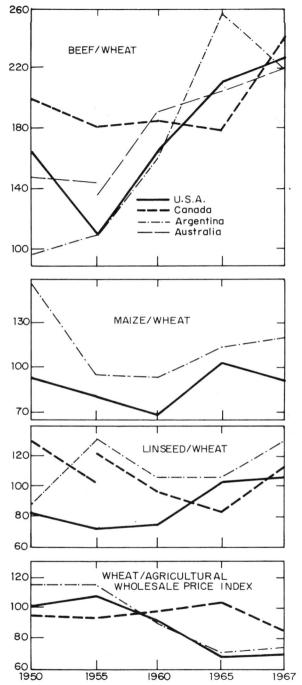

Figure 2-3. Relative prices of major agricultural commodities, 1950–1967 (1934–38=100).

factor in a way which would equate its marginal product to its price, but must use a smaller quantity—then it is legitimate to formulate a supply function in terms of the price of the product, the price of inputs whose supply is limited."[26] He then proceeds to estimate the following equation by simple least squares, in which the variables are expressed as indices:

$$Q_t = -15.24 + .518\, P_{t-1} + .173\, L_{t-1} + .468\, K_t + 13.42\, D_1 - 6.40\, D_2;$$
$$ (20.46)\ (.136) \qquad (.043) \qquad\ (.199) \qquad (4.20) \qquad (3.40)$$

$$R_2 = .784, \qquad DW = 1.81$$

Where:

Q_t = index of volume of agricultural production with 1960–1965 weights and the year 1960 = 100;

P_{t-1} = ratio of agricultural to nonagricultural implicit GDP prices lagged one year with 1960 = 100;

L_{t-1} = index of short-term credits to agriculture;

K_t = index of tractor horsepower used by the sector;

D_1 and
D_2 = dummy variables representing special conditions during the war years 1940–1944 and Perón's early policies during 1948–1953.

The coefficient of the price variable is highly significant, the price elasticity measured from the mean being .48. But the question must be raised as to what extent the correlation may be spurious because of multicolinearity, since both price and output trends have been upwards during the latter half of the period and the variables are measured in terms of indices, not first differences or percentage changes. Reca has helped throw light on this question by including in a second estimation of his model a time trend variable (which is given a value of zero up to 1958/1959 because he considers that technological change was minimal until this year). The new variable is found to be highly significant, raises the R^2 to .875, reduces the serial correlation of residuals, wipes out the significance of the variable K, and reduces the average price elasticity to .31 (and to only .24 at the end of the period).

A more basic criticism of results obtained from total agricultural supply response models must also be mentioned. If as in the pampas there is no more land to be brought under cultivation, increases in total output must be obtained from more intensive working of the soil, either through larger fixed investment or greater use of current inputs and improved techniques of cultivation. Is it reasonable to expect these factors to be reflected in year-to-year variations in output and correlated with annual fluctuations in relative prices, or is it more realistic to assume that such improvements respond to longer run expectations, and that once undertaken they tend to be irreversible over the short run? Institutional changes, the general spread of knowledge about new techniques, and productivity increase "embodied" in machines to replace labor and horses have also exercised great influence on the "efficiency" of Argentine agriculture but clearly are not necessarily related to annual variations in relative output prices. It is of course not necessary to deny the existence of a long-term relationship between increases in productivity and improvement in relative agricultural prices in order to question the policy significance of statistically measured elasticities in such models.

The policy implications of statistically-measured elasticities of supply of individual agricultural commodities in the short run, on the other hand, are not subject to the same kind of criticism. It can reasonably be assumed that the quantity and quality of factors, resources, and production functions remain approximately constant from one year to the next. Quantitative evidence on the elasticity of substitution between commodities competing for use of the same resources would thus be of great help in formulating short-term government price policies. Actual attempts at measuring such elasticities, however, have not met with much success in Argentina. Reca attributes this lack of success to institutional factors by concluding from his own experiments "that producers' decisions closely followed the price signals generated in the economic system in the first period up to 1944, whereas in the second period price influences on land allocation were, at most, weak."[27] This conclusion seems reasonable in view of the market disruptions that occurred during the 1940s and 1950s, the prevalence of great price instability, and the existence of land rent controls, which permitted rates of return to tenants to deviate widely from what would otherwise be expected from changes in relative agricultural prices. [28]

Fortunately more is known about the effect of relative prices on substitution between cattle raising and crops over the cattle cycle. Cattle raising is a particularly important source of agricultural instability in Argentina because (1) the carrying capacity of pastures is highly susceptible to climatic variations, and (2) over the short run the supply function of beef is negatively sloped, that is to say, the larger the increase in price the smaller the supply. The first reason is quite obvious when one recalls that pasture in Argentina is not artificially irrigated, that much of it is natural grassland, and that sources of supplemental feeding during droughts are still very limited. The second reason, however, will not be so obvious to most readers.

As Jarvis says, "the simultaneity involved in the cattle sector must be captured through the competitive bidding process which takes place between consumers and producers."[29] In other words, meat animals are both capital and consumer goods. If consumers want more beef and bid up the price, the first response of cattle raisers is to retain a larger proportion of cows and heifers for breeding and to hold other animals a little longer for fattening before sending them to market. Thus, the relative price of beef should be negatively correlated with changes in volume of slaughter and positively correlated with average slaughter weight. Actual relationships appear to be rather more complicated than implied in this simple statement, but in general it is well confirmed by the evidence. Diaz Alejandro, for example, estimated the following regression equation for the period 1943-1962:[30]

$$b_t = 1.517 - 0.203\ pb_t - 0.359\ pb_{t-1} + 0.062\ pb_{t-2};\ R^2 = .48$$
$$(0.118) \qquad (0.114) \qquad\quad (0.120)$$

Where:

b_t = slaughter of beef in year t divided by slaughter of beef in year $t-1$;

pb_t = index of beef prices relative to wholesale rural prices in year t divided by the same index for year $t-1$; same procedure applicable to pb_{t-1} and pb_{t-2}.

These findings indicate that slaughter is negatively correlated with changes in relative beef prices in both years t and t-1 and becomes positively correlated only in year t-2, thus suggesting a two-year lag in the response of supply. More disaggregated analysis by Jarvis leads to the same general conclusion, although he finds the behavior of different categories of animals vis-à-vis changes in relative prices quite different: the sign of price coefficients in slaughter functions for certain classes of steers and bulls becomes positive in year t-1, whereas the sign remains negative for relative prices of yearlings and heifers right up to year t-3 and in some cases even longer. The R^2's in these disaggregated slaughter functions are also much larger than in Diaz Alejandro's estimate. Finally, Jarvis's slaughter weight functions confirm the hypothesis that the average weight of animals delivered to market is positively correlated with current year relative prices of beef. The positive effect on the supply of beef of the weight increase is far from sufficient, however, to offset the negative effect of the reduction in the number of animals delivered to market.[31]

The inverse correlation between annual changes in cropped area in the pampas and in livestock numbers is indicative of the short-term policy problem created by the cattle cycle. One investigator has estimated that for every increase of two head in cattle stocks, approximately one hectare of land is withdrawn from crop cultivation.[32] This means that a 5 percent increase in cattle herds (in some years actual changes have been substantially larger) would *ceteris paribus* be accompanied by nearly a 10 percent reduction in cropped area; and since in the short run an expansion in cattle numbers leads to a reduction in the supply of beef, the total supply of agricultural products for export and domestic consumption would be drastically curtailed.

Summary and Conclusions

An explanation of the results of Martin Piñeiro's research experiment will help pull together some of the findings in this chapter and bring their policy implications into focus. Based on field surveys of the best technology available at agricultural experiment stations in Argentina in the late 1960's, Piñeiro used a linear programming model to estimate the composition and value of output by major regions that could be produced with an optimal use of resources at 1967 prices. He concluded that "complete adoption of known technology and optimum land use would result in approximately a 28 percent increase in aggregate production over the 1964-66 level." Furthermore, since much of the increase in output was programmed to come from a major reallocation of land to the production of beef, Piñeiro concluded that the out-migration of labor from agriculture would have to be accelerated to avoid rural unemployment and that the existing rate of fixed investment in the sector was more than sufficient to finance the desired transformation of the structure of production.[33]

To give some idea of the adequacy of a 28 percent increase in agricultural production, such an increment would, in the absence of a rise in the share of agricultural output exported, just permit Argentina to reach the $2 billion export target that national planners have projected would be necessary to maintain balance of payments equilibrium with full employment in the early 1970s. The "necessary" rate of agricultural expansion of course depends on the relative rates of growth of GDP, domestic demand for agricultural goods, the demand for imports, and nonagricultural exports;[34] but it is highly unlikely that the 1960-1969 annual rate of rural output expansion of 2.2 percent could support the target rates of growth of GDP included in the last two national development plans (a minimum of 5 percent per year). The conclusion is therefore unavoidable that Argentina must find some way to accelerate agricultural growth so as to prevent the balance of payments constraint from continuing to be a severe limitation on its overall rate of development, at least until nonagricultural exports become more important.

The policy options open to Argentine decision-makers emerge rather clearly from the foregoing analysis and Piñeiro's research results: to sustain a relatively high rate of national economic growth, relative agricultural prices must be permitted to rise quite substantially over time; or cost-reducing technological progress must be greatly accelerated so that the necessary output expansion can be achieved with constant or declining real average costs of production. With regard to the first option, Argentine experience suggests that a substantial increase in relative food prices cannot be achieved under conditions even approximating full employment. Under such conditions rising food prices tend to accelerate the wage-price spiral, which wipes out any initial improvement in the agricultural terms of trade unless real wages are forced down by rising unemployment. It is more difficult to appraise the conditions under which the second policy option might prove practicable. Considerable room for further technical progress beyond that available at Argentine agricultural experiment stations in the late 1960s must be possible, but little research has been carried out on the effect of adopting even already proven technology on average production costs.[35]

Regardless of whether technical progress will be cost-reducing or not, the rate of adoption of new agricultural techniques will be a most important determinant, not only of the overall rate of growth of the economy, but also of the distribution of increased real income between wages and land rents. This conclusion not only underscores the importance of greatly accelerating agricultural research and extension efforts, but it also points to the desirability of doing everything possible to assure that rates of return from the adoption of techniques actually proven profitable under Argentine conditions are sufficient to encourage their rapid acceptance. This would suggest that government policy, as long as it is constrained by limited upward flexibility of relative output prices, should be more concerned than it has been in the past about measures designed explicitly to reduce the cost of innovations, such as by making fertilizer, insecticides, and other modern inputs more readily available at more attractive prices, and by enlarging the selective, supervised credit program begun in the 1960s to expand artificial pasture in the main cattle breeding areas, if not to promote the feed lot method of production on a wide scale.

The analysis in this chapter also suggests that the extreme instability of relative agricultural prices is an important problem. If the chief function of relative prices is to serve as signals for resource allocation—and there is no reason to believe that Argentine commercial farmers are impervious to changes in relative prices, even though quantitative evidence is scanty—then it stands to reason that great price uncertainty dampens the price response of farmers and puts a premium on maintaining maximum flexibility in the use of resources that can be shifted quickly between pasture and different crops. Under these circumstances investments with relatively long pay-out periods in single-purpose equipment or in improvements such as in permanent pasture which promote specialization in land use might be very unattractive to individual farmers, even though they would prove profitable under conditions of greater price stability. Evidence is gradually accumulating that excessive diversification as a hedge against uncertainty may be impeding the adoption of certain kinds of modern technology and the fuller utilization of regional comparative advantages.[36]

It would of course be absurd to consider completely eliminating relative price variations; "permissable" price instability is a question of degree, and like all such concepts it is an exceedingly difficult one to quantify. But as long as the Argentine economy remains partially closed and the government manipulates powerful tools that inevitably influence relative prices, it is preferable that these tools be used in accordance with an explicit price policy instead of assuming incongruously that free market forces will automatically determine correct price relationships. The most important government tools in this context are exchange rate policy and export retentions (taxes), and to a lesser extent agricultural support prices, which in most years have been fixed below actual domestic market prices for all commodities except wheat.

The main objective of exchange rate and export retention management should be to prevent overall agricultural price increases from lagging seriously behind movements in the general domestic price level, while not interfering with world-market-induced trends in intrasectoral relative prices. The danger of explicit official price management is of course that the authorities will be tempted to use differential rates to try to capture "windfall" profits for the treasury from exporters of commodities with rising prices and to grant favored treatment to those with falling prices. Such a policy, unless it is strictly for the purpose of compensating random short-term fluctuations, would obviously impede the desirable reallocation of resources for maximum export growth without producing any other redeeming social benefits. [37]

The cattle cycle poses a unique problem that, because of its great potential impact on the total short-term supply of agricultural goods, must be given special consideration. Measures aimed directly at insulating feed availabilities from the effects of weather variations should be encouraged, such as expansion of artificial pasture sown with drought-resistant grasses, construction of on-farm fodder storage, and the supplemental feeding of animals, which in any event is very likely to beome increasingly attractive to cattle raisers in view of world market trends and projections. It would also be desirable for Argentine authorities to follow conscious policies that help smooth out violent short-term fluctuations in relative beef prices that will probably continue to occur from time to time. Despite the dangers inherent in attempted price manipulation, the reoccurrence of disruptions in agricultural commodity markets caused by the cattle cycle is an even greater threat to the successful management of macroeconomic policy in Argentina.

Finally, even though no firm conclusion can be reached about the economic effects of land tenure patterns in the pampas, it would nevertheless be advisable to strengthen fiscal measures that make it more expensive for large rural property owners to underutilize land. A substantial increase in land taxes would be the most suitable instrument for this purpose. Such taxes have in the past been held at low levels because the power to tax land is vested exclusively in the provinces, where the political influence of landowners tends to be strong. Action by individual provinces has also been severely limited by their understandable reluctance to create tax differentials with neighboring jurisdictions on adjacent land. Krieger Vasena attempted to get around this problem by introducing a national tax on the presumptive income from farm land partly in lieu of income tax, but evidence on the results of this experiment is still too sketchy to judge its success.

The importance of fiscal reform for assuring more satisfactory agricultural performance cannot be overstressed. Because provincial land taxes have been so low and income taxes are difficult to collect from farmers, the national government has felt justified in levying taxes on agricultural output and exports. The incidence of taxation has therefore served to discourage the fuller utilization of land. Higher taxes on rural property, offset by a reduction in taxes on output and exports, would in contrast serve as a positive stimulus to farmers to raise output per hectare, by increasing their net income from incremental sales. At the same time the fiscal authorities would be assured of capturing an appropriate share of unearned income from agriculture as land became scarcer and rents rose. Fiscal policy that promotes a broader distribution of farm income and land utilization might also help, in the absence of a very unlikely major land reform, convince large numbers of Argentines that policies aimed at accelerating export expansion are not politically biased in favor of *agro-exportador* interests but are really in the common good.

3 Industrialization and Foreign Trade

Industrialization as a natural outgrowth of development has a long history in Argentina. As a specific development strategy, promoted by strongly protectionist measures, special incentives, and direct government action, it dates from the beginning of the Great Depression. Not that tariffs were negligible prior to 1930, or that the bias toward maintaining a relatively depreciated exchange rate in earlier years did not provide considerable protection for certain domestic manufacturing activities; but the level of protection was much closer to that prevailing in advanced countries at the time, and quantitative trade controls had not yet come into use.[1]

By the turn of the century about 20 percent of the nation's labor force was already engaged in manufacturing, which accounted for between 10 and 15 percent of total gross domestic product.[2] Argentina had therefore reached by this time a degree of industrialization that the "average" developing country did not attain until well after World War II. According to the 1914 census of manufacturing, over 50 percent of gross value of industrial production was generated by the food and beverages subsector, although the rest of output was rather widely diversified. The relative importance and structure of the industrial sector did not change very much up to 1930: total GDP, manufacturing, and foreign trade grew at similar rates (between 4.5 and 5.5 percent per year), and the value of imports remained at about 25 percent of GDP (measured in prices of 1950).[3]

After adoption of the strategy of forced industrialization at the advent of the Great Depression, both the relative rate of growth and the structure of manufacturing changed markedly. In the thirty years following 1925-1929, the quantum of imports is estimated to have declined absolutely by approximately one quarter, and relatively to about 8 percent of GDP (also at 1950 prices). At the same time, value added in manufacturing grew at a rate 40 percent faster than total GDP, so that by the late 1950s the sector had increased its share of gross product by at least one half (from 14 to 21 percent in prices of 1935, and from 19 to 30 percent in 1960 prices). This impressive industrial take-off was, however, more firmly rooted in the pre-existing manufacturing establishment than might be imagined. As late as 1948 the census of manufacturing revealed that over 60 percent of output was still produced by firms started before 1930.

Despite frequent allegations to the contrary, international comparisons of economic structure do not indicate that the accelerated pace of Argentine industrialization created an "excessively" large manufacturing sector in relation to the country's size and per capita income.[4] Such comparisons, however, say little about the optimum allocation of resources in any particular country, that is, whether a different use of a nation's resources could have generated more rapid growth. It can be argued that during the Great Depression and World War II Argentina had little alternative but to force the pace of industrialization.[5] Had the government followed a more energetic policy of pushing agricultural exports into weak international markets, the country's terms of trade might well have declined even more abruptly and produced a slower rate of growth. Development alternatives were also severely limited during World War II, when large amounts of grain had to be burned for lack of shipping capacity. It was only after the war that the country's development policy can be faulted for not adjusting rapidly enough to the opportunities provided by the unexpected boom in world trade.

Contrary to popular belief, however, Perón's postwar policies were not strongly proindustry and antitrade biased up to 1948. Foreign trade (and to a lesser extent construction activity) again became the main engine of economic growth for a brief period: between 1945 and 1948 commerce and transportation were the leading economic sectors, agricultural crop production almost kept pace with manufacturing output, and the change in the share of industry in GDP was negligible. Some Argentine industries in fact suffered a cutback in output due to renewed import competition, notably a number of rolled iron and steel products, textile machinery, most kinds of marine vessels, and a variety of other consumer and producer durable goods. It was not until after the balance of payments crisis of 1948 that the push toward greater industrial autarchy was renewed in directions quite different from those of prior years. It was largely this difference that led to the later debate about the possible "exhaustion" of import substituting possibilities in Argentina and cast doubt on the external viability of Frondizi's "developmentalist" industrialization strategy.

Import Substituting Industrialization (ISI), 1930-1970

By any definition of the term, the two decades between 1930 and 1950 were a period of strong import substitution. It has been estimated that imports of manufactures fell from 45 percent of the

Table 3-1 Import coefficients, total and by sector, 1925–1929 to 1945–1949. (valued in constant pesos of 1950)

Years	Total imports as percent of GDP	Imports of consumer goods as percent of total con- sumption	Imports of intermediate goods as percent of final demand for manu- factures	Imports of machinery and equipment as percent of total domestic investment in machinery and equipment
1925–29	24.8	13.3	21.0	35.3
1935–39	14.8	6.8	17.4	26.4
1945–49	9.8	3.2	13.4	19.7

Source: ECLA, *El desarrollo económico,* Part I, tables 16 and 17, pp. 82–83. These coefficients are of course distorted both by general overvaluation of the peso in 1950 and by the existence of multiple exchange rates, but they are thought to reflect trends fairly accurately.

total domestic supply of industrial goods in 1929 to only 15 percent in 1950, at this time one of the smallest shares for all medium-sized countries outside of the socialist bloc.[6] Import substitution was most significant in final consumer goods, but the share of imports in total domestic supplies of capital goods and intermediate products also declined steeply (see table 3-1). This evidence of the broad sectoral impact of import substitution is at variance with the widely held belief in Argentina that at least until the early 1950s, if not until the advent of Frondizi, industrialization policy emphasized "light" instead of "heavy" industries, or activities producing final goods rather than intermediate or "basic" products. Even by the end of the 1960s the share of intermediate goods in total manufacturing output still had not changed appreciably despite the expansion in basic steel, chemicals, paper, and pulp production.[7]

It is much more revealing to analyze changes in the structure of industry and import substitution by product groups instead of according to broad end-use categories. In table 3-2 the composition of industrial GDP is given separately for the periods 1925-1929, 1948-1950, and 1967-1969. Changes between the first two periods were strongly influenced by the textile revolution, which succeeded in reducing imports of textiles (both final and intermediate goods) from over 25 percent of the total value of imports in 1928-1929 to less than 10 percent after 1950.[8] Subsequent changes in the structure of production are more difficult to characterize, because aside from the decline in the share of textiles, the same groups of industries contin- ued to lose and to gain in relative importance.

Table 3-2 Structure of manufacturing GDP, 1925–1929 to 1967–1969. (percent of total at factor cost)

Product	1925–29	1948–50	1967–69
Food, beverages, and tobacco	37.4	26.1	19.3
Clothing and leather	13.4	10.6	5.3
Stone, glass, and wood	10.1	7.2	6.7
Printing and publishing	9.8	4.0	3.5
Handicrafts	9.6	8.7	6.0
Subtotal	80.3	56.6	40.8
Textiles	2.9	11.7	7.4
Vehicles and machinery	2.9	9.6	16.5
Metals	4.5	6.5	9.7
Petroleum refining	1.6	5.3	8.7
Chemicals	5.7	5.8	7.9
Electrical machinery and appliances	–	2.0	5.8
Paper and rubber	1.9	2.6	3.2
Subtotal	16.6	31.8	51.8
Total mannufacturing	100.0	100.0	100.0

Source: Diaz Alejandro, *Essays*, table 4.8, p. 224. The figures for 1967–69 are from the Central Bank.

To understand the significance of Argentine industrialization during the second period it is necessary to subdivide the period and disaggregate the composition of output further (see table 3-3). The big push in the manufacture of machinery, equipment, and electrical apparatus occurred in the 1950s when consumer durable imports were rapidly replaced by domestic production. Once this process was largely completed, local output stablized or actually declined: for example, peak production was reached for washing machines and stoves in 1957, sewing machines in 1959, bicycles and motorcycles in 1960, and television sets in 1961. Production of railway and agricultural machinery and equipment also reached a high point in 1960. During the subsequent decade, output of the subsectors producing these goods (with the important exception of automotive vehicles and their components) grew by substantially less than the overall industrial production index.

The fast growers in the 1960s were basic metals and chemicals, notably iron and steel, industrial chemicals, synthetic fibers and resins, and petroleum derivatives. Also in this group were internal

Table 3-3 Industrial production indices, 1950-1969.

Industry	1950	1955	1960	1965	1969
"Traditional" Industries					
Food, beverages, and tobacco	87.5	93.2	100	122.9	145.8
Textiles, clothing, and leather	90.7	99.2	100	109.6	115.9
Wood products	84.7	107.4	100	129.9	144.1
Paper, printing, and publishing	85.7	96.2	100	138.9	160.8
Nonmetallic minerals	86.1	87.4	100	127.3	178.0
"Growth" Industries					
Chemicals	53.2	76.6	100	156.7	202.6
Industrial chemicals	54.6	87.8	100	258.3	332.4
Synthetics and plastics	48.3	69.2	100	402.1	452.3
Petroleum derivatives	136.6	161.6	100	161.0	414.7
Basic metals	37.4	73.9	100	180.2	230.5
Iron and steel	31.1	72.0	100	199.9	255.9
Machinery and equipment	37.7	56.8	100	145.2	181.8
Motors	12.1	27.9	100	469.6	750.7
Automotive vehicles	23.8	31.7	100	200.8	251.7
Radio and T.V.	10.2	19.7	100	113.2	127.0
Electrical household goods	25.8	78.1	100	109.3	133.3
Motorcycles and bicycles	5.2	26.4	100	33.9	24.0
Agricultural machinery and equipment	15.7	44.4	100	88.8	79.8
Total index	66.8	81.1	100	134.5	163.7

Source: Banco Central, *Origen del producto*, table 47.

combustion engines and scientific control and measuring instruments, the demand for which was stimulated by the obligation of the automotive industry to use an increasing share of locally manufactured components. The automotive industry itself also continued to expand considerably more rapidly than the overall production index after 1960, but more irregularly than before.

The growth industries enumerated above, which by 1965 represented about half of total manufacturing GDP (as against only about one fourth in 1950), share certain common characteristics. In the first place, most of them require more modern technology than Argentina's traditional industrial activities. Since most of this technology was not available locally, foreign-controlled enterprises became increasingly important during the period, particularly in the production of automotive vehicles, a number of other consumer durable lines, agricultural equipment, the manufacture of components, industrial chemicals, and to a lesser, though still important extent, in basic metals.

Second, many of the new industries apparently benefit from increasing returns to scale. Although this tends to be true internationally for basic metals and chemicals, the larger scale required for assembling and finishing modern engineering goods under conditions of strict quality control must be understood in relation to the very small scale of operation that on average previously existed in Argentine engineering production. The larger scale requirements of new industries has in turn tended to concentrate increased output in a smaller number of firms.

Finally, partly as a result of the two previously mentioned characteristics, the new growth industries have tended to be more capital and/or skilled labor intensive. Whereas these industries as a whole accounted for over 50 percent of total manufacturing value added in 1969, they employed only about 37 percent of the industrial labor force. In 1950, in contrast, their shares of manufacturing value added and employment were approximately the same. This shift is all the more impressive in that the rest of Argentine industry was also becoming less labor intensive: between 1950 and 1969 the other, slower growing sectors increased their total output by over 50 percent with a negligible increase in employment (see table 3-4).

The shift in overall production functions brought about by development of these new activities, the revision of foreign investment and import policies, and institutional changes affecting the organization of labor (particularly measures taken after the overthrow of Perón to weaken labor unions and ease the mobility of labor between occupations and within plants) was so abrupt that the periods before and after the mid-1950s have been described as belonging to different technological epochs.[9] Whereas industrial employment between the 1930s and mid-1950s increased by a good deal more than output, during the next fifteen years it grew only one fourth as much (and after 1958 hardly at all). The output/capital ratio in manufacturing changed in exactly the opposite way, although the magnitude of the earlier rise and the subsequent fall in the ratio varies greatly depending upon the particular capital estimates used. It is thus difficult to reach any conclusion about the long-term trend in total factor productivity. According to one source, the opposite movements in labor and capital/output ratios were largely offsetting, whereas another serious researcher maintains that only about 10 percent of the increase in industrial output between 1954 and 1961 can be explained by increases in the quantity of labor and capital inputs.[10]

There is nevertheless no doubt that industrial development after

Table 3–4 Industrial employment, 1950–1969. (thousands of paid employees)

Industry	1950	1955	1958[a]	1960	1965	1969
"Traditional" Industries						
Food, beverages, and tobacco	301	308	331	294	279	313
Textiles, clothing, and leather	305	277	268	252	264	262
Wood products	85	68	70	63	64	78
Paper, printing, and publishing	60	63	67	65	77	91
Nonmetallic minerals	87	76	79	74	71	89
Other industries (mainly handicraft)	173	175	183	174	181	187
Subtotal	1,011	967	998	922	936	1,020
"Growth" Industries						
Chemicals	75	91	110	111	118	114
Basic metals	135	157	165	152	164	195
Machinery and equipment	195	245	309	321	326	303
Subtotal	405	493	584	584	608	612
Total	1,415	1,460	1,582	1,506	1,544	1,631

Source: Banco Central, *Origen del producto*, table 36.

[a]Year of peak employment not exceeded until 1968.

the mid-1950s was on average increasingly capital-intensive. The expanding role of foreign enterprise also seems to be pretty well documented. Private United States investment in Argentine industry amounted to almost half a billion dollars between 1956 and 1966 and exceeded that invested in manufacturing in any other Latin American country during the period.[11] By the late 1960s foreign controlled enterprises are estimated to have accounted for 25 to 30 percent of the Argentine market for domestically produced manufactured goods; and out of the ten largest firms in Argentina, which together account for about 10 percent of total industrial output, seven are subsidiaries of foreign companies. Foreign firms also tend to be concentrated in technology-intensive industries.[12]

It is much more difficult, on the other hand, to document the skill intensiveness or the prevalence of increasing returns to scale in Argentina's new growth industries. If it is assumed that average wages and salaries per employed person are a good proxy for skill intensity, then all of these industries require more skilled labor than manufacturing as a whole, some such as petroleum derivatives, chemicals, and electrical machinery and apparatus very substantially more. These same activities also employ a larger than average share of executives, professionals, technicians, and administrators (what are called "employees" in contrast to "workers" in Argentine labor statistics).[13]

Many references can be found in the technical literature to "minimum economic scales of production," although quantitative evidence on the relation between size of plant and average production costs is extremely hard to come by. In those manufacturing processes utilizing large nondivisible installations such as cylindrical towers and spheres (petrochemicals is a good example), the engineering rule of thumb is that productive capacity increases in proportion to the volume of these installations whereas costs increase only in proportion to their surface area. Empirical research carried out in other countries indicates furthermore that not only petrochemicals but also most other rapid growth industries in Argentina tend to enjoy increasing returns to scale.[14] Research carried out in Argentina, although sparse, at least does not appear to contradict this impression.[15]

It can therefore be concluded with a reasonable degree of confidence that Argentine industry entered an important new phase in the 1950s. After many years of semiautarchical industrialization in which expansion was achieved mainly through additional physical inputs with little change in technology, the country suddenly opened the door to the technological revolution that had been passing it by. This development had very profound repercussions that have also been widely observed in other countries passing through a similar stage of industrialization: (1) the gap between the rate of expansion in industrial output and employment has widened and has therefore contributed to the problem of urban unemployment; (2) many of the new technology industries appear to enjoy increasing returns to scale, with the apparent result that output expansion is becoming concentrated in a fewer number of large firms which have an incentive to install capacity in excess of current domestic market needs; and (3) much of the new technology has been imported from abroad via direct private investment, so that a relatively large proportion of new output is controlled by foreign enterprises. The implications of these developments for the Argentine balance of payments and for policy will be analyzed in the remainder of this chapter.

ISI Policy and the Demand for Imports Since 1950

Promotion of the kind of industrialization that took place beginning in the 1950s required some major changes in Argentine commercial policy. As in most industrializing countries, the structure of protection in Argentina, whether by means of tariffs, import surcharges, quotas, or exchange controls, has traditionally been scaled in accordance with two discriminating criteria: (1) protection of activities already existing in the country against the threat of import competition, usually on an ad hoc basis at urging of interest group lobbies; and (2) more favorable treatment of so-called "essential" imports over "nonessentials," particularly during periods of balance of payments stringency. This dual system tended to encourage what might be called "incremental" import substitution—diversification of existing capacity to manufacture goods that could be produced with similar plant and equipment—and it was biased in favor of the production of "nonessential" goods. Because of severe import shortages in Argentina, particularly during World War II and after the balance of payments crisis of 1948, domestic production of a broad range of machine tools and other standard types of machinery and equipment also received strong stimulus.

The recent history of special industrial promotion legislation in Argentina began with the adoption of Decree-Law 14,630 of 1944, which enabled the government to grant special credit, tax, and import privileges (for imports of special machinery and raw materials) to activities declared to be in the "national interest." The three main criteria applied were that these activities should produce "essential" goods for the domestic market, contribute to national defense, and utilize mostly domestic inputs. Partly because of these restrictions and partly because initiative for taking advantage of these incentives was left entirely to private domestic initiative, the law did not lead to any important changes in the overall structure of industry.[16]

Responsibility for developing larger scale, high technology activities was entrusted mainly to specially created mixed or state enterprises. The prime mover in this process was not a development corporation like those common in many other countries but an organization of Military Factories (*Fabricaciones Militares*). The most important industrial activities entrusted to military initiative and management were implementation of the *Ley Savio* of 1947, which provided for establishment of a mixed enterprise (SOMISA, in which private investors never owned more than 1 percent of the equity) for the integrated production of iron and steel; promotion of metallurgical and engineering development, including production of the first tractors, automobiles, and even airplanes and ground to air missiles on a small scale, under an organization attached to the Air Force and first called IAME, later renamed DINFIA; expropriation of thirty German firms (mainly in the pharmaceutical and chemical industries) at the end of World War II, and establishment of a petrochemical enterprise under the National Directorate of State Industries (DINIE); and finally the expansion of naval construction under an organization attached to the Navy Ministry and called AFNE.[17]

These organizations may have had a significant effect in preparing the ground for later rapid development of large scale, technologically complex industries—particularly by providing special training for the labor force, such as at the DINFIA plant in Córdoba next to which a large segment of the automobile industry later decided to locate—but with few exceptions they never increased their own production on an important scale. In the absence of more detailed research, one can only speculate about the reasons for their limited performance: lack of capital funds due to tight fiscal budget constraints, inappropriateness of military administrative procedures for managing industrial enterprise, or perhaps excessive reliance on developing independently technology that was already available abroad.

The impressive technological take-off of Argentine industry in the 1950s was instead the direct result of opening up the economy to massive foreign investment and almost unrestricted imports of capital goods, and of the willingness of the government to enter into special deals concerning individual firms or products. This change of policy was initiated by Perón when he began to liberalize foreign investment controls and negotiated special arrangements with foreign tractor, automotive, and television firms. It was strongly reinforced by Frondizi when he eliminated all remaining barriers to foreign capital and provided powerful new incentives for the wholesale renewal of domestic industrial machinery and equipment. The chief policy instruments used for this latter purpose were tax exemptions for reinvestment of up to 100 percent, unlimited official bank guarantees for credits obtained abroad, and free importation of entire "production lines" and many individual pieces of machinery and equipment that were presumably not produced in the country. Thus, between 1959 and 1963 over half of all imports entered the country free of import surcharges, a large share of the capital goods and other industrial inputs under special industrial promotion regimes.[18]

The policy of protection was therefore completely turned around from one that was responsive to existing interest group lobbies and relied on highly selective or restrictive special promotional legislation, to almost completely free access to foreign capital and technology and generalized protection of newly created activities from import competition, mainly by means of extremely high import surcharges and some outright import prohibitions. These general measures were complemented by special deals and arrangements designed chiefly to protect the market share of new industries that could not completely satisfy existing domestic demand, and to oblige producers of new products to rely progressively on domestic sources of supply for their inputs. Examples of the first kind are the complicated arrangements by which the output and prices of the SOMISA steel mill were not allowed to be adversely affected by competition from supplementary imports, and the special provisions adopted to oblige rubber users to purchase an increasing share of their needs from a recently established synthetic plant as it gradually came into full production. Examples of the second kind of special arrangement are the tractor and automotive industries, both of which were subjected to a progressive reduction in import surcharge exemptions on components and parts (and at one time, prior official approval of their production and import plans) to induce them to play an active role in the development of domestic suppliers.

Far from reducing the demand for imports, the new industrial policy led to a rapid rise in the overall import coefficient during the 1950s and generated considerable speculation about the possible "exhaustion" of import substituting possibilities. In a widely discussed research paper David Felix found that current import requirements per unit of final demand rose by 11 to 16 percent between 1953 and 1960, and that between 29 and 56 percent of the total increase was attributable to only two industrial subsectors: vehicles and machinery and electrical apparatus and equipment.[19] These were of course precisely the subsectors in which new product development, requiring heavy initial imports of materials and components, was most intensive. The central question was therefore whether the sharp increase in the import coefficient represented merely a temporary indigestion of the import substituting process, or whether it signified that development of high technology industries would over the longer term have a smaller (or even a negative) net import replacement effect.

The answer to this question does not depend mainly on the production or supply side, for if the composition of final demand were given, the substitution of domestic for foreign value added would clearly reduce the foreign exchange content of demand even if all materials inputs for new industries were imported.[20] To the extent that "domestication" of high technology industries is more difficult or time-consuming than it was for traditional industries, net import substitution might of course occur more slowly. The subsequent rapid growth of domestic component manufacture in Argentina does not, however, indicate that domestication of these new industries need be a slow process. Industrial goods imports in fact did not increase at all between 1960 and 1968 despite the more than 40 percent growth in manufacturing production. In the latter year merchandise imports represented only 6 to 7 percent of GDP at 1960 prices, the lowest level of all time except for the severe import restriction year of 1953 and during World War II. The large increase of imports in 1969 and 1970, however, kept alive the import substitution exhaustion hypothesis, although Krieger Vasena's tariff reductions and inventory accumulation set off by renewed balance of payments uncertainties may have been the main causes.

Changes in the composition of demand undoubtedly played an important role in the import boom of 1953-1962. The relaxation of import controls permitted Argentines to redirect a larger share of their demand abroad after many years of severe import rationing, and special promotional policies cleared the way for a flood of capital goods imports. The latter led to reduced utilization of existing domestic capital goods production capacity, and the general deepening of fixed industrial capital in substitution of labor contributed to redistributing national income and expenditure in favor of upper income groups. Increased demand therefore shifted toward more income-elastic goods, such as those produced by the new high technology industries, at the expense of common wage goods with a lower import content. Even by the end of the 1960s, production of commodities such as flour mill products, clothing, and shoes had not yet recovered to the levels reached in the mid-1950s.

It would thus appear that Say's Law was at work in Argentina, in the sense that the distribution of income generated by expansion of the new capital and import-intensive industries helped increase demand for their output. To the extent that derived import demand put additional pressure on the balance of payments, the shift in income distribution and expenditure was further reinforced by policies adopted to correct external deficits, since these policies (as will be seen in Chapter 4) also had regressive income effects. If to the above is added at least part of the $150 million increase that occurred in the annual remittance of profits and financial services abroad, and also that proportion of the increase in foreign debt service corresponding to the activities of the new industries, their overall net foreign exchange saving effect may have been quite minimal even after 1960.

The so-called "exhaustion" of ISI possibilities in Argentina does not therefore appear to arise so much from the alleged difficulty of domesticating more sophisticated manufacturing activities as it does from the shift in the composition of demand and the increase in external financial obligations that have accompanied the process. Doubt has also been growing as to whether an industrialization strategy can be justified if it leads to the installation of activities that under prevailing conditions carry a heavy burden of underscaled plants, idle capacity, oligopoly profits, and large payments abroad for new technology that neither sustains growth nor creates many jobs. Since most of these drawbacks could be alleviated by increasing the country's foreign exchange income, attention has increasingly turned in recent years to the possibility of accelerating expansion of manufactured exports. Export expanding industrialization (EEI) might indeed be viewed as a necessary alternative or complement to ISI to make Argentina's recent industrialization strategy viable.

Export Expanding Industrialization (EEI)

The Argentine manufacturing sector was initially quite export-oriented: it has been estimated that before 1930, 15 to 20 percent of the gross value of industrial production was exported, mostly in the form of processed foodstuffs. During World War II exports of manufactures became more diversified (although textiles played a particularly important role) when traditional sources of supply of other Latin American countries were cut off; at this time manufactures accounted for over 13 percent of total Argentine exports. Renewed competition from traditional suppliers and increasing overvaluation of the peso, however, severely curtailed industrial exporting after the war. Official concern with this turn of events finally resulted in the establishment of a Commission for the Promotion of Exports in 1952, followed in 1954 by the formation of another Commission for the Popularization of Argentine Products, and then by the strong recommendation for encouragement of

Table 3-5 Nontraditional exports, 1966–1970. (millions of U.S. dollars)

Export groups	1966	1967	1968	1969	1970
Iron and steel sheets, bars, wire, and profiles	5.6	8.6	17.9	17.0	29.1
Calculating, accounting, card-punching machines, and their components	7.6	12.7	11.6	14.9	20.3
Canned and processed beef	3.1	2.0	3.3	8.2	15.1
Automotive vehicles, tractors and their components	3.9	7.1	9.0	13.0	14.0
Textbooks, pamphlets, and magazines	9.3	10.9	13.1	16.3	12.4
Mixed animal feed	0.1	0.1	2.1	9.7	9.8
Automobile tires and synthetic rubber	0.6	1.0	4.4	8.1	7.3
Antibiotics	1.9	2.2	2.6	3.6	5.4
Machine harvesters and earth-moving equipment	0.2	0.3	1.5	2.1	5.2
Other	62.7	62.3	91.8	116.4	124.6
Total	95.0	108.1	157.3	209.3	243.2

Source: Ministry of Industry, Commerce, and Mining, *Exportaciones argentinas clasificadas según grado de elaboración y tradicionalidad, 1966-1970* (Buenos Aires, 1972). Nontraditional exports are defined as those that "began to be exported on a significant scale after 1960."

nontraditional exports contained in the Prebisch report to the Provisional Government in 1956. It was not until President Frondizi's administration, however, that the first important steps were taken toward implementing Argentina's present nontraditional export incentive system.

This system relies fundamentally on four financial inducements: (1) export credit, first adopted in 1959 and extended in 1963 to help finance production of nontraditional export goods; (2) exemption from payment of sales taxes (Decree 3969 of 1960); (3) drawbacks, or refunds of duties paid on imported inputs (Decree 8051 of 1962, although generalized drawbacks actually began in 1960); and (4) *reintegros,* ostensibly reimbursement of other domestic taxes paid by exporters but in actuality a variable, ad valorem export rebate (Decree 46 of 1965). A number of other export promotion measures have also been adopted, such as establishment of permanent product exhibit centers abroad, creation of a consular market information service, and more recently provision of export insurance. Establishment of regional trade preferences in 1962

Table 3-6 Nontraditional exports, 1966–1970, by destination. (millions of U.S. dollars)

Destination (percent of total)	1966	1967	1968	1969	1970
LAFTA	52.6	58.7	53.7	56.6	52.9
U.S.A.	22.1	21.6	24.6	17.3	18.3
European Economic Community	9.4	7.1	9.7	15.1	15.3
Other	15.9	12.6	12.0	11.0	13.5

Source: Ministry of Industry, Commerce, and Mining, Exportaciones argentinas clasificadas según grado de elaboración y tradicionalidad, 1966–1970.

under LAFTA (Latin American Free Trade Association) was also a most important step toward expansion of Argentine exports of manufactures. Of the more than seven-fold increase in nontraditional exports between 1962 and 1968, over half was accounted for by LAFTA trade.[21] It is also noteworthy that by the end of the 1960s Brazil ranked along with the United States, Britain, and Italy as Argentina's most important trading partners. By the end of the decade total nontraditional exports recovered to about 10 percent of the total value of Argentine exports (including processed foodstuffs).

Judging by this recent rapid growth it would appear that the incentive system was quite effective. Efforts to correlate the increase in nontraditional exports with variations in the "real" exchange rate adjusted for export subsidies have, however, proved unsuccessful. David Felix found that "with two exceptions all the elasticities have the 'right' sign, but their values are low and statistically insignificant at even the 10 percent level."[22] Henry Bruton reached similar conclusions not only for Argentina but also for Brazil and Colombia.[23] The significant explanatory variables for nontraditional export expansion instead appear to be excess domestic productive capacity and LAFTA trade concessions (Felix), or variations in foreign demand and in competitive domestic demand (Bruton).

It would be unwise to try to reach any definitive conclusions on the basis of this research, particularly in view of the problems of aggregation and the short time period analyzed in these studies. Export price incentives in Argentina have also been very irregular, both between commodities and over time. In recent years Argentine export subsidies are estimated to have averaged between 20 and 30 percent ad valorem (for drawbacks and *reintegros*), but they have varied between 6 percent for low value-added products to about 70 percent for seamless steel pipes; and after each major devaluation they have been reduced or withdrawn and thereafter gradually restored.[24] Manufacturers could therefore hardly count on the permanence of export price incentives to justify development of export capacity. It would be more reasonable to assume instead that these incentives made it more attractive for them to exploit export opportunities when they appeared. In other words, export subsidies may very well have been a necessary condition for rapid nontraditional export expansion during the 1960s, although as indicated by the regression results they do not appear to have been a sufficient condition.

Another significant feature of manufactured export expansion during the 1960s is that most of the increase came from the more recently established, technologically complex, larger scale industries. Fully one half of the increase in manufactured exports between 1962 and 1968 was contributed by engineering products (metals and metal products, machinery, transport, and electrical equipment) and another 13 percent by chemicals. The so-called traditional industries (food and beverages, textiles, clothing, printing and publishing, nonmetallic mineral products, leather, and wood products), on the other hand, accounted for only 30 percent of the increase.[25] Only a few new product categories exceeded two million dollars a year—calculating machines, tires, automotive spare parts, seamless tubes—but the range of sophistication of engineering exports was quite impressive: lathes (up to 25 percent of production exported), electric shavers (the major producer exported 40 percent of output to Brazil), automatic bottling equipment, grain seeders, telephone equipment, washing machines, record players, and other products, among which are items that have usually been considered relatively expensive in Argentina. As a matter of fact comparative price studies indicate that relative domestic prices of these new "dynamic" industries are higher compared to United States prices than those of most "traditional" industries in Argentina.[26]

Special reasons undoubtedly explain the export performance of some individual products—such as the very high subsidy given seamless tubes, industrial complementation agreements providing for the exchange of automotive components, and the decision of IBM to establish its computer equipment manufacturing facility for Latin America in Buenos Aires—and examples of individual items produced by new industries at internationally competitive prices can be found. But these exceptional cases do not appear pervasive enough to explain in general how activities recently established with effective rates of protection of up to 800 percent, and utilizing production functions that in general take advantage neither of the country's rich agricultural resources nor its relatively cheap labor, have become the nation's most rapidly growing nontraditional exporters.[27]

The apparent disadvantage of industries using relatively scarce factors more intensively may be offset however by other considerations, such as the quality, effective utilization, and relative prices of different categories of manpower. It has been suggested, for example, that Argentina should possess a comparative advantage in industries using a relatively large proportion of skilled labor, not only because the country is relatively well endowed with this kind of manpower (at least in comparison with other developing countries), but also because of exceptionally small wage differentials between skilled and unskilled labor.[28] It should be noted in this context that many engineering industries, such as machine tools and electrical apparatus and equipment, usually employ a relatively large proportion of skilled manpower and they are not particularly capital-intensive.

Some new Argentine industries with rapidly growing exports, however, definitely appear to be capital- rather than skill-intensive. A plausible explanation for the export performance of these industries could be the especially strong incentives they have to export at less than full cost prices so as to utilize their productive capacity more fully. Such an incentive would presumably exist in activities subject to steeply diminishing average costs of production (or increasing returns to scale) and chronic excess capacity. This situation is illustrated in figure 3-1, in which AC and MC represent a firm's average and marginal cost schedules respectively, and AR_d and MR_d are the average and marginal revenue curves for domestic sales. If a firm sells only in the domestic market it will maximize profits (the shaded area) by producing OQ_2 at price P_d; but if it can export at price P_x, the firm can increase its profits by raising production to OQ_3, selling OQ_1 in the domestic market at price P'_d and exporting the rest.[29] This is true even though P_x is below the average cost OB of producing Q_3, as long as the "loss" $FGHI$ on foreign sales is more than offset by the increase in profits on domestic sales ($P'_d BFC$-$P_d AED$).

A necessary condition for marginal cost exporting to be an important explanation of recent industrial export performance

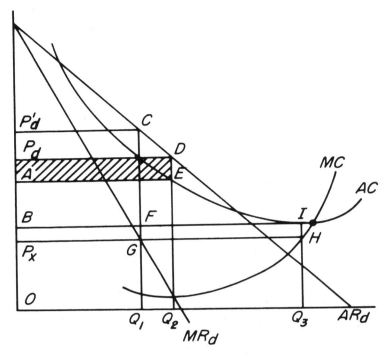

Figure 3-1.

would be the prevalence of decreasing costs and idle capacity. The
likely importance of scale economies in new Argentine industries
was discussed above; evidence of very substantial and persistent idle
capacity in advanced technology enterprises is even more persuasive,
both from capacity utilization surveys and from studies of individual
industries.[30] The prevalence of idle capacity has not only been due to
the stop-go behavior of the Argentine economy; even during peak
years such as 1965 engineering industries have typically worked at
two thirds or less of capacity, and more than one-shift work
schedules in individual firms have been exceedingly rare. This
situation appears rather common in the current stage of
industrialization of major countries in Latin America, so common in
fact that in his study of productivity growth Bruton was able to
conclude that "the principal empirical result of this investigation is
that virtually all of the variance in productivity growth in
manufacturing in Latin America can be explained by variation in
the degree of utilization."[31]

A sufficient condition for greater capacity utilization to be an important incentive for marginal cost exporting would be that underutilization in decreasing cost industries should be caused by "insufficient" domestic demand rather than by supply limitations, such as shortage of labor or of imported raw materials. Although supply constraints were undoubtedly an important explanatory factor in Argentina prior to 1959 when imports were subjected to quantitative controls, more recent reliance on income and price variations to maintain balance of payments equilibrium, and sizable levels of labor unemployment, create a presumption that the main constraint has been on the demand side during the 1960s. "Umbrella pricing"—larger, more efficient firms maintaining prices that permit smaller, less efficient firms to retain a share of the market to prevent what is commonly referred to in Argentina as "disloyal competition"—would also contribute to restricting the volume of domestic demand.[32]

A final probable explanation for the export performance of new Argentine industries is market organization. Recent studies have tended to show that developing countries find it easier to export highly standardized products that do not require setting up special marketing and servicing facilities abroad, or speciality products on order from large foreign firms that have their own marketing outlets. It is therefore relatively easy to dispose of surplus petroleum derivatives, basic chemicals, iron and steel, and other standardized intermediate products abroad at going world market prices. The ease of selling differentiated intermediate or final goods, on the other hand, usually depends on the ability of local firms to produce large lots of individual items according to strict specifications of foreign manufacturers or distributors who are often organized to sell the final products under their own brand names. Larger scale, foreign controlled local enterprises thus have an initial export marketing advantage, which has been enhanced by the creation of preferential regional trading associations such as LAFTA. One of the main barriers to the expansion of trade between members of such associations is the instability of exchange rates: the profitability and even the direction of trade can fluctuate wildly according to movements in the relative value of trading partner currencies. If regional trade is organized between branches of the same multinational firm located in different member countries, however, fluctuations in relative currency values are less likely to disrupt the pattern of trade, because losses on exports from the country with relatively overvalued currency can be offset by exceptional profits on exports from the country with a relatively undervalued currency. As a matter of fact, recent research indicates that market control exercised by multinational oligopolies is becoming an increasingly important determinant of the pattern of international trade.[33]

In summary, then, a number of plausible reasons exist to explain why Argentina's new technology activities have responded more readily than traditional industries to export incentives adopted during the last decade. The introduction of modern equipment in new growth industries may have helped to reduce factor productivity differentials between Argentina and other countries. Some rapidly expanding export goods appear to require a relatively large proportion of skilled labor in their manufacture, and Argentina may well enjoy a comparative advantage in this factor of production. Evidence is also strong that marginal cost exporting by firms benefiting from scale economies (or sharply decreasing unit costs) may be another important explanation. Finally, certain new commodities and multinational enterprises have access to international marketing channels that old established firms are less able (or more reluctant) to take advantage of. It is therefore probably fair to conclude that during the 1960s EEI policies had a rather selective impact on the manufacturing sector and that they raised some new problems for Argentine industrial policy.

Implications for Policy

In a country like Argentina with a tight balance of payments constraint, slowly growing primary exports, and a manufacturing sector that accounts for over one third of total GDP (compared with less than 10 percent for total imports), the future rate of growth of the economy will depend critically on the net foreign exchange impact of further industrialization. The small import-substituting effect of Argentine industrialization after the mid-1950s was due largely to the fact that many new consumer goods were in effect substitutes for goods already manufactured domestically instead of for goods formerly imported. A large part of the acquisition of machinery and equipment, both for new industries and for replacement and modernization in existing plants, also represented the substitution of imported for domestic sources of supply. A certain amount of negative import substitution is a necessary cost of the diversification of wants and technological change in a growing economy, but government policy, far from impeding negative ISI, tended to reinforce it without sufficient concern for its balance of payments implications.

Import duty exemption strongly encouraged negative ISI, especially through the subsidization of capital goods imports. Even in 1969 it was estimated that almost two thirds of imported machinery and 45 percent of imported transport equipment were still admitted into the country duty free, about half of which was on government account. A considerable proportion of these capital goods is not therefore required to meet the specialized needs of high technology industries but is acquired for public works and infrastructure projects. A significant share of the latter kind of machinery and equipment could most probably be supplied by domestic industry at competitive prices if duties were charged on imports, but government agencies have tenaciously defended their privileged position. Early in 1970 official duty exemptions were eliminated for a brief period, but the government was unable to resist vested interest pressure and they were soon restored.

One of the main reasons for official agency insistence on tariff exemption is of course that they are thereby enabled to stretch their individual investment budgets further, but there are also other important reasons. Credit for capital goods purchases is generally much easier to obtain abroad than in Argentina, and foreign suppliers are often better organized to provide even custom made equipment more promptly and to handle large, complex orders. Local firms, on the other hand, are seldom tooled up to take care of large orders expediently, and few of them are diversified enough to bid for package contracts that require the bidder to supply a broad range of equipment for complex projects. Most of these obstacles to local procurement are of the vicious circle variety, in the sense that they could be overcome if appropriate government policies made it possible for local industry to compete more effectively with foreign suppliers.

Government policy has also impeded ISI balance by permitting too many firms to compete for the limited domestic market for a number of new technology products. As a result, plants have been unnecessarily underscaled, chronic excess capacity has developed, and prices have not come down as rapidly as they might have to tap new customers and broaden the market, once the cream was scooped off the top. The automotive industry is the most dramatic example: at one time there were twenty producing firms sharing a market of less than 150,000 units. Over time the number of firms has been reduced through a painful process of rationalization and consolidation, and relative prices of automotive vehicles have declined appreciably; but domestication could have been achieved much more rapidly and efficiently if only a few brands and models had been selected for production and standardization of parts manufacture had been facilitated. The usual argument made against adoption of a discretionary government policy is that it would impede competition and lead to graft and corruption. The existence of a few more firms in an industry does not, however, assure greater competition, and once government establishes special privileges and regulations for the conduct of a business, the opportunity for graft and corruption exists regardless of the number of firms involved. It is in fact more likely that public scrutiny of government regulation of industry might be somewhat easier if fewer regulations and firms were involved.

Finally, ISI balance could be assisted by a more rational tariff policy. Indiscriminate import substitution certainly contributed to the rapid peaking and subsequent stagnation or decline of a number of consumer durable goods industries during the 1950s and 1960s, and protection of high-cost production of basic industrial inputs has had serious cascade effects on the price structure of user industries. The technical advice that emerges from the large and growing literature on ISI tariff policy is that import duties should be rationalized to equalize the effective protection of value added in different activities so as to minimize the domestic resource cost of saving foreign exchange. If it is unfeasible to establish a uniform level of tariffs for all imports, however, no good method exists for equalizing effective protection through selective tariff adjustments unless strong assumptions are made about the absence of scale economies, the inelasticity of substitution between industrial inputs, the "normal" level of profits, and other controversial matters. Proper discussion of this subject far exceeds the scope of this study, but it is the opinion of the authors that, although more uniform protection would be desirable, progress toward a more rational tariff policy will depend primarily on how the central issue of ISI is resolved.

This issue is the extent to which industrial autarchy should be the objective of national policy. All the discussion about "exhaustion" of import substituting possibilities notwithstanding, there is little doubt that the country could substitute domestic production for imports of just about every manufactured good necessary to sustain the present standard of living in Argentina. Movement toward autarchy, if this were the objective of policy, could also be carried out much more scientifically than in the past. Industrial complexes could be developed systematically and integrated from the raw material stage right through to the final product, much in the way it has been done in some socialist countries. With such a strategy the issue of relative efficiency or comparative advantage would become largely irrelevant in the determination of resource allocation unless the cost of autarchy in terms of more restricted consumer choice and a much greater domestic savings and investment effort obliged policymakers to consider trade-offs between autarchy, trade, growth, and the introduction of new technology. In this event, however, it is highly unlikely that policy trade-offs would soon be debated again at the decision-making level in terms of a major shift in relative prices in favor of agriculture. With at least three times as many Argentines directly dependent on industry as on agriculture, a drastic redistribution of income from the former to the latter would be intolerable unless the country were ruled by a repressive liberal dictatorship. The issue of comparative advantage in trade is much more likely to be decided, either explicitly or *de facto*, in terms of the relative roles of ISI and EEI in the country's future development.

Some advocates of EEI argue in effect that Argentina should seek to do what the old colonial powers were accused of doing: export sophisticated manufactures in exchange for cheap raw materials. This mercantilist approach would of course not generate much trade because most other developing countries are just as eager as Argentina to possess sophisticated manufacturing activities. Advocates of a more open economy, on the other hand, are willing to accept a certain degree of international specialization or division of labor in manufacturing, although such a division of labor would encounter serious opposition if it prevented the country from broadening its capacity to produce "basic" and high technology goods. How can this apparent contradiction of policy objectives be resolved?

One answer can be found in the experience of advanced countries: although the United States, Western Europe, and Japan each possess virtually the full range of basic and high technology industries, trade among them has expanded much more rapidly during the last couple of decades than between industrial and primary exporting countries. This trade has been based on a high degree of product differentiation: each of them manufactures steel, machine tools, electronic equipment, shoes, and just about every other industrial product line, but each country has developed a comparative advantage in producing and exporting different kinds or styles of steel, machine tools, electronic equipment, and shoes. Trade expansion has not therefore promoted sophisticated industries in some countries and relegated others to producing traditional products; it has enabled all trading partners to take better advantage of economies of scale and specialization in a broad range of manufacturing activities. For example, there are several hundred different types of steel products; any country, except perhaps one of continental size, that tried to develop self-sufficiency across the board would in all likelihood end up with a steel industry far less capable of taking care of national requirements, for defense as well as for civilian purposes, than a nation that concentrated on the more efficient production of a few dozen types.

EEI is therefore quite compatible with broad industrial diversification in each trading partner. The principal controversial issue about open economy industrialization that emerges from the recent experience of developed and semideveloped countries alike concerns the ownership of new technology. Because of their earlier start and vast investment in research and new product development, giant multinational firms have tended to control expansion of new technology industries throughout the world. To the consternation of many host countries they have often been able to do this with a minimum use of their own funds and a maximum use of local financing, thereby generating claims for profits remittances abroad far exceeding the amount of capital brought in. These claims would not produce balance of payments problems, however, as long as ISI and EEI were properly balanced. The chief policy problem is therefore how to induce local branches of multinational firms to help achieve such a balance while at the same time assuring adequate national participation in their oligopoly profits. Equally important, because multinational enterprises are concentrated in new growth industries, their influence has been expanding so rapidly that host countries have become alarmed about the threat they pose to national sovereignty.

A further complication of an open-economy, EEI development strategy, at least for those who take central planning seriously, is that there is much less scope in such a strategy for highly selective policies. The main reason is that it is very difficult to predict which individual manufactured products may enjoy a comparative advantage in trade. This is true not only for the reasons mentioned previously—the limited relevance of general relative factor prices and resource endowments, opportunities for marginal cost exporting, special marketing situations, and the role of multinational firms—but also because intercountry differences in comparative advantage appear to be relatively small over a broad middle range of products. Furthermore, export opportunities open to any particular country depend not only on conditions and policies in that country but just as much on the unpredictable and frequently irrational policies of potential trading partners. Thus, leaving aside a few obvious manufactured products such as processed beef, Argentina might, if strong general export incentives are provided, become a major exporter of false teeth or rubber bones for dogs instead of expanding sales of some already existing export commodity. For this and other reasons mentioned above, policies affecting the role of industrialization in foreign trade must be analyzed in the broader context of Argentina's prospects for achieving sustained growth with external equilibrium.

4 Toward Sustained Growth With External Equilibrium

The period from the balance of payments crisis of 1948 to the fall of the Ongania administration in 1970 embraced at least eight major external payments adjustments. During this time Argentina was a kind of laboratory for balance of payments policy experiments, ranging from the general or selective use of quantitative exchange regulations, various forms of price rationing of imports by means of surcharges, prior import deposits and devaluations of up to 150 percent, to crawling peg or freely floating exchange rates and compensated devaluations. Balance of payments difficulties have also occurred under almost every conceivable domestic economic situation: over-full employment inflation in 1948 and 1958, relatively little inflation in 1955 and early 1970, and rapid inflation with less than full employment in 1962 and 1967. Balance of payments problems have indeed been so persistent under such varying conditions and policies that one is tempted to conclude that unless agricultural export expansion again becomes the main engine of growth of the Argentine economy—a very dim prospect at least in the medium run—the country is condemned to continue suffering from the semistagnation of stop-go development.

Such a conclusion cannot, however, be justified on grounds that Argentina lacks the economic potential to follow an alternative growth strategy. The problem is that since the late 1940s the country has not been able to escape the short run for a sufficiently long time to pursue a growth strategy. It is easy to attribute responsibility for this state of affairs to the high degree of political and institutional instability, but this instability is in turn closely related to the difficulty Argentina has had in resolving short-run balance of payments problems. This difficulty is due mainly to the short-run unresponsiveness of exports and imports to changes in relative prices, so that policymakers have been obliged to rely on restrictive measures that reduce and redistribute income to solve external payments crises. Such measures have subsequently either failed to provide incentives for moving the economy toward greater longer term equilibrium, or the incentives initially provided have rapidly evaporated once economic recovery was underway. A longer term growth strategy cannot successfully be pursued unless macro-economic policy management is based on a recognition of the limitations of the balance of payments adjustment mechanism.

The Short-Run Balance of Payments Mechanism in Argentina

As a very marginal buyer in world markets, Argentina can exercise little influence on the prices or other conditions under which imports are supplied, but the country possesses significant market power in several of its major exports. Sales of linseed oil account for about 75 percent of world trade (mainly via the Rotterdam entrepot market), and Argentina has traditionally supplied about half the beef sold in Great Britain's principal wholesale meat market at Smithfield. Private Argentine exporters have thus long followed the practice of trying to regulate the volume of beef shipments to England so as to avoid violent price fluctuations. Establishment of the variable levy on beef imports into the European Common Market provided an even greater incentive for attempted price manipulation by Argentine exporters, at least prior to Great Britain's joining the Common Market. Because the levy was equal to the difference between the support price in Common Market countries and the free import price in Britain, the higher the latter the lower the variable levy and thus the greater the price received by overseas exporters.[1]

These are the clearest examples of Argentine export market power, although international markets for a number of other commodities are also sufficiently imperfect to permit significant variations in the volume of Argentine exports to affect prices. The important point to grasp, however, is that Argentina's export market power is fundamentally a short-term phenomenon. If its supplies are held off the market for any significant period of time, competing exporters have abundantly demonstrated in the past that they can and will pick up the slack and replace Argentine sources. Because market losses are often quite difficult to recuperate, over the longer run Argentine authorities would in general appear to be well advised to avoid trying to manipulate international market prices on their own.

Among the balance of payments variables that can, and indeed must, be influenced by Argentine policymakers are the demand for imports and the supply of exports. With regard to the former variable, one would expect the price elasticity of demand for imported goods to be rather low, at least over the short term, insofar as Argentine imports are noncompetitive with domestic production because of the highly discriminatory tariffs and surcharges levied on competitive imports. Also, about 95 percent of total imports are composed of raw materials, intermediate products, capital goods, and fuels (see table 4-1), so that the effect of changes in relative import prices on domestic prices of final goods is substantially dampened. Less substitution in final demand should therefore be expected to result directly from an exchange rate devaluation than if a larger proportion of final consumer goods were imported.

The quantitative evidence on the behavior of Argentine imports amply confirms the above expectations. Although after 1955 direct controls were progressively replaced by other measures to regulate imports, and in 1959 import controls were almost completely lifted, no researcher has to the knowledge of the authors ever found relative prices to be a statistically significant determinant of import demand in Argentina.[2] The chief determinant has instead been found to be the volume of output in domestic user industries. It is possible, for example, to explain over 90 percent of the variation in the demand for imports of raw materials and intermediate products during the period 1953-1964 (the period for which a carefully estimated deflator for this category of imports was available) solely by fluctuations in the volume of production of rapid growth industries (see table 4-2).

Changes in foreign exchange reserves during the previous year were also found to improve regression results. Diaz Alejandro, who first used this variable in estimating import demand functions for Argentina,[3] considers that it is a proxy for quantitative import restrictions. In view of the continued significance of the variable after 1958, however, it may also stand as a proxy for variations in inventories of imported goods in anticipation of balance of payments difficulties and exchange devaluation. Inclusion of a relative price variable, on the other hand, does very little to improve the explanatory power of the regression equations. In fact, if this variable is excluded, fluctuations in the volume of production of rapid growth industries and changes in exchange reserves in the previous year together "explain" 97 percent of variations in the demand for imports of raw materials and intermediate products, and this specification of the estimating equation also reduces the likelihood of bias due to the serial correlation of residuals (see column 6 of table 4-2).

Bias is of course introduced in single equation estimates of price elasticities if fluctuations in imports are largely caused by shifts in the import demand schedule; in this case actual observations would tend to trace out the import supply curve. In Argentina this possibility appears unlikely in view of the very large year-to-year changes in relative import prices in domestic currency induced by the country's periodical massive devaluations and the rapid rate of

Table 4-1 Composition of merchandise imports, 1955–1970. (millions of U.S. dollars)

Import	1955	1956	1957	1958	1959	1960	1961	1962
Raw materials and intermediate products	703.3	562.8	673.9	701.4	576.2	650.3	795.0	667.3
Capital goods	196.7	237.3	259.2	218.7	181.7	419.7	493.8	556.4
Consumer goods	69.4	76.8	59.8	61.1	23.7	23.4	41.9	41.2
Fuels and lubricants	203.2	250.7	317.5	251.4	211.4	155.9	129.7	91.6
Total	1,172.6	1,127.6	1,310.4	1,232.6	993.0	1,249.3	1,460.4	1,356.5

Import	1963	1964	1965	1966	1967	1968	1969	1970
Raw materials and intermediate products	527.6	752.8	882.9	764.5	738.8	778.9	1,074.1	1,059.6
Capital goods	372.0	208.9	154.6	202.9	217.7	257.5	332.0	365.0
Consumer goods	23.7	31.8	45.8	48.4	45.5	48.3	69.0	82.0
Fuels and lubricants	57.4	83.7	115.3	108.5	93.5	84.5	101.0	79.0
Total	980.7	1,077.4	1,195.0	1,124.3	1,095.5	1,164.2	1,576.1	1,684.6

Source: Banco Central, *Comercio exterior*, supplement to *Boletín Estadístico*, no. 3 (May 1969), and Economics Ministry, *Informe Económico*.

Table 4-2 Import demand functions for raw materials and intermediate products.

	(1)	(2)	(3)	(4)	(5)	(6)
Constant	−584	−795	−726	−167	−51	−292
Total industrial production	12.0 (9.23)	13.1 (11.9)	13.1 (11.4)	−	−	−
Production of rapid growth industries	−	−	−	7.90 (10.0)	8.19 (9.71)	8.20 (16.3)
Foreign exchange reserves $t-1$	−	.373 (2.82)	.358 (2.54)	−	−	.321 (3.99)
Relative prices of imports	−	−	−54.9 (0.47)	−	−113 (0.98)	−
R^2	.88	.93	.93	.91	.92	.97
D–W statistic	1.01	1.08	1.03		1.16	1.70

Source: The regression equations were estimated from annual data for the period 1953–1964, the years for which comparable data were available. The figures in parentheses are "*T*" values (ratios of standard errors to the coefficients), and the last row gives the Durban-Watson statistics.

Imports of raw materials and intermediate products: see Appendix table E–1.

Industrial production: Total manufacturing production in 1960 pesos, from CONADE, *Distribución del ingreso y cuentas nacionales*, vol. III, table III–19.

Dynamic industrial production: ibid.; included are the subsectors pulp and paper, chemicals, petroleum derivatives, rubber products, stone, glass and ceramics, metal products, machinery and vehicles, and electrical apparatus.

Foreign exchange reserves: gross gold and convertible exchange reserves of the Central Bank at the end of the previous year, from Diaz Alejandro, *Essays*, Statistical Appendix, table 73, p. 486.

Relative import prices: ratio of wholesale price of imported goods to implicit price deflator for manufacturing production; the first is from DNEC, *Boletín Estadístico*, various numbers, and the second is from CONADE, *Distribución del ingreso*, vol. III, table III–49.

internal inflation. The negative correlation between shifts in the import supply and demand schedules, caused by the synchronization of devaluations with restrictive monetary and fiscal policies (and conversely, the greater stability of exchange rates during periods of domestic income expansion), would in fact tend to give an upward bias to statistically measured import demand elasticities.[4]

The price elasticity of total supply of Argentine primary export goods is, as was observed in Chapter 2, limited in the short and even the medium run by the length of the growing season for agricultural crops, the perverse cattle cycle, the high degree of regional specialization in production, and by the lag in agricultural research and extension. It is still possible that domestic demand for export commodities could be sufficiently elastic to enable the supply of exports to respond quickly to changes in relative prices, even though total supply remained constant. Because Argentine exports are largely composed of foodstuffs, however, one would expect a priori that the price elasticity of domestic demand for export goods is fairly low. Nevertheless, Larry Sjaastad found that the cross-elasticity of demand for agricultural products is over -0.8 in Argentina, and the implicit average elasticity revealed in Jeffrey Nugent's regression work also appears surprisingly high. Diaz Alejandro, on the other hand, estimated the price elasticity of domestic demand for "exportables" to be -0.35, and Willy Van Rijckeghem's estimate for agricultural goods was only -0.23. The price elasticity of demand for beef, whether compared with other food or with nonfood expenditures, has also been found to be quite low in Argentina (generally less than -0.5).[5]

The main explanations for these divergent results are, on the one hand, that Sjaastad assumes that consumption as a proportion of income remains constant, and on the other that Diaz and Van Rijckeghem take explicitly into account the effect of changes in the distribution of income between wage earners and other income recipients. Since variations in the relative prices of agricultural goods have been closely associated in Argentina with devaluations accompanied by deflationary domestic policies, variables representing changes in income and the share of wages in the estimating equations of Diaz and Van Rijckeghem pick up a large part of the explanatory significance attributed by Sjaastad to variations in relative prices alone. It is therefore tempting to discard Sjaastad's conclusion out of hand, but as he himself has pointed out, none of the estimated elasticities are completely satisfactory.

Any increase in relative agricultural prices in Argentina leads ceteris paribus to some real income redistribution, both because a smaller share of farmer income goes to wages and because a larger share of wage income is spent on agricultural goods. It can therefore be argued that the relevant elasticity for policy purposes should include the effect on consumption of this kind of income redistribution as well as the "pure" substitution effect of a change in relative prices. Measurement of such an elasticity poses serious statistical problems, however, since observed income redistribution cannot be attributed only (or perhaps even mainly) to relative price variations and differences in the wage share between agriculture and other sectors. The income redistribution effects of the restrictive monetary, fiscal, and wage policies that have consistently accompanied exchange rate devaluations in Argentina should, for the purpose of policy analysis, be distinguished from those of relative price adjustments. Given the practical impossibility of

partitioning the income redistribution effect between its different
causes, one can only assume the "true" elasticity lies somewhere
between the two sets of measurements.

Even if the price elasticities of demand for imports and of supply
of exports are so low as to make it unwise for Argentine
policymakers to rely exclusively on currency depreciation to bring
about short-term balance of payments adjustments, the responsiveness of movements on capital account should also be considered.
Reference has already been made to the great importance of
short-term capital receipts in solving the external payments crisis of
1958-1959, and they were undoubtedly of immense value in the
implementation of Krieger Vasena's program. Conversely, almost
the entire deterioration in the balance of payments during the crisis
of 1961-1962 was caused by a net adverse movement of half a billion
dollars on short-term capital account. Such movements have been
chiefly of two kinds: compensatory credits from the IMF and other
international agencies, and speculative movements of funds owned
by Argentine nationals or owed to foreign banks and suppliers. If
the country is willing and able to qualify for the first kind of
financial assistance, all well and good; but the second kind—often
referred to as "hot" money—has a very undesirable characteristic.
Just as a speculative inflow of funds from abroad can be of immense
short-term help in improving the balance of payments, so can a
speculative outflow eat up foreign exchange reserves at an incredible
pace once confidence in the economy or in the stability of the peso
has been shaken.

Argentine policymakers who are (with considerable empirical
support) both elasticity pessimists and reluctant to play the "hot"
money game have, however, only one other short-run balance of
payments adjustment alternative: reduce total domestic income and
expenditure. This can be done by means of quantitative controls as
it was after the payments crisis of 1948, or it can be accomplished by
restrictive monetary and fiscal policies as it was during most subsequent crises. In either case, however, domestic income reduction
obviously cannot by itself provide any durable solution; it can only
give a little time for longer-term policies to begin to take effect. It is
therefore essential that appropriate incentives be provided by such
policies and that they be maintained during the postcrisis recovery
period. The permanence of incentives in a pluralistic society in turn
depends on the extent to which they can be protected from the
inevitable political pressures and competing economic claims of conflicting interest groups. This task is difficult at best, but it will

remain unachievable in Argentina as long as incentives depend, as they usually have in the past, on the constancy of economic relationships that cannot realistically be held constant.

Greater Policy Flexibility

One of the most notorious examples of policy rigidity has been in the management of the "real" exchange rate. Because authorities have usually insisted on maintaining the rate at a fixed nominal level for extended periods of time despite the highly variable but persistent rate of domestic inflation, the real purchasing power of the peso has fluctuated violently and unpredictably during most of the period under analysis. It would be hard to design a policy more destructive of incentives for export expansion, rational import substitution, or efficient resource allocation; and yet nominal exchange rate stability has been defended as necessary to generate confidence in the value of the domestic currency. The fact is of course quite the opposite: periodical large adjustments of a pegged exchange rate are the best way of creating uncertainty and rampant speculation in the exchange market. Last ditch devaluations have indeed been such a traumatic experience in Argentina that they have come to be considered symbolic of the general failure of government economic policy, thereby tending to reduce over time the policy flexibility of subsequent economic teams.

A more flexible exchange rate policy has helped assure greater balance of payments stability in countries where it has been adopted. In Latin America a crawling or trotting peg exchange rate—one that is adjusted in small increments at frequent intervals to maintain its real value vis-a-vis the domestic price level—has been adopted in Chile, Brazil, and Colombia. None of them has since suffered an external payments crisis, except after Allende became president of Chile in 1970 and returned to a fixed peg system. It would be absurd to claim that greater exchange rate flexibility alone was responsible for their improved economic performance, but the acceleration in nontraditional export expansion and the more satisfactory rate of growth they subsequently experienced is really quite remarkable when it is recalled that each of these countries previously suffered from cyclical instability and repeated external crises similar to those in Argentina.[6]

No special preconditions must be fulfilled to make a crawling peg exchange rate policy viable: real exchange rate stability can be beneficial independently of the rate of domestic inflation and the level of international reserves. The effect of a crawling peg policy on export expansion and resource allocation in general will be greater, however, the smaller the initial overvaluation of the local currency, because there are definite limits to the speed with which the real exchange rate can be increased through incremental devaluations without generating speculative capital flight. If for example a firm is paying 10 percent interest per year on a foreign supplier's credit and can borrow from a domestic bank at 18 percent, it would be profitable for the firm to take out a domestic loan and prepay the foreign debt if the real exchange rate rose by much more than 7 percent per year (118/110). Similarly, if an investor is obliged to pay income taxes on profits earned at home but not abroad, the break-even rate of real exchange devaluation would be that which equalized the gross rate of return on investment overseas with the domestic rate of return net of taxes. [7]

The main point of these examples is that a crawling peg policy is not an appropriate vehicle for rapid real exchange rate improvement; the permissible rate of such improvement depends on existing differentials between interest, profit, and tax rates at home and abroad. To obtain maximum benefit from real exchange rate maintenance it would therefore be desirable in practice to introduce the policy immediately after an orthodox devaluation. This timing would also help to placate fears that the crawling peg was leading up to another major exchange rate adjustment. With regard to Argentina, restoration and subsequent maintenance of the average real exchange rate prevailing in 1968-1969, when it and relative agricultural prices were close to their prewar parity, would probably be adequate to produce benefits similar to those enjoyed by the countries that have already adopted the crawling peg, if at the same time appropriate domestic policies were introduced. [8]

Improved policy management would also be facilitated if the exchange rate were viewed as a long-term rather than a short-term policy tool. As was argued above, devaluation is not likely to be a very effective instrument in solving short-term external payments crises anyway; in Argentina it is necessary to place greater reliance on domestic income reduction and redistribution. A more appropriate role for exchange policy is to make such painful and socially costly readjustments less necessary by stabilizing export expansion and import substitution incentives. The best of all short-term payments policies would in fact be a long-term policy that enabled the country to get off the razor's edge of just balancing its international accounts, ready to fall at the first stroke of bad luck into another costly recession.

Real exchange rate maintenance would probably be the most effective single policy that could be devised to expand agricultural output and exports, under the assumption that further substantial improvement in the sector's relative prices is ruled out for sociopolitical reasons. As was argued in Chapter 2, agricultural growth will be seriously inhibited unless specialization in production and investment in improvements with relatively long pay-out periods is encouraged through greater relative price stability. Another barrier to the improvement of agricultural productivity is the relatively high cost of many modern, manufactured agricultural inputs that are produced domestically.[9] There is no reason in principle, however, why sales of domestically manufactured inputs to pampean farmers should not benefit from the subsidy that the same goods would receive if they were exported directly. Such indirect export subsidization might well generate even larger additional foreign exchange earnings per unit of domestic resources employed, and insofar as domestic producers of fertilizer and other manufactured agricultural inputs are subject to increasing returns to scale—and as was seen in the last chapter there is strong evidence that this is indeed frequently the case—the export subsidization of farm inputs could lead over time to significant reductions in real domestic production costs.

The Argentine cattle cycle is another major problem that requires greater policy flexibility to reach a solution. It will be recalled from Chapter 2 that the short-to medium-term price elasticity of supply of beef is perverse, so that an abrupt increase in its price relative to that of grains that compete for use of the same land leads to an immediate reduction in export availabilities. The primary effect on the balance of payments of a decline in the volume of beef exports is customarily offset at least partially by an increase in the export price, but the secondary effect of reduction in the area devoted to export crop production can be much more serious. An increase in pasture land sufficient to accommodate a 5 percent expansion in cattle herds is associated with a 10 percent reduction in cropped area in the pampas. This problem of substitution is especially serious because the variability of beef production is higher in Argentina than in any other major producing country.[10]

If the cattle cycle is initiated by an abrupt change in international market prices, the most suitable short-term policy would be offsetting export retentions or subsidies. The purpose of these retentions or subsidies would not be to interfere with longer term relative price movements but to moderate them over time, particularly when the beef/grain price ratio is near its upper or lower critical limits.[11]

A reasonable policy target might be to prevent externally induced variations in the beef/grain price ratio from exceeding 5 or 10 percent per annum. This could be accomplished by operating on the price of beef alone, because fluctuations in the prices of the commodities that enter into the denominator of the beef/grain price ratio tend to be largely offsetting. If massive, periodical devaluations are replaced by a policy of real exchange rate maintenance, the main justification for general export taxes—namely, to soak up windfall profits generated by large devaluations—would be eliminated.

If an abrupt rise in the relative price of beef were of domestic origin, on the other hand, export retentions would not only divert reduced supplies from exports to domestic consumption but they would severely squeeze the margins of the large packing plants specializing in exports. Export packing plants have in fact been one of the principal victims of relative price instability in Argentina, so much so that they have had little incentive to modernize and on occasion have been driven into bankruptcy. A temporary, progressive sales tax by weight of steers delivered to market would in principle be a preferable way of discouraging the speculative retention of animals, but such a tax would be very difficult to administer given the large number of small-scale slaughterhouses that can buy directly from cattle raisers. The only effective way of preventing a drought-induced cattle cycle is thus a more secure feed supply. This can be provided by the replacement of natural grasslands by permanent pasture sown with drought resistant varieties, by an expansion in cut fodder storage capacity, and by development of the feedlot system. But for these improvements to be more generally profitable in Argentina, relative prices would have to be stable enough to encourage investment in specialized improvements that reduce land-use flexibility. Real exchange rate maintenance and stabilization of the beef/grain price ratio are the most suitable policies for this purpose.

A crawling peg exchange rate would also facilitate adjustment of domestic minimum or support prices for export crops more in accordance with world market trends. Except for wheat, support prices have almost always been fixed far below current market prices because of the reluctance of the authorities to run the risk of accumulating large inventories during periods of increasing overvaluation of the peso. Under a policy of real exchange rate maintenance, agricultural commodity stock variations could also be expected to be offsetting as between individual products. It would be wise, however, to base adjustments in the support price of each crop partly on the rate of stock accumulation so as to prevent the system from becoming a method of permanent subsidization of commodities facing a declining world market. Used strictly as a short-term policy tool, inventory movements can play a very useful role in preventing disposal of bumper harvests like that of 1965 from depressing export prices, or in cushioning the effect of production shortfalls on current export revenue.

Accumulation of inventories of imported goods can on the other hand have a very disruptive short-term influence on balance of payments stability. Speculative importing in anticipation of balance of payments difficulties appears to have played a significant role in intensifying Argentina's external payments problems on a number of occasions, the most recent being in 1969. In this year merchandise imports rose by more than 400 million dollars over the previous year's level, due mainly to an increase in iron and steel products (blooms, slabs, laminated sheets, and tubes), automotive parts and components, and other raw and intermediate products far in excess of the corresponding increase in output of user industries. The best prevention is again a more flexible exchange rate policy that reduces expectations of a large crisis devaluation, combined with domestic interest rates that are sufficiently positive in real terms to make idle inventory accumulation costly. The same policy tandem is also the most effective tool for discouraging destabilizing international capital movements.

Compensation of Sector Dualism

Greater policy flexibility also implies some accommodation to existing economic "distortions." The most important distortion that bears on balance of payments policy is the existence of an internationally competitive agricultural sector together with a largely noncompetitive manufacturing sector. If a uniform exchange rate and tariff system were established, this discrepancy would of course disappear: relative domestic and international prices would tend to converge, thereby shifting the internal terms of trade in favor of agriculture and enabling it to bid away resources from manufacturing. Since this outcome is politically unacceptable, as it tends to be in all countries suffering in some important degree from sectoral dualism (in advanced countries it is usually the agricultural sector that is protected from international competition), differential exchange rates and/or tariffs and subsidies would have to be introduced to make both sectors internationally competitive without drastic changes in relative domestic prices. There are many ways of doing this: through multiple exchange rates, by allowing the exchange rate to be determined by the more efficient sector and subsidizing the less efficient one, by fixing the exchange rate at a level needed to make the less efficient sector internationally competitive and taxing the other sector, or by other methods such as the U.S. PL-480 program (which enables the government to support high domestic prices for agriculture and dispose of surpluses abroad on concessional terms).

Argentine policymakers have also been very schizophrenic on this subject. They have been quite willing to protect high relative prices of manufactures in the domestic market, but they have been very hesitant to adopt policies that would permit manufactures to compete in foreign markets. The chief reason for this schizophrenia is probably quite similar to that responsible for their reluctance to give up a fixed exchange rate even though they are unable to stop inflation: the orthodox view is that local industry should become more internationally competitive by increasing its productivity, not by receiving special exchange rate concessions or subsidies. The stubbornness of advocates of this ideal norm of behavior has not been shaken by the facts that few domestic industries are likely to become internationally competitive at an exchange rate just suitable for agriculture as long as high import barriers force them to pay noncompetitive prices for their inputs, and that it is even less likely that these barriers can soon be removed.

Although a variety of possible methods exist for compensating sector dualism, as a practical matter it is usually wise to try to draw on a country's previous experience in the design of new policies. Argentina has experimented with four methods: government marketing boards, multiple exchange rates, compensated devaluation, and nontraditional export subsidies. The most important example of the first method was IAPI, the marketing board established after World War II to capture windfall profits from agricultural exporters and subsidize imports of "essential" goods. In performing these functions IAPI did not of course help compensate sectoral dualism, nor was this its purpose; but a state trading board could in principle be used for doing so, although it is not clear what advantages it would have over other methods except possibly in dealing with other countries that also employ state trading boards to market their products.

Argentina's experience with multiple exchange rates has not been very felicitous either. The main reason is that effective implementation requires a very efficient system of exchange controls and extraordinary resistance to the temptation of progressively differentiating rates to take care of specific commodity problems. With Argentina's wide-open borders and the great skill traders have developed in under- and overinvoicing, it would probably be wiser to avoid using pervasive exchange controls except possibly during brief periods of national emergency.

The objective of compensated devaluation is to raise the exchange rate to a level above that required by agricultural exporters and levy an export tax on them large enough to prevent their domestic relative prices from rising sharply. The simultaneous lowering of import duties is designed to reduce relative input costs which, combined with a higher tax-free exchange rate for nonagricultural products, provides a special incentive for expanding manufactured exports. Insofar as the lowering of import duties actually reduces the divergence between relative domestic and international prices, compensated devaluation has the advantage over straight export subsidization of diminishing sector dualism instead of simply compensating for it. The experience of 1967-1970 appears to demonstrate, however, that effective import duty reduction, unless accompanied by real exchange rate maintenance and rapid expansion in GDP and exports, is likely to be short-lived because of its short-term effect on the balance of payments and vested interest resistance to greater import competition.

The most feasible way to compensate sector dualism, at least until the foreign exchange constraint is eased and the country achieves a higher, more sustained rate of growth, would therefore seem to be nonagricultural export subsidization. The main purpose of such a system should be to provide a stable incentive for the development over time of industrial capacity explicitly intended for export. Given the lead time between the decision to develop such capacity and its coming into production, and the difficulty and expense of converting production facilities from one use to another if markets are not found for the goods they were originally designed to produce, long-term export incentives should be consolidated by combining the subsidy program with a stable or gradually rising real exchange rate. The exact level of export subsidies is in fact probably less important to full cost exporters than confidence in their longer-term stability. Marginal cost exporters would also have a greater incentive to install more adequately scaled plants in anticipation of future domestic market growth if they could count on a supplementary export market free from real exchange rate uncertainty.[12]

The desirable level of export subsidization is not easy to determine. Toward the end of the 1960s it was estimated that the average differential between domestic and international prices of manufactures was a little over 40 percent, although the dispersion of relative price differentials is extremely large.[13] Considering also the potential export capacity of decreasing cost industries, an export subsidy amounting to substantially less than 40 percent ad valorem could be expected to provide an adequate incentive for a substantial number of manufactured products. On the other hand, the upper limit to an export subsidy is that level which would make importing for re-export profitable. To avoid this possibility the following condition must be fulfilled:[14]

$(1 - e_x) (1 + s_x) (1 + e_h) < (1 + c) (1 + t)$, where e_x and e_h are

foreign tariffs and domestic taxes on the export goods,

s_x = export subsidy,

c = international transport costs, and

t = import duties.

If for example, $e_x = .15$, $e_h = .10$, $s_x = .25$, and $c = .15$—quite reasonable values of these variables for Argentina — import duties (t) would have to exceed 11 percent ad valorem to fulfill this condition. Since the unweighted average of Argentine import duties exceeds 50 percent, export subsidies could probably be even larger than the current 20-30 percent without providing an incentive for re-exporting imports.

The danger is greater that export subsidies of this magnitude might enable some processed agricultural goods, or other products which are large users of internationally traded raw materials or intermediate goods, to be sold abroad at prices insufficient to recover the world market cost of traded inputs. This possibility arises if the subsidy represents a significantly larger proportion of the market price of a commodity than domestic value added in processing or production. A valid argument can therefore be made in favor of discriminatory subsidies related to industrial value added, a principle which has in fact been incorporated into Argentine export promotion legislation. Such discrimination has, however, been very difficult to apply in practice and is probably not feasible except for a very few broad categories of products. The proliferation of different kinds and categories of subsidies would instead likely lead to a situation similar to indiscriminate ISI protection or an unwieldly proliferation of multiple exchange rates to take care of specific commodity problems.

Perhaps the most dramatic example of this kind, and one that has surprisingly been praised by some economists (who are perhaps unfamiliar with the details), is Korea's export promotion policy. Initially the Korean government motivated industrial exporters with a realistic foreign exchange rate and exemptions from payment of customs and other indirect taxes, but it subsequently expanded benefits to include accelerated depreciation privileges, a 50 percent reduction in income and corporate taxes, 30 percent discounts on power and transportation charges, subsidized bank loans at 6 percent interest (instead of at the going rate of about 26 percent), grants of one-year monopoly rights for new product or new market development, and other special privileges that have made it virtually impossible to measure the cost of subsidization and must have led to increasing distortions in the allocation of financial, public utility, and other resources.[15]

It seems that part of the explanation for Korea's policy is that proliferation of special export incentives in recent years has been used to compensate for the increasing overvaluation of the won. Real exchange rate maintenance would therefore appear to be a necessary condition for avoiding this kind of experience. Another check on the excessive proliferation of subsidies would be to make it difficult to disguise their fiscal cost. Unlike ISI protection, which does not normally entail direct fiscal outlays and may even provide some additional tariff revenue (unless all protective tariffs are set at prohibitive levels), export subsidies usually require a sacrifice of public funds and should appear as such in the documents that are subjected to budgetary review and control.

A related issue is the relative advantage of subsidies that reduce the costs of export firms compared to those that increase their export revenue. Their different effects can be illustrated by the diagrams in figure 4-1, which are basically the same as the one presented earlier. The increase in exports from a revenue subsidy that raises the export price from Px to P'x (see the first diagram) would equal Q_3Q_5 plus

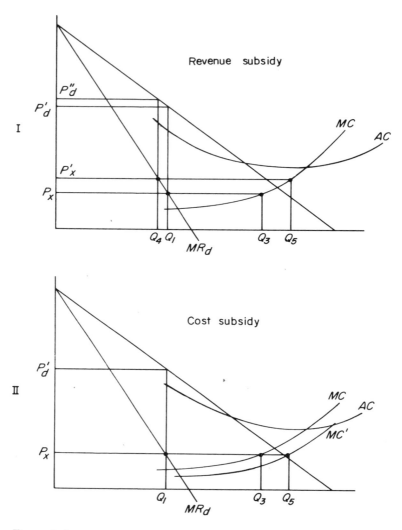

Figure 4-1.

Q_4Q_1, the first arising from an increase in the firm's total output and the second from a reduction in its domestic sales so as to maximize total revenue. This reduction in domestic sales would lead to a rise in the internal price from P'd to P''d. If a cost-reducing subsidy were instead used to generate the same increase in total output by shifting the firm's marginal cost curve downward from MC to MC' (see the second diagram), the firms would have no incentive to reduce domestic sales and the domestic price would remain at P'_d.

Exports would be increased by only Q_3Q_5, however, and the amount of the subsidy per unit of additional foreign exchange earned would be greater insofar as it benefited production for the domestic market as well as for export, a very likely possibility since in practice it is almost impossible to limit cost subsidy benefits to a particular part of the production of a firm.

This kind of cost subsidy was recommended above for pampean agriculture because of the serious problem of upward inflexibility of relative agricultural prices in Argentina, but this position is not inconsistent with the opposite one taken with respect to industry. An input cost subsidy to Argentine agriculture would provide an incentive for increasing the value of output per unit of land (and hopefully promote a shift to the right of the cost curves in the diagram) which, in view of the rather low price and income elasticities of domestic demand for food, should lead to a much larger than proportional increase in export availabilities. Furthermore, one of the purposes of the proposed subsidy is to bias incentives in favor of more intensive utilization of the subsidized inputs, whereas this is clearly not the intent of subsidization of transport and electricity charges and interest rates for industry.

It might also be objected that the fiscal cost of export subsidization would be excessive, especially in view of the serious problems of public finance that have also afflicted Argentina during most of the period under analysis. The net fiscal cost of a subsidy depends on the extent to which additional tax revenue will be generated by increased exports. If the balance of payments is really the binding constraint on the rate of economic growth, as appears to have generally been the case in Argentina, then it is appropriate to offset the cost of subsidization against the increase in tax revenue that more rapid economic growth would make possible. According to one calculation based on somewhat restrictive assumptions, namely, that exports pay all existing taxes at the same rate as domestic sales and that all of the rise in tax revenue can be considered an offset against export subsidies, the maximum allowable subsidy consistent with an unchanged fiscal balance ranged by industrial subsector from 170 to over 700 percent ad valorem.[16]

In conclusion, then, it would appear advisable for Argentina to try to compensate sector dualism by consolidating the existing system of export subsidization. Over time it might become increasingly possible, if the balance of payments constraint is eased and a more rapid, sustained rate of growth is achieved, to accompany crawling peg exchange rate adjustments with equivalent reductions in import duties so as progressively to narrow divergencies between relative domestic and international prices. Although it would be tempting to try to discriminate subsidies in favor of higher value-added activities, caution is recommended because of the difficulty of identifying legitimate cases (for example, value added can be raised simply by padding profits) and because of political and administrative complications. It would therefore be preferable to avoid the risk of introducing further policy-induced misallocations of resources by making export subsidization more uniform than it has been in the past. Finally, because of the danger that a high uniform export subsidy might enable manufactures that are large users of internationally traded raw materials (notable domestic agricultural products) to be sold abroad at prices insufficient to recover the world market value of traded inputs, the amount of total export subsidies should probably not exceed the average level recently in force, namely between 20 and 30 percent ad valorem.

Mediative Policy and Equilibrium with Growth

A disconcerting feature of economic policy analysis is how the same body of evidence can be interpreted in diametrically opposed ways. For example, one interpretation of the great cyclical instability of the Argentine economy is that it demonstrates the unwillingness of Argentines to live within their means by adopting appropriate policies to equilibrate the supply and demand for foreign exchange. Another interpretation is that it is the result of the intransigency of orthodox policymakers who refused to adjust their policies realistically to Argentine conditions. Paradoxically both of these interpretations are correct in the context of the very different premises upon which they are founded.

The basic premise of the first interpretation is that it is the purpose of rational economic policy to root out the distortions responsible for balance of payments disequilibrium. The economic model that most advocates of this interpretation have in mind is one of competitive general equilibrium under the international rules of the game established after World War II at Bretton Woods, which require that each country adopt a fixed parity exchange rate and thereafter defend it with appropriate domestic monetary and fiscal policies. Use of quantitative controls or discriminatory trade practices is considered a violation of these rules of the game, and exchange rate adjustments are supposed to be made only as a last resort after every available domestic remedy has been used and failed.

Alternative approaches that would provide for greater exchange rate and domestic policy flexibility have customarily been looked upon in financial circles, both in Argentina and in some international agencies, as being dangerously permissive of irresponsible government conduct, if not downright immoral. In the absence of the fixed exchange rate discipline, what, they ask, will prevent government from constantly indulging in excessive deficit financing and monetary expansion? The ideal policy solution expressed by several Argentine bankers and businessmen to one of the authors was to make it even more difficult for the country to escape from this discipline by returning to the gold standard.

Advocates of this position are correct in insisting that domestic inflation must be curbed if balance of payments equilibrium is to be maintained with a fixed exchange rate. Supporters of the opposing view do not in general disagree with this proposition; instead they maintain that inflation cannot be curbed quickly by restrictive monetary and fiscal policy and that the attempt to do so in defense of a parity exchange rate has been one of the main causes of cyclical instability. In the absence of domestic price stabilization the struggle to impose a fixed exchange rate discipline on the economy has, they argue, taken on masochistic overtones by obliging the country to pay for its inflationary "sins" with frequent balance of payments crises, periodical massive devaluation, and a very irregular rate of growth.

The balance of payments policy recommendations contained in this chapter are intended to provide a realistic and viable alternative. Their chief rationale is not that by themselves they can remove the balance of payments constraint on the country's future growth, but that they are much more likely to facilitate improved policy management than the attempt to follow an orthodox or a normative policy strategy that cannot be enforced. If in the absence of adequate mediative institutions or the power to impose their will, policymakers are obliged to buy political support for their programs with ad hoc concessions to different interest groups, it makes little sense for them to try to adhere to normative policy goals such as fixed exchange rate or zero inflation. Such an attempt only leads to frustration and failure when political concessions on wage increases, public utility prices, tariffs, and tax exemptions generate a level of inflation, fiscal deficits, and balance of payments pressure inconsistent with the government's program. In the presence of so many divergencies from the behavioral norms assumed in setting such policy goals, it is impossible even to say whether achievement of any single goal would be desirable or whether it might instead produce still more serious distortions.

5   Secular Inflation and Stabilization Policy

The degree of flexibility required for a viable balance of payments policy is determined largely by the degree of stability that it is possible to impart to the domestic price level. If the upward movement of prices cannot be restrained for significant periods of time at or below the international rate of inflation, any attempt to hold the exchange rate at a fixed level will sooner or later lead to an external payments crisis.

This inescapable fact of economic life has been repeatedly demonstrated under persistent inflationary conditions in Argentina. The country holds the unenviable record of maintaining one of the highest rates of prolonged inflation of any country in recent history. During the period 1949-1965 the cost of living index rose at an average annual rate of over 28 percent, which placed it fifth in close competition with four other Latin American countries and Korea.[1] Aside from these six, no other country averaged more than 10 percent during the period, and for the world as a whole the average rate of inflation was well under 5 percent per annum.

Maintenance of such a rapid, sustained rate of inflation that neither explodes nor is brought under control over time is a rather novel phenomenon in economic history that observers have had difficulty explaining. That the Argentine economy has been under almost constant inflationary pressure over the last twenty years is of course not difficult to explain: attempts by Perón to bring about a radical shift in the distribution of income, the slow growth of agriculture, the development of domestic industries behind high import barriers, and other "structural" causes constitute a sufficient condition for generating such pressure. What is uncommon is for this kind of pressure to lead to very high and prolonged *rates* of inflation.

It has therefore been argued that independently of the underlying causes or structural imbalances that may have provided the initial stimulus to a rise in the price level, some kind of propagating mechanism has also operated to reinforce and sustain the rate of inflation. If this mechanism could be brought under control, it might then be possible to moderate inflation sufficiently so that more orthodox macroeconomic policies could be relied upon to preserve external equilibrium. The inflationary propagator most

113

frequently singled out by economists is excessive monetary expansion.

The Monetarist Explanation of Inflation

One important school of thought has taken the position that excessive monetary expansion is both a necessary and sufficient condition for explaining inflation of the Argentine type. The "monetarist" argument runs essentially along the following lines: given the close relationship between markets for goods and for financial assets, overall "excess" demand in the former can only exist if there is "excess" supply in the latter, in the sense that the increase in the stock of money exceeds the demand for holding cash. In this case excess liquidity spills over into the goods market to inflate effective demand and force up prices. Or looked at another way, the cost-push effect of excessive wage demands cannot affect the general price level unless they are "validated" by monetary expansion; if they are not, such wage increases, when passed on in higher prices, would create a gap between the total value of output and effective demand and generate sufficient unemployment to moderate wage demands.

No one would of course seriously argue that high, sustained rates of inflation can occur with no long-term increase in the money supply. The issues at question are instead: (1) whether the demand for real cash balances is sufficiently stable or predictable to allow monetary policy to play an efficient role in controlling inflation, and (2) whether economic agents respond to monetary restrictions in a way that helps restore equilibrium (or at least greatly moderates the rate of inflation) in a reasonable period of time at an acceptable cost in terms of unemployment, bankruptcies, and loss of production. Use of the terms "sufficiently stable," "reasonable period," and "acceptable cost" imply that the answers to these questions (as with most questions concerning economic policy) involve value judgments. This is even more true if, as some monetarists insist, to be effective monetary restriction must also be credible, that is, the public must be convinced that monetary restrictions will be made to stick to induce them to act in the desired way. If confidence were the key to the effectiveness of monetary policy, however, the outcome of policy would depend not so much on the particular policy employed as on who made and tried to implement the policy. It could indeed be argued that severe monetary restriction is either ineffective if employed by authorities who lack credibility, or unnecessary if credible authorities can change price expectations largely by convincing the public that they intend to stabilize the economy.

Analysis of the modern, monetary theory of inflation must begin with discussion of the critical role played by the demand for cash balances. According to this theory the demand for money is not only a function of income and expenditure but also of the price of competing assets and of price expectations. Thus, when the price level rises, the increased cost of holding idle cash balances, which neither yield a rate of return nor appreciate in value, induces the public to replace a portion of its cash by holdings of other assets that provide a better hedge against inflation. The relation between income and the stock of money (or the velocity of circulation) is therefore not assumed constant, as it was in the old theory, but is considered a key variable subject to monetary management: it is the responsibility of the monetary authorities to prevent a flight from money from inflating expenditure on goods and services by making it more attractive to hold financial assets, namely by restricting credit and driving up the rate of interest. [2]

The efficiency of monetary restriction as a short-term policy tool therefore depends critically on the behavior of demand for cash balances and is enhanced by the existence of a well-functioning market for financial assets. More specifically, price expectations must be incorporated functionally into reasonably reliable estimates of the demand for money to guide rational monetary management under inflation. Friedman, Cagan, and others have attempted to develop a methodology for doing this: they hypothesize that expectations are related to past, observed price increases in accordance with some empirically testable model of distributed lags, a methodology that has been tested with data from a considerable number of countries. [3]

Empirical research on the demand for money in Argentina has, however, produced mixed results. Dagnino Pastore found a significant relationship between prices, income, and the demand for money during the early part of the period 1935-1960, but beginning in the 1950s his relationship broke down. Lopez and Damus were also unsuccessful with quarterly and monthly data for the period 1959-1963. Diz, using the Cagan specification for price expectations, was on the other hand able to explain a high proportion of annual changes in real per capita money balances for the period 1935-1962 as a whole, but beginning in the 1950s the average weighted lag of past price increases that best "explained" price expectations increased substantially in length. In other words, Diz's findings would lead us to believe that as the rate of inflation accelerated in Argentina, assets holders based their expectations on the future rate of inflation on price increases in the more distant past.[4] The authors' own experiments with quarterly data for the period 1957-1968 confirm these unsatisfactory results, but when a negative log time trend was introduced into the estimating equation, the coefficients of all variables became highly significant, the coefficient of determination (R^2) rose to .945, and short lags became the most significant proxy of price expectations (see Appendix A). After Krieger Vasena was appointed Economics Minister in 1967, however, the log time trend equation also failed to estimate accurately the demand for money.

These findings imply that instability of the demand for cash balances is a serious impediment to effective control of inflation through monetary policy. The erratic decline in the ratio of the stock money to GDP from .28 in 1954 to .14 in 1963[5] was almost certainly related to rising price expectations and to the reduced attractiveness of holding cash balances, but alternating periods of very tight and somewhat more lax credit also contributed to monetary instability. Monetary authorities have in fact been accused of overkill during this period, of so restricting the supply of money that the economy stagnated and monetary and fiscal policy instruments were undermined by the pressures put upon them by the continued, rapid rise in prices. Credit documents of reputable firms and debt to the public sector (unpaid tax, social security, and other obligations) began to "circulate" on a wide scale as partial substitutes for money; and between 1959 and 1962, the two years of most severe credit rationing, the number of taxpaying companies fell by one third in manufacturing and by 60 percent in agriculture, whereas unpaid social security contributions soared to over half of total obligations.[6] When, on the other hand, Krieger Vasena finally appeared to bring inflation under control in the late 1960s, he did so by imposing price and wage controls while following an expansionary monetary policy. The 44 percent increase in private bank credit permitted in 1968 was the largest on record, but the additional liquidity was used mainly to finance a construction boom and to increase holdings of financial assets (including 20 billion pesos of National Public Works Bonds) instead of generating excess demand and pushing up the price level.

A policy implication that can be drawn from this experience is that monetary policy cannot be relied upon alone to eliminate rapid, secular inflation, especially in the absence of strong fiscal discipline. In the crunch macroeconomic policy is only as effective as its weakest link. It can therefore be argued that Argentine experience does not really disprove the monetary theory of inflation: money as conventionally measured simply ceased to represent accurately the real money supply, and consequently the monetary authorities lost control over the market for financial assets. The log time trend in the demand for money equation referred to above may thus be a proxy for the growth of "black market money," which suddenly began to dry up when Krieger Vasena's policies reduced price expectations and made it more attractive to hold legal financial assets.

Structural and Cost-Push Explanations of Inflation

Another interpretation of stabilization experience in Argentina and other Latin American countries is held by the so-called structuralists. In contrast to the emphasis placed by monetarists on excessive overall demand as the cause of inflation, structuralists maintain that the stagnation of agriculture, the inelastic supply of foreign exchange, and the inability of government to increase real tax revenue make it impossible for a country like Argentina to grow without inflation. Not that inflation resolves the conflict between stabilization and growth, but restriction of demand through the use of macroeconomic policy simply tends to make matters worse.

The pessimistic attitude of structuralists toward the use of macroeconomic policy for stabilization purposes is based on what they perceive to be the effects of the existing distribution of income, wealth, and political power. The problem of inelastic supply is attributed in large measure to the importance of *latifundistas* (large landholders) who, concerned with maintaining their social status by means of conspicuous consumption, neglect their farms, while monopolistic control of industry by powerful domestic and foreign interest groups generates large profits on small turnover. The combined effect of this structure of ownership on supply, income distribution, and the composition of expenditure leads to a kind of inflation-stagnation trap: real wages cannot rise appreciably because wage increases are almost immediately passed on in higher prices, and even if they were not, the increased domestic demand for food would reduce exports, thereby producing a balance of payments crisis. Such a crisis cannot be avoided by redistributing income against wages either, because expenditures out of nonwage income are so import-intensive that their growth also soon leads to external disequilibrium. At the same time, direct government action to help correct this state of affairs is hampered by inadequate powers and fiscal resources. At the root of this dilemma is the conflict between relative prices and factor remunerations as the determinant of resource allocation on the one hand and of distributive income shares on the other: breaking the food and foreign exchange supply bottlenecks and diverting expenditure from imports to domestic goods would allegedly require a transfer of real income to farmers and other entrepreneurs larger than wage earners and the precarious fiscal situation could tolerate. Hence the conclusion that to stop inflation it is necessary to introduce far-reaching institutional reforms that would permit improvement of resource allocation and income distribution simultaneously.

It is immediately apparent even from this oversimplified description of the structuralist position that proper analysis of its implications for stabilization policy would require comparing the behavior of the Argentine economy under alternative institutional arrangements. Such an analysis, however, far exceeds the scope of this book, which is concerned with policymaking under existing pluralistic conditions in which no political group has the power to restructure society according to its own "ideal" model. Within these limitations it is nevertheless possible to consider the structuralist proposition that the persistence of inflation under existing institutional arrangements is due largely to the unresponsiveness of the economy to market price incentives. It has already been noted that farmers seem more responsive to price and investment incentives than structuralists usually assume, and that price incentives have been seriously undermined by great relative price instability; but it is necessary to take a harder look at the closely related argument that Argentine inflation has mainly been of the cost-push variety.

A necessary condition for cost inflation is the existence of factor and goods market imperfections that prevent idle resources from restraining price increases. Wage-push, "administered price," "sellers," and "demand-shift" inflations all depend in varying degrees on strongly organized labor unions, the oligopolistic power of firms, immobilities, and/or adjustment delays to make them work.[7] Most economists will admit that such market imperfections are not uncommon, but many will also insist that these imperfections do not all work in the same direction (for example, oligopolists may be confronted by monopsonists) and that at least in the longer run their inflationary effects will be mitigated unless reinforced by demand inflation. Since few economists will deny that cost inflation can be stopped if unemployment is allowed to rise enough, the whole debate seems to turn on how much unemployment is considered"normal" or tolerable. Indeed, since it is generally agreed that a certain amount of "frictional" unemployment is necessary to assure relative wage-price stability, disagreement could be formally resolved simply by defining full employment as that level which is consistent with price stability.[8]

Regardless of whether such a definitional "solution" is considered to beg the question, it does point up the relationship between market structure, employment, and the price level. The policy implication is also clear: the more competitive are markets for factors and goods, the closer an economy can approach full employment without generating inflationary pressure. This is not a very helpful guideline for policymakers in developing countries where not much can be done quickly to introduce greater competition except by increasing imports, an option that is usually foreclosed by strong protectionist opposition and by a tight balance of payments situation. Policymakers faced by what they consider cost inflation therefore quite naturally want to know which cost or demand-shift factors are most responsible for pushing up the price level so that they can try to adopt more selective countermeasures. This question unfortunately runs up against the very sticky inflation identification problem.

Perhaps the best example of the difficulty of trying to identify the cost factors responsible for inflation concerns the role of wages. The existence of unemployment is clearly not an indication of the absence of wage-push, because as was pointed out above, the amount of unemployment needed to prevent wage-push depends on the degree of imperfection of labor markets. On the other hand, a rise in real wages in excess of improvements in productivity is quite consistent with demand-pull inflation, whereas the reverse may simply indicate that entrepreneurs have been able to offset the effect of wage-push by substituting other inputs for labor. The effect of higher wages on prices will in fact vary between activities and over time depending on the elasticity of substitution between labor and cooperating factors, of the supply of cooperating factors, of demand for the final product, and on the ratio of wages to total cost.[9]

Despite these reservations, however, there is little room for doubt that wage increases played an important role in Argentine inflation during certain periods, particularly up to the early 1950s and again in 1956, 1958, and 1964-1965. Wage adjustments followed with considerable regularity increases in the cost of living index, and wage adjustments were usually followed by further price hikes in the industries in which they occurred. A good case can also be made for the influence of other cost-push or demand-shift factors such as exchange devaluation, import substitution via high rates of protection, and the slow and uneven growth of agricultural production.[10] The behavior of profit margins at least in foodstuff markets was quite consistent with markup pricing practices, and the role of manufacturers associations in price setting and industry-wide wage bargaining with large labor unions suggests wide interference with market forces.[11] It is very difficult on the other hand to make a strong case for the existence of demand-pull inflationary conditions. Brodersohn has estimated that during the decade following 1958 a substantial proportion of total productive capacity remained unutilized in every year except perhaps 1961, and periodical employment surveys conducted since 1963 show that unemployment has usually been over 5 percent in Buenos Aires and generally higher in other urban centers.

Econometric Models of Price Behavior in Argentina

The impossibility of resolving the conflict between different theories of inflation on the basis of casual empirical observation has led several economists to test more rigorously the dynamics of Argentine inflation by incorporating monetary, wage, exchange rate, and other variables into econometric models of price behavior. One of the earliest attempts was by Diz, inspired by the work of Harberger.[12] Using percentage changes in quarterly data for the period 1946-1962, Diz found that by far the most important determinant of price changes was price expectations (measured as the weighted average of past price increases), whereas the influence of wages was insignificant and of the exchange rate quite small. Variations in money supply with different time lags were also tested, but only instantaneous changes were found to be very significant statistically.

These findings would be very discouraging for policymakers if interpreted to imply that the rate of today's and tomorrow's inflation has already been determined by the rate of past price increases. On the other hand Diz's model is also consistent with an "expectations" explanation of inflation according to which the success of stabilization policy depends on its impact on anticipations. Whatever one's interpretation, however, Diz's findings do not appear to be very well substantiated by later work.

Diaz Alejandro, using half-yearly percentage changes in variables for the period 1950-1965, tested the relationship of price variations to lagged values of wages, the exchange rate, and money supply. In contrast to Diz, Diaz found that the only statistically significant coefficients were for changes in wages and the exchange rate, so that: "these regressions imply that on the whole cost-push elements (wage increases and devaluations) have played an active role in the inflationary process, with monetary expansion taking a more passive role . . . We can say that cost-push elements drove the price level upwards even when money was not expanding in proportion."[13]

A third attempt to develop a model of price behavior in Argentina was made by Maynard and Van Rijckeghem using annual percentage changes in variables also for the period 1950-1965. They concluded that both lagged money supply and current wages appear to be important determinants of the price level, but also that expansion of bank credit to the private sector was inversely correlated with the rate of inflation. This result is explained by the positive correlation between increases in bank credit and variations in nonagricultural output, which all investigators agree are also significantly and inversely related to changes in the price level.[14] Thus, despite the fact that all three studies "explain" between two thirds and three fourths of fluctuations in the rate of inflation, their only point of common agreement is that changes in prices and output are inversely related. The principal explanation for this anomaly appears to be multicolinearity, that is, interdependence between the supposedly independent or explanatory variables in the estimating equations. This should of course come as no surprise, because during prolonged, rapid inflation all variables move up together and fluctuations in their values tend to be synchronized with changes in the overall price level and thus with each other. To the extent that such synchronization is strong, it is impossible to estimate accurately the independent influence of individual explanatory variables on the rate of inflation through simple regression analysis.

The econometric studies cited have therefore employed percentage changes in variables in an effort to reduce multicolinearity, under the assumption that rates of change of independent variables are more likely to be truly independent and to vary in ways that reflect cause and effect relationships more accurately than absolute values or indices. The inclusion of the same independent variable lagged one or more times in a single estimating equation is, however, likely to reintroduce multicolinearity because of the serial correlation that frequently exists between changes in variables like money supply in successive time periods, particularly if the time period chosen for regression analysis is relatively short.

These kinds of problems showed up very clearly when Diaz Alejandro's regressions were rerun by stepping in independent variables one at a time: the money supply coefficients were highly significant until the wage and exchange rate variables were stepped in. Upon examination of the correlation matrix it was found that the simple R between money supply and the exchange rate with the same lag was .67 and that multicolinearity between other pairs of independent variables also appeared to be disturbingly high (although no statistical test exists to tell us what is "too" high). Since the structure of Diz's estimating equations is similar and the time period is shorter, it must be assumed that the same problem distorts his results. The Maynard-Van Rijckeghem equations have a somewhat different structure and use a longer time period, but multicolinearity still appears to be strong (for example, the simple R between variations in wages and in lagged money supply is .63).

Another impediment to the use of econometric price determination models is the occurrence of structural breaks or discontinuities in behavioral relationships. As a check on this possibility, the period covered by Diaz Alejandro's study was split in half, and the two subseries were rerun separately with substantially different results. The most interesting finding was that during the later period (beginning in the first half of 1957) fluctuations in the exchange rate were the overriding determinant of the rate of inflation. The relationship was a bit stronger for wholesale prices than for the cost of living, but in both cases the R^2 was superior to .8 and no other independent variable came even close to being statistically significant.[15]

It was therefore decided to carry out a rather large number of independent experiments with a similar model using quarterly data for the period 1957-1968. A sample of the results is given in table 5-1 (more details appear in Appendix B). They indicate that changes in the price level are significantly related to all of the explanatory variables previously mentioned. The corrected R^2 are similar or slightly higher than those reported on above, the statistical significance of the coefficients is in general higher, the Durban-Watson statistics do not indicate serial correlation of residuals, and at least for some of the cost of living equations the constant terms are not significantly different from zero (indicating that no important explanatory variable has been left out of the

Table 5-1 Regression results on price behavior. (quarterly percentage changes 1957–1968)

	Cost of living					Wholesale prices (excluding agriculture)			
	(1)	(2)	(3)	(4)	(5)	(6)	(7)	(8)	(9)
Constant	1.36 (1.29)[a]	1.96 (1.90)	1.24 (1.03)	1.82 (1.77)	1.83 (1.43)	-2.12 (1.50)	-0.59 (0.43)	-1.40 (0.89)	-2.52 (1.46)
Exchange rate t	.20 (4.13)	.18 (3.40)	.22 (4.27)	–	–	–	–	–	.15 (2.06)
Exchange rate $t-1$	–	–	–	.23 (3.38)	.26 (3.72)	.29 (3.50)	.35 (4.07)	.34 (3.95)	–
GDP t	-1.23 (4.90)	-1.42 (5.67)	-1.14 (4.80)	-.95 (2.87)	-.67 (2.12)	-.95 (2.39)	-.98 (2.31)	-.80 (2.07)	-1.59 (4.70)
Wage rate t	–	.14 (1.64)	.19 (2.31)	.18 (2.10)	.24 (2.79)	.18 (1.76)	.16 (1.50)	.22 (2.14)	.25 (2.10)
Wage rate $t-1$	.18 (2.40)	–	–	–	–	.24 (2.47)	–	–	–
Money supply $t-1$	.64 (3.96)	.64 (3.70)	–	.52 (2.74)	–	.74 (3.21)	.74 (3.02)	–	–
Money supply $t-1.5$	–	–	.31 (3.56)	–	.19 (1.79)	–	–	.41 (3.18)	.63 (5.05)
$\bar{R}^2$	.74	.72	.71	.72	.69	.77	.74	.73	.66
D-W statistic	1.62	1.71	1.83	1.42	1.59	2.03	1.93	1.74	1.90

[a]The figures in parentheses under the coefficients are T values, which for 40 degrees of freedom indicate the following: 2.71, significant at the 1 percent level; 2.42, significant at 2 percent level; and 1.68, significant at the 10 percent level.

equation). The correlation matrix in table 5-2 does, however, reveal that there is still a problem of multicolinearity, although it appears to be less serious than in the other regression studies analyzed above.

The regression results presented in table 5-1 imply that the most important determinant of the rate of inflation is the relationship between monetary expansion and the rate of growth of real GDP. Money supply can be increased at least 50 percent more rapidly than GDP while prices remain stable, as long as wage rates rise *pari passu* with GDP and the exchange rate remains unchanged. The higher the rate of inflation, however, the lower the permissable rate of expansion in money supply relative to that of GDP (given the rate of increase in real GDP and wages). In other words, the relative rate of monetary expansion becomes more inflationary the higher the rate of increase in prices. This implication is quite consistent with the expected behavior of the demand for cash balances under inflation, as was pointed out earlier. Changes in money supply in the previous quarter appear to be more closely related to current variations in the price level than changes in other periods, although it was not possible to test the relative importance of different lagged values by including them in the same estimating equation because of multicolinearity (the simple R between changes in money supply in periods t-1 and t-1.5 is .84).

The coefficient of the wage variable in the previous period is also larger and more statistically significant than it is in other quarters, but in this case the very low correlation between successive wage adjustments permitted inclusion of the variable with different lags in the same estimating equation (see equation 6 in table 5-1). The results suggest that wage increments over time may act independently and cumulatively on the price level, which if true would give greater support to the wage-push explanation of inflation than is provided by the other equations.[16] The influence of changes in the exchange rate on the price level is also highly significant statistically, but it is not clear how this influence should be interpreted. If it represents cost-push, one would expect the lagged value of the variable to have a more significant coefficient, as in the case of wages, but the reverse is true in the cost of living equations. In the wholesale price equations, on the other hand, the size of the exchange rate coefficient implies that a much larger proportion of devaluation is almost immediately passed on in higher nonagricultural prices than internationally traded goods represent in the cost of production.[17] It is therefore quite likely that increases in the exchange rate also generate changes in price expectations. If

Table 5-2 Correlation matrix.

	$P_{c. \text{ of } 1.}$	P_{wh-ag}	ER_t	ER_{t-1}	Y_t	W_t	W_{t-1}	L_{t-1}	$L_{t-1.5}$
$P_{c. \text{ of } 1.}$	—	.85	.70	.80	-.50	.43	.43	.49	.51
P_{wh-ag}		—	.57	.82	-.48	.39	.47	.50	.61
ER_t			—	.55	-.24	.42	.18	.45	.34
ER_{t-1}				—	-.55	.29	.41	.40	.51
Y_t					—	.07	-.25	.22	-.02
W_t						—	.07	.45	.25
W_{t-1}							—	.16	.35
L_{t-1}								—	.84
$L_{t-1.5}$									—

Definitions

$P_{c. \text{ of } 1.}$ percent change in cost of living index.
P_{wh-ag} percent change in wholesale price index excluding agriculture.
ER_t percent change exchange rate, current quarter.
ER_{t-1} percent change exchange rate, previous quarter.
Y_t percent change three quarter moving average GDP in constant prices.
W_t percent change wage rate index, current quarter.
W_{t-1} percent change wage rate index, previous quarter.
L_{t-1} percent change primary liquidity, previous quarter.
$L_{t-1.5}$ percent change primary liquidity, average last two quarters.

true this is very important for policy purposes, because a more flexible exchange rate might generate less expectation of future price rises and thus have considerably less inflationary impact than implied in the regression results, which reflect the periodical massive devaluations that occurred during most of the period analyzed.

Implications for Stabilization Policy

Empirical research on Argentine inflation thus seems on balance to indicate that, despite evidence of substantial idle capacity during most years since 1958, monetary expansion has played a very significant role in determining the rate of increase in the price level. It would be naive, however, to view the relationship between money supply and prices as one of simple cause and effect. Empirical findings are also consistent with the hypothesis that the prime movers in Argentine inflation can be found on the cost side, but that the actual *rate* at which prices are forced up by autonomous increases in costs depends on the rate of monetary expansion relative to the rate GDP is growing, which is influenced by the rate of expansion in bank credit to the private sector in relation to the increase in costs. Thus the chain of cause and effect comes full circle and we end up with a chicken and egg situation.

To break through this circularity it might be more helpful to approach the problem from the point of view of the policy variables that appear to influence the rate of growth of GDP. Maynard and Van Rijckeghem divided total real gross output between agriculture (Z_A) and "rest" (Z_R) and, using annual percentage changes for the period 1950-1964, estimated the following equation (standard errors in parentheses):[18]

$$Z_r = 2.30 + 0.13 \ (B_r - N) + 0.22 \ m_{0-1/3} + 0.13 \ Z_a, \ R^2 = .81$$
$$ (0.04) (0.05) \phantom{m_{0-1/3} +} (0.09) D\text{-}W = 1.74$$

where:

B_r = bank credit to the "rest" sector,

N = wages paid by the "rest" sector, and

$m_{0-1/3}$ = dollar value of noncapital goods imports lagged one third of a year.

In view of the significance of private bank credit expansion relative to the increase in wages as a determinant of domestic output, policymakers, if they are concerned about stabilization but do not think they can impose enough recession on the economy to hold down wages (or believe that other policies are more appropriate for this purpose), should consider the possibility of applying monetary restrictions in a way that affects private bank credit as little as possible.

The other major determinant of monetary expansion (excluding changes in foreign exchange reserves) is of course Central Bank financing of the government deficit. Increases in the money supply would therefore presumably be less likely to have inflationary repercussions *ceteris paribus* if they were accompanied by a tighter fiscal policy. The analytical explanation for this differential effect of monetary expansion is not immediately clear, however, if it is considered that money is fungible and that its point of injection into an economy makes no difference except possibly in the very short run. The role of bank credit in the financing of firms is, however, very different under conditions of secular inflation than it is in a stable economy with well-developed financial markets. The excess demand for bank credit over generally limited supplies at legally controlled interest rates leads to tight credit rationing, so that firms, which naturally keep their cash on hand at a bare minimum, are obliged to finance their current operations mainly through the adroit juggling of accounts payable and receivable. The leverage of bank credit is therefore extraordinarily high. Any further credit restriction is bound to cause a general scramble for solvency that in the short or medium term may add to inflationary pressures. Firms facing a less elastic demand for their product will attempt to improve their cash flow by raising prices, and those facing a more elastic demand may, unless they are able to borrow in the parallel money market at extremely high interest rates, be obliged to cut back production or go into bankruptcy. As one observer of the Brazilian experience observes, "Bank credit is the narrow apex of the pyramid which supports a substantially multiplied volume of interfirm credit, as well as consumer credit. If the authorities try to contract bank credit, a domino theory is applicable."[19]

The other variables found by Maynard and Van Rijckeghem to be significant determinants of the rate of nonagricultural growth are fluctuations in imports and agricultural production. A key policy needed to assure sustained expansion of agricultural output and the capacity to import is, as was argued in previous chapters, maintenance of the real exchange rate. Policymakers should therefore keep in mind that adjustment of the exchange rate to keep pace with the increase in the domestic price level, although it might at first seem from empirical research and common sense to contribute to inflation, is an important determinant of the rate of growth of GDP, which in turn appears to be a much more important factor affecting the rate of inflation than devaluation. This is likely to be even more true if, as was pointed out above, a more flexible crawling peg exchange rate policy is adopted that will have a smaller impact on price expectations than the less frequent, large devaluations of the past.

Perhaps the "model" that in the final analysis comes closest to capturing the essential nature of the Argentine phenomenon is what might be called "income" or "expectations" inflation.[20] In such a model, long experience with inflation is built into the behavior of economic agents through markup pricing, cost of living escalation of wage rates, and other rules-of-thumb designed to protect incomes against the constant erosion of rising prices. In a sense this represents a sophisticated system of barter in which indices and margins serve as the numeraire in transactions instead of bags of wheat or pounds of salt. Under this system the principles of marginal productivity and utility tend to give way to real income maintenance and security as guidelines for pricing of factors and products, and hedging against possible disaster replaces more rational expectations and extrapolations as the criterion for decision-making.[21] In such a society any effort to bring about immediate stabilization is almost bound to disrupt the economy instead of eliminating inflation.

"Neutral" Inflation as an Objective of Policy

The foregoing analysis has underlined the great difficulty of moving quickly to zero inflation (or inflation at "international rates") in a country like Argentina, regardless of the combination of stabilization measures adopted. The importance of lags between changes in causal factors and their effect on the price level shows up very clearly in econometrical studies, which in general probably underestimate the cumulative inflationary effect of past changes in such factors for reasons already explained. Even more important, a number of important prices and factor remunerations are bound to be "out of line" at any moment a new stabilization program is initiated. It has of course been frequently argued that a temporary freezing of the status quo is the only way to stabilize an economy, and that those who happen to be at a disadvantage in the inflationary struggle over distributive income shares at that moment must necessarily sacrifice themselves in the common good.

This kind of argument might be acceptable in an economy in which inflation has been relatively mild and of short duration, and consequently one in which inflationary distortions in relative prices and factor remunerations do not greatly affect the allocation of resources or the distribution of economic welfare. As will be seen in Chapter 6, however, this is clearly not the case in Argentina. In most years when stabilization programs were initiated, what was most needed to put the economy on a sounder footing was a strong dose of "corrective" inflation to raise real public utility tariffs, tax collections, exchange and interest rates, and other key prices relative to the general price level so as to improve the distorted allocation of resources. The most common counterargument is that once the economy is stabilized such adjustments can be brought about more easily and made to stick. It has never been possible to put this tactic to the test, however, because whatever stabilization was achieved through freeze has soon come unstuck, permitting the rate race to begin all over again with most of the same relative price distortions still intact.

It is frequently heard that such stabilization program failures are simply due to lack of will power or political guts or to the existence of weak governments. It is of course indisputable that no government can carry out a stabilization program without a minimum of determination, efficiency, and authority, but it seems passing strange if not downright patronizing that the question of the feasibility of rapid stabilization under conditions of high secular inflation has not received more serious attention. When prices are rising at over 2 percent per month, a sudden freeze soon imposes such severe economic hardship on some frozen groups that resulting sociopolitical tensions become increasingly uncontainable. If despite these tensions a freeze is maintained for a fairly prolonged period of time—say, longer than a year—it is also almost inevitable that some exogeneous disturbance, such as a crop failure or change in the international market, will require corrective adjustments that prove inconsistent with the conditions of the freeze. In short, freezes under conditions of trotting or galloping inflation tend to be too rigid and too prolonged to accommodate necessary adjustments to sociopolitical tensions, exogenous disturbances, and the distortions that have to be corrected before the economy can safely be unfrozen.

If quick stabilization is not feasible, then what alternative is there to uncontrolled or runaway inflation? As has been illustrated by Maynard and Van Rijckeghem, it is possible within the constraints imposed by the lagged effect of causal inflationary factors to bring about a progressive decline in the rate of inflation over a period of years while allowing for some increase in real wages and without necessarily reducing the real income of other groups. Such a solution would almost certainly require the explicit or tacit consent of powerfully organized interest groups to an incomes policy. It would of course be idle to expect such groups to do so voluntarily unless some attractive incentives (as well as some effective penalties) were attached.

One of the most powerful inducements the government could provide for agreeing to an incomes policy would be to demonstrate convincingly that it would not permit exhorbitant wage and price increases to change the distribution of real income. Although initially the rate of inflation might thereby be accelerated, the government could make sure that the exchange rate, public utility tariffs, interest rates, and other key prices over which it has control increase at least *pari passu* with the general price level. At the same time the government could apply pressure selectively on those who violate incomes and stabilization policies by scrutinizing their tax records, restricting their access to official bank credit and public contracts, and by other measures well within existing governmental powers. Cooperating firms and labor unions could similarly be rewarded, and new inducements—such as longer-term public contracts, expecially prompt payment for services rendered, and escalator clauses to protect wage and price contracts against inflationary depreciation—could be adopted exclusively in their favor. The arsenal of public power is in reality quite formidable in Argentina if the government cares to use it for a purpose and is prepared to demonstrate its credibility by living up to its own guidelines.

It would probably take much less muscle than one might think to dissuade interest groups from committing extravagant breaches of incomes policy guidelines if the government demonstrated its own commitment to live by the same rules. The public sector cannot expect private entrepreneurs to strike any tougher bargain with their labor unions than it is able to work out with its own, and the same criteria for price adjustment in the public sector would have to be applicable to the private (for example, if real public utility tariffs were updated in relation to some base period, the same basis for updating should be allowed private firms). Perhaps the most important (and at the same time the most difficult) government commitment would be to fulfill its part of the annual financial plan by not using any more Central Bank credit than provided for therein. Given uncertainties about the proper amount of new money that should be injected into the economy at different rates of inflation, the authorities should be willing to be quite pragmatic about the target for private bank credit expansion, but it is impossible to conceive of any important progress toward stabilization without the public sector restricting its own claims to (or reducing them progressively toward) 1 percent or so of GDP.

This rather flexible *quid pro quo* approach to stabilization policy, together with the uncertainties of public finance and the need to adjust policy realistically to accommodate sociopolitical tensions, exogenous disturbances, and correction of important relative price distortions, suggests that progress toward price stability would be slow at best and perhaps quite irregular. A better term for such a policy strategy might therefore be "neutral" inflation, in the sense that the price level might continue to rise faster than international rates for an indefinite period and that policy would be aimed primarily at correcting inflation-induced distortions, or at preventing them from recurring. With such a strategy the aim of policymakers would be to try to assure that the rate of inflation was more predictable and that key prices rose at roughly the same rate.

This kind of policy would be more likely to succeed if conventional rigidities were rooted out of the economy as rapidly as possible. In the public sector, for example, it would be necessary to make the tax base more price elastic by converting specific taxes to an ad valorem base and by adjusting delayed payments for the loss in real value from the time the liability was incurred; and greater access of the public sector to the capital market could be assured by indexing issues of government securities (that is, adjusting their value to compensate for the rise in the price level) so that they would be attractive to private savers. On the expenditure side the government could also try to adjust its investment criteria and budgeting procedures to the new rules of the game.[22] Similar rigidities in the private sector would have to be broken down by indexing, greater use of escalator clauses, and the like to protect the weak against the ravages of inflation and to promote redevelopment of financial markets. A positive real interest rate policy is a "must" for this purpose; bringing savers and investors, lenders and borrowers, more effectively together in a healthy financial market would help prevent driving smaller, domestic firms into the hands of usurers in the extrabank money market.

6 Inflation, the Distribution of Income, and the Financing of Growth

The conflict between stabilization and growth is closely related to that between equity and growth in an inflationary economy. Secular inflation almost inevitably produces longterm shifts in relative prices and factor rewards, and periodic stabilization efforts also frequently bring about even sharper changes in the distribution of income. Such changes tend to follow a pronounced cyclical pattern synchronized with the stop-go behavior of the economy. These fluctuations in relative prices, income shares, the level of economic activity, and liquidity tend to have strong repercussions on the level and composition of savings and investment and thus on the rate and direction of growth. It is the purpose of this chapter to explore the dynamics of these interactions and to analyze their implications for macroeconomic policy in Argentina.

The Sectoral Distribution of Income

With a rapidly rising general price level, the distribution of income among economic activity sectors depends to a large extent on the behavior of relative prices: those activities less able to adjust their prices flexibly will tend to fall behind in the race. This is more likely to be the case with sellers subject to officially administered prices, those operating in more competitive markets, and those which are less able to shift the composition of their output quickly according to changes in the terms of trade. Agriculture is a good example of a sector extremely dependent on government price policy, since domestic prices of exported products are determined by the prevailing exchange rate and export taxes. Officially administered prices are also more likely to work to the disadvantage of sellers of mass-consumed goods and services who cannot easily evade official prices: public utilities are probably the most obvious example. Utilities and agriculture are also less able to defend themselves against relative price swings by quick changes in the composition of output. Competition, on the other hand, will be disadvantageous for sellers who, unprotected by the oligopolistic price leadership of a large firm, are unable to organize themselves into strong trade associations that can effectively limit price competition during periods of less than full employment.

These a priori expectations seem to be confirmed by the actual behavior of relative prices in Argentina during the period of rapid inflation. If the economy is divided into primary, secondary, and tertiary activities, it can be seen from figure 6-1 that relative prices of the secondary sector (dominated by manufacturing) varied less than those of the other two sectors.[1] This is consistent with the presumption that industry is in general less competitive and can more easily evade official price controls. In this regard it is significant that the largest and most sustained deterioration in relative industrial prices occurred during the Krieger Vasena stabilization program beginning in 1967, when manufacturers were obliged to enter into price restraint agreements with the government.

Relative agricultural prices, on the other hand, improved substantially after the later 1940's in line with the increase in the real exchange rate. The wide fluctuations in relative agricultural prices were also closely associated with swings in the real exchange rate adjusted for export retentions. The most surprising aspect of the chart, at least for those who have viewed the relative price struggle in Argentina as mainly between agriculture and industry, is that the entire improvement in the agricultural terms of trade was brought about at the expense of the tertiary sector (services and construction). This is what should have been expected during a

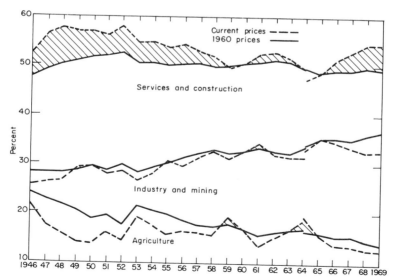

Figure 6-1. Composition of GDP in current and constant price.

period of rapid inflation, however, in that the service sector includes activities that are especially prone to officially administered prices and others in which price competition is particularly difficult to avoid.

The services which suffered the most severe drop in relative prices between the late 1940s and the end of the 1950s were general government services (almost 50 percent), construction (20 percent), electricity, gas, and water (about 25 percent), and rents on urban property. The deterioration in relative prices of these last two groups of services in fact started during World War II, so that by 1959 their prices relative to the general price level had fallen to less than 20 percent of prewar. Official price policy had in effect led to the virtual euthanasia of rentiers and public utilities, with consequent serious effects on both home construction and the government budget. Later administrations were therefore obliged to try to raise the relative prices of these services very substantially, a task which in the short run reinforced inflationary pressures and even by the end of the 1960s had not yet been completed.

A special word should be said about the construction sector, both because of its importance as a source of employment and because somewhat different factors influenced trends in its terms of trade. Between prewar and 1948 the relative prices of construction doubled as a result of Perón's policies of raising real wages and expanding public works, but thereafter they followed fairly closely trends for the rest of the tertiary sector. Fiscal austerity and a more moderate wage policy were the initial causes for the change in direction of relative construction prices, but deterioration was subsequently strongly reinforced by lack of demand for construction of rental property and especially by the drying up of the mortgage market. Both of these latter factors were largely the result of official price and monetary restrictions until Krieger Vasena's change of policy led to a revival of mortgage financing in the late 1960s.

Distribution of Income by Socioeconomic Groups

The effect of inflation on the distribution of personal income could be expected to be determined (assuming constant production functions) by changes in the sectoral distribution of income on the one hand and by the nature of the contracts that fix the level of remuneration of different socioeconomic groups on the other. The remuneration of labor would *ceteris paribus* be favored relative to that of capital if changes in relative prices favored more labor-intensive sectors. However, the sectors in which wages and salaries have consistently represented half or more of value added are (in order of wage share size) general government services, construction, electricity, gas and water, transport, and communications. The first three of these sectors were among those that suffered the worst deterioration in their terms of trade up to the 1960s. On the other hand, agriculture, which enjoyed the most pronounced improvement in relative prices, is the sector with the lowest share of wages and salaries in value added.[2]

To the extent that contractual rates of remuneration of an income group tend to remain fixed over extended periods of time, it will of course inevitably lose ground in the struggle over distributive income shares. Rentiers and pensioners constitute the most prominent examples of this kind of "fixed" income group in Argentina, the first for reasons explained in the previous section and the second because of the increasingly slow rate at which pensions were adjusted when the social security system fell into deficit. Thus between 1953 and 1961 (the years for which detailed figures are available) the share of rentiers in total personal income declined from 5 to 2 percent whereas the proportion of retired persons and pensioners in the lower 20 percent of family income recipients increased from under 2 percent to over 28 percent.[3]

Among recipients of earned income in the active labor force, one would *ceteris paribus* expect the self-employed to do better than wage earners during periods of rapid inflation, because wage contracts are usually subject to renegotiation at intervals of one year or longer whereas price contracts are typically more flexible. An attempt was made to test this hypothesis by correlating annual variations in real wage rates in Argentina with year-to-year changes in the rate of inflation, but the correlations were not very significant. Improvements in real wage rates are strongly associated with periods of declining rates of inflation and vice versa, but annual variations appear to be influenced also by a number of other factors. One of the most important of these factors is changes in the level of economic activity, which in sectors with important fixed costs of production are closely correlated with short-term fluctuations in labor productivity. To test this relationship, year-to-year variations in real industrial wage rates were plotted against changes in real industrial product per worker. These results are presented in figure 6-2.

This chart confirms that annual variations in real wage rates, at least in manufacturing, have been correlated with changes in labor

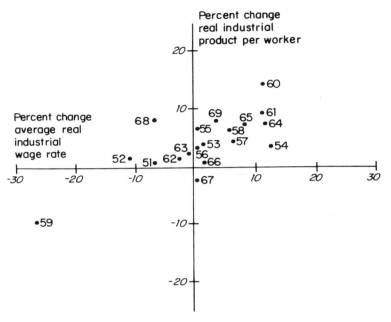

Figure 6-2. Relation between real wage rates and labor productivity.

productivity, which in turn have been closely related to swings in the level of economic activity: the extreme observations in the northeast quadrant are all years of rapid economic expansion, whereas those in or near the southwest quadrant correspond to recession years. Another interesting fact revealed in figure 6-2 is that, although years of accelerated inflation and recession have been almost as frequent as good years during the period covered, real industrial wage rates have clearly improved over time. This improvement did not prevent the wage share of manufacturing income from declining very substantially, however, because the effect of higher real wage rates was more than offset by the rapid substitution of capital for labor in industry.

The share of wages in fact declined in most sectors of the Argentine economy after the mid-1950s. This was particularly true in the agricultural, mining, electricity, gas, and water sectors in which, like manufacturing, technical innovation and/or changes in the composition of output were especially laborsaving. In those sectors where savings in labor were more difficult to effect, the wage share either did not decline or, as in construction and banking in which strongly organized unions were able to push up wages despite the deterioration in relative sectoral prices, the wage share actually rose.[4] This is an important finding for price policy to the extent that if a sector cannot offset the competitive bidding up of real wage rates by improvements in labor productivity, it will have to increase its relative prices to attract new capital and expand output. This may very well explain part of the rapid increase in relative prices of the construction and services sectors in the 1960s.

Sectoral wage shares are shown by pairs of years in table 6-1 to help throw light on the role of attempted stabilization policies on their evolution over time. The first year of each pair represents the last in a period of economic expansion, whereas the second shows the effect of government stabilization policies, which without exception have been accompanied by a reduction in the share of wages in total national income. During periods of economic expansion, on the other hand, the total wage share has increased, except during 1952-1955 and 1966-1969 when economic growth was accompanied by effective wage restraint policies. Wage shares in individual sectors have in some important cases deviated from this overall pattern, but it can in general be concluded that changes in the share of wages in national income have been closely related to the economic cycle, and that the long-term decline in the total wage share has been caused mainly by the fact that increases during years of economic expansion have been insufficient to offset reductions during periods of economic retrenchment and attempted stabilization. Thus, the decline in the wage share would probably have been much less, or might not have occurred at all, if the economy had not been so cyclically unstable.

The progressive decline in most sectoral wage shares did not, however, result in a fall in average real income per wage earner, even though total per capita income in Argentina rose very slowly during the period under analysis. The decline in wage shares was completely offset by a reduction in the relative importance of the wage earning population from over 70 percent of all families in 1949 to less than 62 percent in 1965.[5] Thus, wage earners in general, like those in industry in particular, were able during periods of economic expansion to recoup the losses they suffered in real wage rates in years of accelerated inflation and economic retrenchment. Workers in sectors experiencing a relatively rapid rate of increase in labor productivity appear to have been able to do somewhat better than others, although the competitive pushing up of wages was in general so irresistible that sectors unable either to improve labor

Table 6-1 Share of wages and salaries in sectoral incomes at factor cost.

Sectors	1952	1955	1957	1958	1959	1961	1963	1966	1969
Declining wage shares									
Agriculture	35.0	32.8	25.9	30.7	22.4	24.8	21.0	27.4	29.4
Manufacturing	50.0	44.2	42.1	39.4	33.5	35.3	32.0	35.9	36.5
Mining	45.7	43.0	41.7	40.9	30.8	29.0	25.3	38.2	33.0
Commerce	32.6	33.6	26.7	24.4	20.8	22.9	27.4	25.1	22.7
Transport and communications	60.9	59.9	58.0	60.2	57.5	54.9	50.3	52.9	46.1
Electricity, gas, and water	68.2	57.7	67.3	72.6	65.2	48.0	46.4	45.4	40.3
Government and other services	60.7	60.7	57.7	60.4	54.4	57.7	56.1	59.1	56.9
Increasing wage shares									
Construction	65.8	65.0	66.3	72.4	62.8	64.5	71.9	74.9	74.4
Financial services and housing	20.0	18.3	22.1	28.3	29.6	34.5	39.2	46.9	38.2
Overall average	46.5	44.1	40.5	41.7	35.2	38.1	36.6	41.0	39.9

Source: Banco Central, *Origen del producto*, tables 3–20. Employer social security contributions are excluded from wages and salaries.

productivity or pass wage increases along in higher relative prices were obliged to accept a substantially larger share of wages in total sectoral income.

Since rentiers and retired persons were net losers and wage earners did little more than maintain their real per capita income in the inflationary struggle, it stands to reason that the self-employed must have been net gainers. This was true only to a minor extent for per capita income of the self-employed as a group, however, because the ranks of the self-employed grew quite significantly during the period. The number of pensioners also increased so rapidly that, despite the severe reduction they suffered in real per capita income, they absorbed a much greater share of total personal income at the end of the period than they did at the beginning. Thus the most significant income redistribution affecting the self-employed occurred, not between it and other groups, but within the self-employed group itself.

Within this group entrepreneurs in the industrial, commercial and transportation sectors appear to have improved their real per capita incomes quite substantially at the expense of those self-employed in miscellaneous services and to a lesser extent in agriculture. Between 1953 and 1961 the proportion of the self-employed in services appearing in the lower 20 percent of total Argentine family income recipients rose from only 1 percent to over 38 percent. It seems that this deterioration is explained by new entrants into the labor force and migrants from agriculture who could not find employment as urban wage earners and were forced to eke out a living in low productivity service activities. The shift in income distribution among the agricultural self-employed was more complicated: per capita income in this sector has been extremely unstable, but it appears that over time the proportion of farm owners in the upper deciles of family income distribution declined, the proportion in the lower deciles increased, and the proportion in the middle deciles also increased, but not enough to offset the other shift.[6]

In summary, then, analysis of the effects of complex interactions between inflation and other variables on the distribution of income by socioeconomic groups reveals the inadequacy of characterizing the struggle over distributive income shares simply as competition between wages and profits. Argentine wage earners demonstrated an ability to defend their real incomes over the longer run and, in sectors where labor productivity was rising rapidly, actually to improve them. The struggle for survival during rapid inflation accompanied by severe cyclical instability appeared in fact to favor the strongly organized, both workers and entrepreneurs, who were able to exploit imperfect markets. The losers in the struggle tended to be the unorganized and the politically weak, particularly retired persons, small businessmen, independent vendors of personal services, and sellers who were especially vulnerable to government price regulations. The income they lost appears to have been transferred mainly to large entrepreneurs in the modern, well-organized business sector: the only income group to increase its share of personal income between 1953 and 1961 (the extreme years for which detailed information is available) was the upper 5 percent, mainly in the manufacturing and commerce sectors.

It is very difficult to draw any firm conclusions about the significance of this redistribution of income. Most of the quantitative measures of income dispersion between these two years indicate growing inequality, but this phenomenon has also been observed in recent years in a number of other countries such as Mexico and Puerto Rico, and income distribution in Argentina is still considerably more "equitable" than in these last mentioned countries. Furthermore, one of the measures of income dispersion in Argentina shows less inequality in 1961 than in 1953: it is the coefficient of variation, which indicates that average incomes rose sufficiently between the recession year 1953 and the peak year 1961 to offset the effect of a widening in the distribution of income.[7] Any judgment about the welfare implications of inflationary income redistribution, however, must also take into account its effect on savings and investment and the financing of economic activity.

Consumption, Savings, and Investment

The effect of inflation on savings and investment is a controversial subject about which there is conflicting empirical evidence in the literature. On the one hand, inflation at least initially can be expected to lead to some "forced saving" through a redistribution of income from fixed income groups to entrepreneurs, as was observed in the previous section with respect to Argentina. On the other hand, inflation, especially if accompanied by a fixed exchange rate subject to periodical violent readjustments, should logically provide an incentive for savers to invest a larger share of their resources in assets that are likely to appreciate rapidly in value, such as inventories and foreign exchange. The net result of these conflicting influences on the behavior of consumption, savings, and investment in Argentina is not immediately apparent from available data.

In figure 6-3 trends in gross domestic savings and investment are expressed as percentages of gross national income and of total available goods and services respectively.[8] Gross domestic savings have fluctuated rather widely, but in current prices (the best measure of actual saving effort) they have exhibited no trend, averaging out at approximately 19 percent of gross domestic income for the two-decade period as a whole. Furthermore, the fluctuations observed bear no particular relationship to changes in the rate of inflation, although most of the peaks represent years when policy was aimed at curtailing consumption in an effort to stabilize the economy. The figures in the chart of course represent savings that are measurable ex post, so that it could be argued that savings in fact might have been larger if there had been less inflation, and that a smaller proportion would have been channeled into holdings of foreign exchange, inventories, and other "unproductive" assets that are more difficult if not impossible to measure. To the extent that this is true, the adverse effect of inflation on savings would have to be judged, not in terms of changes in the observed savings rate, but with respect to the loss of potential savings that could otherwise have been channeled into more productive investment to accelerate the rate of growth of the economy. In other words, the social cost of the inflationary redistribution of income might not have been manifested so much in an increase in domestic consumption levels of the well-to-do as in a misallocation of savings.

The same figures expressed in prices of 1960, however, reveal that real gross domestic savings have tended to increase over time. This

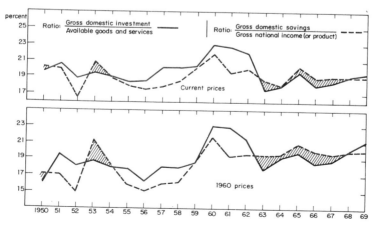

Figure 6-3. Relation between domestic savings and investment.

difference between current and constant price series is explained by
the increase in the relative prices of consumer goods and (the reverse
side of the coin) by a sharp decline in the relative prices of
investment goods. The shift in relative prices occurred especially
after 1959. Up to this year the fall in relative construction prices was
offset by the rise in relative prices of capital equipment, caused
especially by the effect of the increase in the real exchange rate on
domestic prices of imported goods; but during the subsequent
decade the relative prices of capital equipment declined by no less
than 30 percent, led by a more than 40 percent reduction in transport equipment. This trend was probably due in part to a change in
the composition of investment (since implicit GDP prices have been
used in this analysis) and to a deterioration in the real exchange
rate, but the most important explanatory factors appear to be the
lifting of quantitative import controls, the reduction of import duties
and surcharges on noncompetitive foreign equipment, and the improvement in efficiency of domestic producers, especially in the
automotive industry which was just getting started in the mid-1950s.
Despite this reduction in the relative prices of producer durable
equipment, however, it is estimated that in 1969 they were still
approximately 40 percent above the pre-World War II level in
Argentina and also at least as far out of line with respect to relative
international prices.[9]
     It should also be pointed out that the increase in relative prices of
consumer expenditures affected socioeconomic groups differential-
ly. Lower income groups generally spend a half or more of their
income on food, which was particularly affected by the policy of
trying to improve the domestic terms of trade of Argentine agriculture. A larger share of the expenditures of upper income groups, on
the other hand, is directed toward consumer durables, the relative
prices of which have on the whole tended to decline for the same
reasons mentioned in the previous paragraph with respect to capital
goods. Thus it is estimated that between 1950 and 1963 relative
consumer prices increased by about 12 percent for lower income
groups, whereas they fell by 15 percent for higher income
consumers.[10] This differential movement in consumer prices was
sufficient to wipe out any progressive income redistribution effect of
fiscal policy during the period. It can therefore be surmised that
during the 1960s the well-to-do in Argentina could have increased
their savings rates quite substantially even without reducing their
real level of consumption.
     The difference in trends between current and constant price series

is not as pronounced for gross domestic investment. The reason is that in most years up to 1962 a significant share of capital expenditure was financed by net foreign investment, the importance of which is indicated by the shaded area between the domestic savings and investment curves in figure 6-3.[11] In later years the need to rebuild the country's depleted gold and foreign exchange reserves and heavy service payments on foreign obligations accumulated in previous years made it necessary to maintain a surplus between exports and imports of goods and services (the reversal in 1969 was caused, it will be recalled, by the speculative flight of capital and increase in imports caused by the resignation of Krieger Vasena). Thus, if the investment boom years of 1960-1962 are excluded, the share of real gross domestic investment in available goods and services rose from an average of 17.8 percent in earlier years to only 19.3 percent in the later period (compared to an increase of from 17 to 20 percent in the share of real gross domestic savings in gross national income).

Along with the rise in fixed capital formation a significant change also occurred in its composition. This change especially affected new construction, which fell from about 60 percent of total fixed capital formation in the 1950s to not much more than 40 percent in the 1960s. This was the result not only of diminished private construction activity but also of a reduction in the relative importance of government investment in public works. Thus an increasing share of investment in Argentina was carried out by private business enterprise. To the extent that larger enterprise investment was financed out of profits, the increase in the profit share of national income may have represented a change in the method of financing capital accumulation instead of a redistribution of welfare in favor of the wealthy.

Financing Private Enterprise Investment

The private share of total fixed investment is estimated to have risen from around 70 percent during the early 1950s to over 75 percent at the beginning of 1955, and to over 80 percent in the peak years 1956-1957 and 1962.[12] There is some evidence that the private share of fixed investment may have declined somewhat in recent years, but the swift rise in private capital formation (which more than doubled in real terms between 1953 and 1961) must have called for a major effort to mobilize the necessary financing. The sources of financing enterprise investment can most conveniently be broken

down between those external and those internal to the firm. Possibilities for external financing depend upon the degree and
sophistication of financial market development, which in Argentina
was already quite advanced in the 1930s and early 1940s.[13] During
the Perón regime, however, government decided to take over or
closely control financial markets, with the result that many financial
instruments either ceased to exist (for example, the *cédula
hipotecaria*) or declined in relative importance (the stock market).
This process was greatly accelerated by inflation in combination
with usury laws that placed ceilings on interest rates, so that fixed
interest securities almost disappeared along with life insurance as
outlets for savings. Virtually the only important vehicle that survived
to bring savers and investors together in the market was the banking
system.

In the early part of the Perón administration the expansion of
bank credit to the private sector, usually at interest rates that were
negative in real terms, was probably sufficient to offset the drying up
of other sources of external enterprise financing. In the
manufacturing sector, for example, total bank credit outstanding is
estimated to have risen from 12 percent of industrial GDP in 1943 to
over 19 percent in 1948.[14] Such a rapid expansion permitted those
enterprises with ready access to bank credit to rely less on internal
sources of financing and to tolerate the reduction in the profit share
of enterprise income that took place at this time. Even after the rate
of credit expansion was cut back by Perón after introduction of his
stabilization program, financing the rather steady rate of real
private fixed investment still did not meet with a serious funding
constraint: between 1950 and 1954 the rise in retained earnings was
accompanied by a decline in income tax payments out of profits.[15]

The private investment boom that began to gather momentum
after 1954 coincided, however, with even greater restriction of bank
credit, particularly beginning in 1959. Between 1956 and 1962
foreign credits were of increasing importance in financing enterprise
purchases of capital goods, but retained earnings also rose swiftly.
As a share of total personal income they doubled between 1953 and
1961, reaching the equivalent of about 5 percent of the income of the
top 10 percent of families.[16] The rise in retained earnings, however,
did not represent a real net addition to the internal financing of
enterprise, because depreciation allowances, which were legally tied
to original purchase prices, did not keep pace with inflation. It has
been estimated that if depreciation of equipment were recalculated
at replacement cost, the difference would have amounted to between

1.5 and 2 percent of the personal income of the top decile of income recipients.

The enterprise sector was therefore obliged to search for additional sources of external financing, a search which became more desperate when foreign credit began to dry up in 1962. Analysis of corporate balance sheets (although notoriously unreliable) throws some light on where they were able to find additional funds. According to this information the fall in the relative importance of bank credit was offset mainly by an increase in what is euphemistically classified as "other debt." This debt was presumably constituted mainly by credits from the extra-bank money market which, as was seen earlier, was expanding rapidly at this time.[17] This shift in sources of external financing may therefore have had an important effect on raising the financing costs of enterprise.

The corporate enterprise sector does not appear to have suffered from the credit squeeze as much as noncorporate enterprise. Banks preferred larger corporations during the period of credit rationing, and certain nonbank intermediaries such as the *financieras,* which became engaged in placing promissory notes of business firms with savers, usually insisted that such notes be backed by bank guarantees, a very difficult condition for smaller firms to fulfill.[18] Credit from banks and other financial intermediaries to noncorporate enterprise therefore declined from almost half the latter's total financial liabilities in 1955 to only 20 percent in 1965. This gap was partly filled by increasing indebtedness with other enterprises in the corporate sector, but the most important new source of financing was in the form of delayed payments (or nonpayment) of taxes and social security contributions to the public sector. This method of financing could in a sense be considered indirect bank credit financing, because as current fiscal revenue declined the government was itself obliged to replace its lost income with larger bank credit. It has in fact been estimated that between 1959 and 1965 the debt of enterprises to government grew by a larger amount than government borrowing from the banking system.[19] To the extent that this is true, it certainly leads to a different interpretation of the causes of "excessive" credit expansion during the period and demonstrates once more that the effectiveness of monetary policy depends a great deal on the effectiveness of fiscal and other policy instruments.

In summary, then, it can be concluded that inflation and the credit squeeze not only forced enterprises to raise and retain more profits to finance a greater proportion of their needs from internal resources, but interest rate controls also undermined the organized money market and helped push smaller firms to the wall. Between 1955 and 1965 the share of noncorporate enterprise in total financial liabilities of all enterprises declined from almost 70 percent to less than half.[20] This was occurring precisely during a period when the private sector was being called upon to finance a significantly larger share of national investment. At the same time the public sector, due largely to the withering away of tax revenue, was absorbing an increasing share of credit from the banking system, thereby compounding the problem. This combination of circumstances must have also helped give foreign firms with better access to external sources of financing a substantial competitive edge in expanding production.

Financing the Public Sector

Government financial policy should pursue two major objectives: raise the resources the community desires to devote to public goods and services, and compensate fluctuations in the rest of the economy so as to assure greater stability. The Argentine government has seldom managed to pursue either objective successfully. Lack of fiscal control has in fact become such a traumatic experience for Argentines that government profligacy is widely considered to be the main cause of inflation as well as many other ills that have afflicted the country. There is no doubt that fiscal mismanagement has contributed to the inflationary problem, but the reason is not that the government taxes and spends too much. On the contrary, it can be argued that the Argentine public sector has been starved of funds, and that this starvation, unaccompanied by any important reduction in government responsibilities, has made it impossible to put fiscal management on a sounder footing.

International comparisons can be misleading, but it has been found that for countries with a per capita income of between 300 and 750 dollars, a strong positive correlation exists between per capita income and the government revenue share. Assuming that Argentine per capita income is between 500 and 600 dollars (safely below what is usually assumed), the share of government revenue in national income would be expected to be about 22 percent.[21] This is approximately what revenues of the consolidated public sector did in fact amount to up to 1957, but after this year its share declined precipitously. It is therefore necessary first to explore the question of what relationship might have existed between the decline in government revenue and inflation.

Because of the lack of reliable statistical series for the provinces and municipalities, this question will be analyzed using figures for the national government, which accounts for about 75 to 80 percent of the total government sector. As can be seen from figure 6-4, current net fiscal revenue averaged close to 15 percent of GDP until 1957, but during the following eight or nine years it declined to between 10 and 12 percent (except for a partial and transitory recovery in 1960-1961). It will be recalled that this was also the period of the fiercest struggle over distributive income shares; clearly the public sector was also a loser along with the other weaker and more vulnerable members of the society. The most important single explanation was the fall in social security contributions from about one third to only one quarter of national fiscal revenue. At the same time social security payments were rising rapidly, so that on balance the system switched from being a net contributor of fiscal revenue equal to 3.6 percent of GDP in 1953 (and still over 2 percent in 1957) to a net drain beginning in 1963 (see again figure 6-4). Thus if both revenue and expenditure trends are considered, the turnaround in the social security system alone fully accounts for the entire deterioration in the fiscal situation.

Another important factor in the decline of net fiscal revenue during this period was the increase in transfers of central

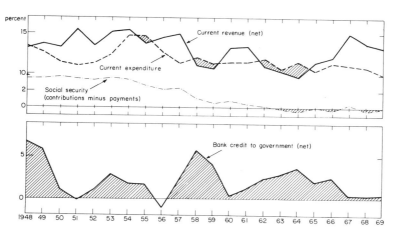

Figure 6-4. National government revenue, expenditure and financing as a percentage of GDP.

government revenue to the provinces under the tax-sharing scheme. Part of the increase can be explained by a relatively slower decline in receipts from taxes in which the provinces participated, but the real pinch was felt when, as a result of the crisis of 1962-1963, the fiscal situation of the provinces so deteriorated that the central government was obliged to increase their participation rate from 33 to 40 percent. As a consequence provincial tax transfers reached almost 22 percent of total national government revenue in 1964, compared with only 12 to 14 percent prior to 1956. The situation got so bad that in some months of 1964 the national treasury, after deducting debt cancellation certificates that were issued on a large scale during the recession and were later received in lieu of tax payments, barely had enough cash on hand to cover provincial tax-sharing transfers before attending to any of its other current obligations. The plight of the provinces also obliged the central government to increase quite substantially other financial transfers appearing on the expenditure side of the ledger. Thus, similar to what occurred with social security, the national treasury found itself struggling to bail out another fiscal system that in theory was supposed to be largely self-financing.

Otherwise the fall in tax pressure appears to have affected both direct and indirect taxes about equally, although taxes on foreign trade increased in relative importance. The erosion of the income tax base (caused by investment exemptions legislated at the beginning of the 1960s and by the inflationary reduction in the real value of delayed income tax payments) seems to have been just as much offset by the shift in income tax incidence against lower income groups (caused by the slow adjustment of personal exemptions to take account of inflation), as the erosion of the indirect tax base (due to the inflationary loss in revenue from specific excise levies) was offset by more price elastic ad valorem taxes. It is important to point out, however, that the effect of inflation both on income tax collections (through the lag in adjustment of personal exemptions) and on indirect tax receipts (through the decline in the real value of excise levies on nonessential goods) has been to make the tax system more regressive. This result might have been at least partly justifiable if these offsets to inflationary erosion of the tax base had imparted greater stability to the tax system; but regression experiments reveal that not only are fluctuations in real government revenue negatively and significantly correlated with changes in the price level, but that fiscal revenue is quite elastic with respect to changes in the rate of inflation (an elasticity of the order of -1.3 around the mean).[22]

On the expenditure side no significant trends can be observed in the share of current national government outlays: except for the temporary increase in 1954-1955 and a small decline at the end of the period, they have fluctuated between 11 and 13 percent of GDP. This relative stability does, however, mask some important changes in the composition of expenditure. The increase in current outlays after 1952 reflects mainly the rise in subsidies paid to consumers of agricultural goods to protect them against the effect of improvement in the agricultural terms of trade. These subsidies were later gradually removed, particularly after 1959, with the results that were already pointed out on the differential increase in relative consumer prices. At the same time the deficits of state enterprises began to absorb a rising though irregular share of national government expenditure. It is not really accurate to use the plural: the state railway accounted for most of the deficits. By 1965-1966 the operating losses of this enterprise alone absorbed about 20 percent of current expenditures of the national treasury and, together with treasury-financed railway investment, amounted to an incredible 2 per cent of the nation's total GDP.[23]

Part of the railways' financial problem is attributable to the lag in adjustment of tariffs, which between 1952 and 1963 declined by one third in relation to the general price level. During the same period, however, railway freight traffic (in ton-kms.) fell by an even larger proportion as road transport began to compete more intensively. In the decade following the mid-1950s the number of trucks licensed in Argentina grew by almost two and one half times, reflecting not only dissatisfaction with the notoriously poor service provided by the railways but also a worldwide shift in modes of transport. The result was that the railway network became increasingly overdimentioned relative to effective demand so that by the early 1960s total revenue of the enterprise did not even cover the wage bill.

Efforts to rationalize and cut back railway operations nevertheless faced formidable obstacles: the shortage of funds to modernize and replace equipment led to further deterioration in the quality of service; suspension of losing lines was vehemently opposed by many communities that lacked adequate alternative means of transportation and/or were dependent on the railway as a principal source of income and employment; and railway labor was extremely well organized in support of work rules that had long condoned featherbedding. An example of the frustration suffered by those attempting to cope with the problem was the effort in 1961 to induce railway employees to accept early retirement by offering generous benefits, but those who accepted included a large proportion of skilled workmen and officials who later had to be rehired as consultants in order to keep the enterprise functioning.

The railways were of course not the only state enterprise that was a thorn in the side of the treasury: few of them generated resources sufficient to cover more than a small fraction of their investment needs, and a number of others—the river fleet, Buenos Aires subway, the shipyards, the government airline, and so forth—also suffered from chronic current account deficits. The general problem was in fact so serious that a quick solution was one of the principal declared policy objectives of General Ongania when he assumed control of the government after the coup d'état of mid-1966 and used military force to break resistance to reform. It is therefore interesting to observe that even though the burden of the railway deficit was reduced significantly, by 1969 it still amounted to approximately 6.5 percent of total treasury disbursements (compared with 15 percent in 1966), and the reduction of employment in state enterprises amounting to about 11 percent was mostly offset by an increase in employment in the rest of the public administration.

Since this was a period of subsiding inflation, it is possible that at least part of the increase in government expenditure can be explained simply by the smaller loss in the real value of outlays between the time they were budgeted and when they were actually spent. From regression experiments it indeed appears that the elasticity of real government expenditure with respect to changes in the rate of inflation is higher than that for real government revenue, although the difference between the elasticities is not very significant in view of the relatively small explanatory power of price variations in both cases.[24] If other factors had not been so important in influencing the behavior of revenue and expenditure, however, it is significant that the effect of variations in the rate of inflation alone appears to be partially compensating, in the sense that its differential effect on current revenue and expenditure reduces government savings somewhat less when prices rise more rapidly (and similarly increases them when the rate of inflation declines) than would otherwise be expected.

In any event, the improvement in the fiscal situation after 1966 was due entirely to the swift increase in government revenue back to the pre-1958 share of GDP (see again figure 6-4). This was accomplished by a general improvement in tax and tariff collections and social security contributions (although the latter deteriorated again in 1968), assisted by large additional revenues from export retentions levied in conjunction with Krieger Vasena's compensated devaluation and by increased payments of back taxes under another *blanqueo* or partial tax waiver agreement with debtors. Assuming that the stronger revenue position of the government will be able to be maintained despite the transitory nature of recent windfall tax receipts, and that it is possible to keep the fingers of state enterprises, provinces, and the social security system from digging deeper into the treasury till, the question must now be asked whether the problem of financing the public sector can be considered solved.

If there is no major change in existing institutional arrangements that oblige government to assume greater responsibilities, the sufficiency of a 14 to 15 percent revenue share will in the first instance depend on the portion of public sector investment the national government will be called upon to finance. According to the national development plans of 1965-1969 and 1970-1974, the public sector should stand ready to carry out about one third of gross fixed capital formation, which at prevailing relative prices of capital goods should on average amount to something over 20 percent of GDP to assure a minimum 5 percent rate of growth of the economy. The two plans differ with respect to the portion of public sector investment that the national government would be asked to finance, but the portion in both plans ranges between the equivalent of 4 and 5 percent of GDP.[25]

If current national government expenditure is prudently assumed to absorb from 11 to 12 percent of GDP, then national government savings would be sufficient to finance between 40 and 100 percent of its public investment financing obligations. This is a wide range and does not take into account other capital account expenditures, such as capital transfers to government financial institutions for lending to the private sector or amortization payments on the public debt. The national government could of course expect to be able to obtain some credit from the banking system without generating excessive monetary expansion or competing with the legitimate credit needs of the private sector, say at least the equivalent of 1 percent of GDP per year if the economy is growing at 5 percent or better. Then there is the possibility of public borrowing from nonbank sources: the inflationary demise of the securities market has prevented the public sector from tapping domestic savings, but foreign credit has at times been an important source of government credit. Because of the accumulation of large external obligations in the past, however, amortization payments on the existing public external debt at the end of the 1960s were running at between 1.7 and 1.8 percent of GDP, so that Argentina will be lucky if disbursements from new foreign credits simply offset amortization payments.

One is therefore obliged on balance to reach the conclusion that even under favorable (and perhaps excessively optimistic) assumptions regarding the behavior of current expenditure and of other current claims on the treasury, a national government revenue share of 15 to 16 percent of GDP does not by any means assure that it can meet its direct public sector investment financing obligations without "excessive" borrowing from the banking system. Much depends upon what is considered "excessive" bank borrowing, but it is unlikely that the government will be able to stay out of financial troubles unless the domestic market for government securities is resurrected. Not only the national government but also the provinces, municipalities, and state enterprises should under normal circumstances be able to finance a portion of their own investment by borrowing from nonbank sources. There appears to be no dearth of savings capacity in Argentina to meet the investment needs of both the public and private sectors: during periods of economic expansion, public and private consumption have together typically absorbed less than two thirds of the increment in available goods and services (with the notable exception of 1963-1965). What have been lacking are appropriate instruments to mobilize and channel these savings efficiently to investors in productive assets.

Conclusion

The picture that emerges from the foregoing analysis of income distribution and the financing of investment under inflation is one of growing inequity and isolation: inequity in the distribution of income favoring well-organized members of the community able to exploit imperfect markets, and isolation of savers from investors that has forced each tub to stand more and more on its own bottom. The latter trend benefited those organizations and people, either national or foreign, who were most able to generate their own resources for expansion and development. The retired person, the unemployed or semiemployed laborer, the small businessman, and the public sector, who in well-organized and fairly advanced societies usually depend to a large extent on transfers from the rest of the community for their sustenance and/or growth, have had to shift increasingly for themselves. Inflation and the policies followed by the government have in short permitted the economically powerful to appropriate an ever larger share of the national economic surplus but have prevented them from using their larger share either to increase their real consumption level substantially or to compete effectively with foreign enterprise in the expansion of domestic production.

The process by which this state of affairs came about is, however, far from inevitable under inflation. The losses of fixed income groups are in large measure attributable to inflexible government controls and to the virtual collapse of the social security system, both of which could have been avoided by more realistic policies. The tax system, which under noninflationary conditions is considered to be moderately progressive in Argentina,[26] was allowed to become more regressive mainly because of the differential efficiency with which taxes were collected from different socioeconomic groups during inflation accompanied by severe credit restriction. Interest rate ceilings emasculated the capital market and forced enterprises to rely increasingly on internal sources to finance investment; at the same time they reduced construction activity and thereby curtailed a major source of employment while eliminating inflationary domestic sources of credit financing of the public sector. Finally, the fixed peg exchange rate policy encouraged savers to hold a larger proportion of their assets in foreign currency and in inventories of imported goods, thereby diverting resources away from more productive investment. Even in a second best world which for lack of consensus must learn to live with inflation, it must be possible to improve on past Argentine performance.

7 A Mediative Approach to Macroeconomic Policymaking

This book has dealt with the persistent crises in Argentine economic policy that followed seven decades of substantial, if not always spectacular, economic growth. Until 1930 this growth was based mainly on the dynamic expansion of agricultural production for export; but even after the advent of the Great Depression, the Argentine economy recovered rapidly and continued to grow quite satisfactorily, at least compared with most other countries during the period, by accelerating the pace of domestic industrialization. At the end of World War II the country was therefore in a very strong position: it possessed a per capita income at least as high as that prevailing in southern Europe, a rather diversified production base with great potential for future expansion, convertible gold and foreign exchange reserves sufficient to pay for more than a year's normal imports, and a foreign market eager to buy up its exports at the highest prices ever recorded. During the subsequent quarter of a century, however, instead of moving toward the ranks of the advanced industrial powers, Argentina was barely able to increase its real per capita income by a trifling average of 1 percent per year.

Explanations of why Argentina was not able to take better advantage of its opportunities have ranged widely but have usually centered on the search for a scapegoat: the mismanagement of Perón, the existence of weak governments in later years, the orthodoxy of the IMF, the inability to carry out a thoroughgoing reform of existing socioeconomic institutions, the intransigence of national character, foreign plots, or simply the inability of Argentines to live within their means. All of these explanations may contain some elements of truth, but in this book it has been argued that the fundamental cause of the semistagnation and great cyclical instability of the economy was that policymaking was not properly adapted to the conditions of a conflict society. In such a society generally accepted procedures or rules of the game do not exist for reconciling conflicting claims on limited resources generated by sectoral clashes and the struggle over distributive income shares. It therefore follows that monetary, fiscal, and exchange policies—the macro policies upon which governments must rely to establish some balance between the use and availability of resources—will continue to fail to attain their objectives as long as they are not designed in

154

accordance with the nature and degree of political support received by the administration charged with their implementation. In other words, in the absence of a repressive dictatorship—which would clearly represent a backward step in the development of stronger mediative institutions in Argentina—macro policies should be consistent with the ad hoc rules of the game that each successive government is able to negotiate with a pluralistic, largely alienated constituency.

Sociopolitical Alienation of Argentine Society

The change in Argentine economic development strategy toward more rapid industrialization and urbanization after the advent of the Great Depression naturally shifted the locus of economic power increasingly away from so-called agro-exporting interests. This shift was also accompanied by a strengthening of national populist sentiment against the liberal metropolitanism of the elite that had guided the country during the previous period of export-oriented growth. The shift in the locus of economic power and the rise of national populism did not, however, coalesce into a coherent effort to mobilize the new industrialist, urban labor, and related interest groups in support of a new national consensus. Perhaps the paternalistic heritage of elitist rule, the largely immigrant composition of the population, the great dependence of the country on foreign capital and entrepreneurship, and/or other sociohistorical factors had ill-prepared the society for this difficult task. Whatever the more deeply rooted reasons may have been, the immediate cause of the failure to provide an organized political outlet for these new forces was the decision of the military to assume direct control of the government.

Alienated from direct participation in government and freed from the need to build a broad-based political coalition capable of assuming responsibility for the exercise of power, the majority of these new forces withdrew into small associations or groups dedicated to lobbying for their narrow economic or ideological interests. When a charismatic leader then finally emerged to become the standard-bearer of national populism, he proceeded to impose a personalistic, semiauthoritarian rule in favor of some interest groups largely at the expense of others. The Peronist experience not only reinforced passionate political divisions in Argentine society but persuaded many of its members that improvement in their own condition could only be achieved by worsening that of their adversaries. This is the psychology of a primitive, tribal society, not of a responsible, pluralistic one.

The escalation of intransigent group conflict also tended to reinforce nonpragmatic attitudes toward problem-solving and policymaking. The substitution of philosophy for analysis not only impeded the quest for more rational policies but often fostered curious contradictions. Thus, the reaction of those who felt injured by the abuse of state power during the Perón regime was to try to make government incapable of future abuse by destroying records, cutting back statistical and technical staff services, diluting central authority, and otherwise reducing the public sector's capacity to function efficiently, thereby contributing to the fiscal malaise that later afflicted the Argentine economy. Similarly, the ideal of the unfettered market as neutral arbiter of resource allocation came to be embraced by many agro-exporters and industrialists alike, who saw no contradiction between special concessions on tariff protection, tax exemption, and other discriminatory favors on the one hand, and the free play of the market price mechanism on the other. The strong appeal of economic ideology, reinforced by the common attitude of technocrats that the economics of compromise is trivial and ineffectual at best, if not a prostitution of professional ethics, also undoubtedly contributed to the stubbornness with which policymakers insisted on breaking the same lances against old walls.

No government of the period in fact demonstrated by its actions a keen awareness that, in pluralistic societies with weak mediative institutions, conflicts between political and economic vested interest groups must be reconciled in each major macroeconomic policy decision. Prominent examples of such unawareness in recent Argentine experience are the failure of Perón to renegotiate coalition support for his shift to a policy more favorable toward foreign capital in the early 1950s, and the measures taken by the Aramburu regime that alienated organized labor even though its support would be essential for fulfilling the government's objective of restoring effective electoral democracy. Frondizi then made a complete break in policy in 1959 but did not allow himself enough exchange rate and other policy flexibility to take care of later balance of payments and employment problems that eventually undermined the economic and political viability of his program. The shock therapy monetary restrictions adopted in 1962 coincided with a brief period of civil war when feasible alternative policy strategies were admittedly difficult to implement, but they left the country's monetary and fiscal systems in a shambles that greatly handicapped subsequent administrations. The Illia government demonstrated greater economic policy flexibility than previous regimes but steadfastly refused to broaden its political base sufficiently to remain in power. When this government was overthrown, Ongania decided that he could solve the country's economic, social, and political problems in separate stages. He entrusted the first stage to Krieger Vasena who again boxed himself into a wage-price "freeze" with a fixed exchange rate that proved too rigid to cope both with later economic developments and the sociopolitical tensions generated in part by the freeze itself. After the fall of Ongania his successors have continued to struggle, so far unsuccessfully, to pull together an economic program acceptable to a viable political coalition.

This lamentable experience can only be comprehended in the context of the great difficulties of economic policy management faced by semi-industrialized countries like Argentina. These problems are extremely resistant to quick, neat solutions. For example, the attempt made in the second half of the 1950s to restore stronger price incentives by means of devaluation and decontrol ran into serious difficulties because of lags in the response of the economy to changes in relative prices, the persistence of pent-up import demand, and unanticipated shifts in the composition of domestic expenditure and the distribution of income. Other factors that disrupted the quick and smooth implementation of economic programs in these and later years were periodic swings in the perverse cattle cycle, unpredictable changes in inflationary price expectations and the demand for money, the deterioration in fiscal discipline and control, and exogenous fluctuations in climatic conditions and the external terms of trade. Similar factors are of course common occupational hazards of policymakers everywhere, but the peculiar characteristics they present in Argentina make them especially difficult to handle.

Economic Dilemmas of Semi-Industrialized Countries

Most semi-industrial countries in the world today, like many advanced industrial powers during their earlier stages of growth, reached their present status by attempting to force the pace of domestic development through import substitution. At the same time they had to try to adjust their economic and political systems to accommodate broader participation by new, increasingly well-organized interest groups, accelerated urbanization, and those profound changes in consumer habits that accompany "modernization." The reconciliation of these transformations within existing institutional and resource constraints so as to assure a tolerable degree of external and internal economic stability called for a high order of political dexterity and macroeconomic policy management skill that few governments have been able to achieve without restricting effective political pluralism.

With regard to external stability, one of the chief sources of difficulty is that the balance of payments adjustment mechanism of semi-industrialized countries is less automatic than in more open agrarian societies, whereas it is less price responsive than in advanced industrial economies. In the former kind of society, changes in domestic income and expenditure tend to be synchronized with the balance of payments through fluctuations in primary production. Expansion in output generates additional exports to pay for increased imports arising from higher incomes, and vice versa when output declines. In advanced industrial societies, on the other hand, there is no such linkage between domestic income and export expansion, but the short-term elasticity of the balance of payments with respect to exchange and interest rates tends to be rather high. Not only is a large proportion of home goods production internationally competitive or can be made so by moderate changes in relative prices, but international capital movements are very sensitive to changes in relative interest rates. This close economic interdependence of advanced Western industrial nations can be a source of friction and embarrassment, but there is no denying its great efficacy in assuring rapid and relatively painless short-term balance of payments adjustment in countries other than those with reserve currency status.

In semi-industrialized countries, however, neither of these situations generally prevails. The effect of primary output expansion or contraction is asymmetrical: it is extremely important for the balance of payments because these countries still rely mainly on exports of primary goods (and some of them are also quite dependent on supplementary food imports), but variations in primary production are no longer a very important direct determinant of total domestic income and expenditure. The short-term elasticity of the balance of payments with respect to the exchange rate, on the other hand, tends to be rather low. The main reasons are the generally low short-term elasticity of supply of most primary goods and the fact that home production of most other goods is so noncompetitive internationally, and most imports are so noncompetitive with domestically produced goods, that moderate changes in relative prices provide little inducement to increase exports or to substitute imports. International capital movements are also rather insensitive to interest rate variations in these countries; short-term capital flows instead respond almost exclusively to local "confidence" in the value of the domestic currency.

Semi-industrial countries seem in short to be suffering from a new form of economic dualism: they are not yet full-fledged members of the international financial community, and their economies are divided into an internationally competitive, primary exporting sector that coexists with a much larger but noncompetitive group of activities producing almost entirely for domestic use. This noncompetitive sector is composed not only of activities that provide so-called nontradable goods and services (that is, items that no country normally exports such as nonfinancial services and goods with prohibitively high transport costs), but also of a broad range of industries producing behind high protective barriers erected to promote the substitution of imports. This situation is so prevalent that at least until very recent years almost no middle income country with a substantial domestic market exported finished manufactures worth more than 3 percent of its total exports. [1]

A large proportion of these middle income countries have other significant common characteristics: they are located mainly in the Mediterranean area or in lands of recent settlement outside of Asia and black Africa; they have relatively favorable population-resource ratios and temperate or mixed climates; and they are often specialized in the export of primary agricultural products that compete with the protected output of advanced countries and their overseas associated territories. These advanced countries still provide the main markets for trade in agricultural produce, but their demand tends to be residual: imports cover the difference between variable protected supplies and total demand at domestic support prices. The remainder of exports from semideveloped nations must be sold to other developing or socialist countries often under special trading arrangements. Important variants to this pattern exist for different commodities, but in general it can be said that import demand for primary agricultural products is determined in very imperfect markets and is greatly influenced by import substitution and other protective policies of developed countries. This is undoubtedly one of the reasons why between 1937-1938 and 1955 the volume of world trade in commodities exported chiefly by middle income nations remained practically stagnant, and the volume of world trade in those exported by Argentina declined by an average of 12 percent.[2]

Another important reason for the unsatisfactory growth of primary exports from semi-industrialized countries has been their own policy toward domestic export producers. An unfortunate characteristic of such producers is that they are often large landowners and/or foreign companies whose political leverage has been declining progressively in recent decades. If in addition exports are largely composed of popular consumer goods, as is the case with Argentina, it is quite understandable why governments have been hesitant to provide more attractive price incentives for export expansion except when balance of payments crises forced a reluctant (and often temporary) change of policy. Reluctant middle income exporting countries have not, on the other hand, been obliged to take drastic corrective action by the threat of being cut entirely out of the world market, because the demand facing any particular unprotected exporter is largely determined by his competitive position vis-à-vis other unprotected suppliers who are often following similar policies.

Argentine policymakers have therefore had to cope with quite different, and in several ways more difficult, balance of payments problems than their colleagues both in more advanced and in less developed countries, or in those nations that are major producers of petroleum, some metals, and a few other primary commodities that have benefited from a relatively rapid expansion in total world trade. They have also had to understand that the impediments to exporting manufactures developed to supply a highly protected domestic market are of a quite different order of magnitude than those of small nations that have succeeded in developing export-oriented industries from scratch.

These balance of payments difficulties have been matched by equally serious and closely related problems with the maintenance of internal stability. During the quarter of a century after World War II, the domestic price level in Argentina rose by an average of over 20 percent per year, and in one year exceeded 100 percent. The problem of inflation is of course universal, particularly in semi-industrialized countries, but in conflict societies like Argentina the struggle over distributive income shares has made it next to impossible to reconcile conflicting claims on limited resources through appropriate macroeconomic policies alone. All Argentine administrations have nevertheless sooner or later felt obliged to try to stop inflation, usually by means of orthodox monetary and fiscal restrictions or through attempted wage and price freezes. Most of these efforts had the effect of reducing the level of economic activity instead of slowing down the increase in the price level, but even those attempts that began to show some signs of success eventually broke down in a renewed wage-price-exchange rate spiral. Even more serious, the unsuccessful preoccupation of successive governments with the elimination of inflation instead of with protecting economic institutions and policy instruments from serious inflationary erosion led to the virtual destruction of previously well-developed capital markets, loss of government control over the money market and the fiscal system, tremendous distortions in relative prices and factor remunerations, and a redistribution of income against the more poorly organized and weaker groups of the society, thus producing further alienation among important segments of the population.

Under such circumstances it serves little purpose to debate whether inflation is mainly demand-pull or cost-push. Over the years rising price expectations become built into the behavior of individuals, firms, and other organizations, whose success or even survival depends on their ability to develop contract, pricing, and resource allocation practices that protect them as much as possible from the inflationary erosion of real income and wealth. The conventional concepts of forced saving and money illusion are of little relevance in a secular inflationary environment, and the links between monetary and "real" economic variables are even more obscure than in noninflationary societies. Balance sheets and budgets, the control variables that monetary and fiscal authorities mostly rely on, reveal only the apex of the large and complex pyramid of transactions that actually take place.

Decision-makers in this kind of pluralistic conflict society are therefore faced with a job of reconstruction resembling that of a country emerging from a long, destructive civil war. Their priority tasks are to rehabilitate basic services that have been seriously damaged, such as public utilities and markets for foreign exchange and financial assets; to assure as equitable a distribution as possible of essential goods and services until output recovers; and to help provide productive employment for refugees from the conflict, such as supernumerary government employees. These tasks cannot be achieved without growth, growth cannot prosper without a stable government, and a stable government cannot be formed without reconciling or suppressing conflict.

The major groups whose disagreements would have to be reconciled or suppressed to implement a viable economic program in Argentina have been referred to repeatedly in this and previous chapters. The most important numerically are of course organized labor and the middle classes, although young people are emerging as an important (though amorphous) new source of power that cuts across traditional interest group lines and signifies a shift of the political center of gravity to the left. The most representative voices of these groups are still Peronism and the Radical party, both of which have neither a clear ideology nor a fixed policy platform. The basis therefore exists in principle for negotiating their joint participation in a coalition government with a popular nationalist flavor, once it is made clear that neither of them is able to win sufficient power to rule unilaterally. Such a coalition would probably be welcomed by a substantial segment of the armed forces, but the military leadership in particular would have reservations and would in all likelihood insist on direct participation for themselves and a role for that part of the business community not associated with the CGE (which would probably be able to reach an understanding with a popular nationalist coalition on its own). To win over these powerful holdouts it would therefore be necessary to make further concessions, such as the inclusion of some planks from the developmentalist platform in the economic program and the granting of greater voice in decisions than would otherwise be justified by their numerical strength.[3]

This scenario for putting together a broad political coalition is sketched only to illustrate the possibility of doing so and to indicate the nature of the policy compromises that would probably be required. Any viable economic program under such a coalition would have to be based either explicitly or implicitly on an incomes policy that would make rapid attainment of zero inflation quite unlikely. Disputes over fiscal and foreign investment policies would also probably occupy center stage, and the issue of greater provincial autonomy could well become an important bargaining point in the struggle to maintain broad enough support from diverse, shifting alliances to maintain a coalition government in power without the use of naked force. Whether the stresses and strains generated by this kind of institutional solution could be reconciled with the implementation of a consistent set of macroeconomic policies would depend on the possibility of adopting a more mediative approach to policymaking than Argentines have been accustomed to in the past.

Mediative Policymaking

The most popular scenario for resolution of the kind of conflict described above is installation of a "strong" government capable of imposing rational economic order. In practice such a government usually turns out to be either a personalistic, a one-party, or a military dictatorship. The main problem with this kind of institutional "solution" is that those who are most adroit at seizing power are seldom as adept at managing an economy, and once established there is seldom any way to get them out except with the help of political adventurers even more adroit at seizing power (and perhaps even less adept at economic management). Furthermore, the use of force instead of compromise to impose policies is almost bound to polarize sectoral clashes and the struggle over income shares into extremist political ideologies. This outcome can only be avoided by broadening effective political and economic participation which, even if carried out by a benign one-party or military dictatorship, requires the strengthening of mediative institutions capable of resolving interest group conflicts. The search for mediative policy alternatives is therefore likely to continue at least on the part of those who do not see any possibility for the immanent appearance of a philosopher king or for the introduction of a social system that completely sublimates human conflict.

It is easier to advocate a role for nonnormative economic policymaking than it is to provide a cogent explanation of how to put it into practice, since neither economists nor political scientists have yet developed practical decision models for this purpose. The economist's chief traditional concern at the macroeconomic policy level is to determine what monetary, fiscal, and balance of payments policies can most efficiently raise the income of a society, given its preference between present and future consumption, its natural and human resource endowments, and other attributes that both define the tradeoffs between different economic objectives and constrain society's capacity to achieve them. This approach can be very powerful in situations where it is meaningful to speak of the objectives of society as a whole and where some minimum agreement exists with respect to the economic and institutional relationships that can and should be affected by policy.

The familiar approach of political science to policymaking, on the other hand, is to try to explain decisions in terms of the distribution of power among pressure groups, government agencies, and important personalities, and of the tactical techniques and political skills they employ in pursuit of their aims. This approach provides useful insights for policy analysis but is not of much help in measuring the tradeoffs between policy alternatives. Some day political scientists may find a way of using the economist's notion of cost-benefit to quantify the impact of policies on changes in social hostility and instability, support for the system, policy options foregone or truncated, and on other factors affecting the political feasibility of decisions.[4]

Though no formal model suitable for mediative policy analysis has yet been devised, some economists and political scientists have ventured generalizations about the policymaking process in pluralistic societies. A promising point of departure is that body of literature that emphasizes the importance of compromise, adjustment, negotiation, and bargaining among competing power groups, none of which exercises overriding control. In this literature it is suggested that the concept of satisficing should replace optimization as a criterion for practical policymaking. Satisficing involves acceptance of a level of goal accomplishment short of the optimum perceived by the decision-maker, who often finds it convenient to avoid clarification of goals so as to facilitate agreement among factions with quite different motives and expectations. A satisficing policy would therefore have to be designed in accordance with the relative strength of support for a multiplicity of often conflicting and vaguely specified goals.[5]

Within a mediative context policy decisions tend to be tentative, with further steps in the same direction or policy reversals determined by response or adaptation of the economy to previous decisions. Policymaking is thus typically serial or sequential, "a never-ending process of successive steps in which continual nibbling is a substitute for a good bite."[6] Since policymakers are obliged to be as concerned with the process of adjustment to new policies as they are with end results, they require more information on the probable impact of policies than is provided by static "before and after" comparisons. According to Simon's well-known metaphor, if one is interested in the final state of equilibrium of molasses poured into a bowl, one only needs to know the shape of the bowl and the fact that over time it will minimize the height of its center of gravity. But if the bowl were constantly jiggled, or if one wanted to know about the behavior of the molasses before equilibrium were reached, it would be necessary to know more about its internal structure.[7] The logical result of a satisficing approach to goal achievement and seriality or successive approximation in policy tactics is an incrementalist policy strategy. Except on unusual occasions, new policies will tend to be only incrementally or marginally different from existing policies, so as to permit the decision-maker to concentrate his analysis on familiar experience, reduce the number of policy alternatives to more manageable proportions, and facilitate gaining acceptance from his political coalition.[8]

These decision-making rules for pluralistic societies seem in general well adapted, with some modifications, to conditions in middle income, conflict societies. They first imply that macroeconomic policies should be formulated in a way that facilitates the formation and survival of coalitions broad enough to maintain a government in power. The severity of this policy constraint depends, of course, on the degree of fragmentation of power among interest groups and on the breadth of participation in the political process that a government is willing or obliged to concede. Bargaining over alternative policies, none of which necessarily commands majority support, may result in unexpected compromise. Agreement can often be reached only in terms of outcomes that are considered in general either desirable or undesirable, not in terms of policy means. The policymaker may therefore enjoy by default more immediate freedom of action than his counterparts in more stable, structured societies as long as his constituency is satisfied with the apparent consequences of his decisions.

Given the frequent lack of specific policy consensus within coalitions and the tendency for coalitions in conflict societies to shift frequently and unpredictably, major policies tend to be subjected to continuous reappraisal and can seldom be assumed "settled." In one sense this also gives the policymaker more scope, since he is able to tamper with policies that in more stable societies constitute the cornerstones of long-agreed upon political compromises, alterations of which would require difficult renegotiation among affected interest groups to keep them in line.[9] In another sense conditional policy flexibility, in addition to generating uncertainty, imposes a very severe time constraint on the decision-maker: even his longer-term policies will be judged largely by their immediate effects. This constant jiggling of the bowl—to use Simon's metaphor—obliges policymakers to view the long term largely as a sequence of short terms.

Since it is difficult to envisage policy consistency and continuity under a system of shifting political alliances, logrolling has been suggested as a more desirable policymaking tactic. Logrolling is more compatible with continuity in the executive branch and with the incorporation of divergent opinions into a smaller, more manageable number of political parties. This policy tactic would undoubtedly facilitate more coherent macroeconomic policymaking, but it is not likely to be feasible in a society that considers compromise a questionable trait of human character. Even among Latin societies Argentina has been considered the nirvana of intransigents, where "social forces confront each other nakedly, no political institutions, no corps of professional political leaders are recognized or accepted as the legitimate intermediaries to moderate group conflict, and no agreement exists among the groups as to the legitimate and authoritative methods for resolving conflicts." The judicial and legislative branches of government have traditionally been weak, so that fundamental decisions are made in the executive establishment "under the influence of pressure groups of importance that extend their heads directly into the governmental structure." This praetorian style of conduct allegedly reaches also into the management of private enterprise and labor unions and of relationships between them. In fact, the image of conflict is painted so grim in Argentina that it is difficult to conceive how any law could possibly be implemented except that of Darwin.[10]

The Argentine style of political conduct is therefore likely to continue to depend more on shifting alliances and on the more or less charismatic leadership of a strong political figure than on logrolling. During periods of national emergency such a figure may be able to sublimate interest group conflict for a time and mobilize majority support for important new policy departures. But during more "normal" times, decision-making will usually have to obey the incrementalist principle, according to which policies are subject to constant reappraisal in terms of their apparent short-term effects. Since the unpredictability of leads and lags in policy responses and slippage in implementation are considerably greater in Argentina than in countries with more stable economies and institutions, "fine tuning" is out of the question and new decisions will depend more on the outcome of previous decisions than on any fixed guidelines that may be laid down in national economic plans and programs. The inescapable conclusion is that the design of policy must take into account the contingent nature of decisions, that policymakers should thus build greater flexibility into their programs, and that they must stand ready to revise them when political expediency makes it the lesser of evils to do so.

The arguments usually raised against this kind of flexibility are that a general revision of targets would be tantamount to a confession of the failure of a government's economic program, that such action would undermine confidence, or that by making concessions policymakers would soon lose control over the economy. A clear distinction should be made, however, between policy flexibility and policy drift. Flexibility is necessary as a hedge against uncertainty and slippage in the implementation of one or more key policy variables when failure to fulfill some policy target makes achievement of others counterproductive. To accommodate to this frequently encountered situation, programs should be formulated in terms of the relative values of key variables, not in terms of absolute levels or fixed percentage changes, since it is relative prices and relationships between economic variables that influence resource allocation. This kind of flexibility would make policy programming more meaningful and would provide a better check on policy drift by focusing attention on timely policy adjustments needed to maintain program consistency. The argument that rigid adherence to fixed policy goals discourages slippage is certainly not confirmed by Argentine experience; on the contrary, decision-makers faced by inevitable slippage in the implementation of inflexible programs have often tried to play down the importance of interpolicy and intertarget relationships, an attitude that is about as conducive to policy drift as no program at all.

Efficiency Versus Feasibility in Mediative Policy Programming

The chief recommendations contained in this study for a satisficing, sequential, incrementalist approach to policymaking in Argentina have as their main objectives the assurance of greater policy consistency and the protection of economic institutions, policy instruments, and incentives from inflationary erosion. Even if previous arguments are accepted that these are indeed the most appropriate feasible objectives of macroeconomic policy under existing institutional constraints in Argentina, the question can legitimately be raised as to whether achievement of these limited goals is likely to improve the country's economic performance appreciably over time. In other words, what tradeoffs does the recommended policy strategy involve between economic efficiency and political feasibility? Before attempting to answer this question, however, it may be useful to remind the reader of the chief policy suggestions made in earlier chapters.

With respect to balance of payments policy, it was argued that the most important objective is protection of the exchange rate from wild fluctuations in its real value, that is, preservation if not a gradual improvement in the value of foreign currency relative to the domestic price level. If domestic inflation cannot be completely eliminated or brought down to, and maintained at, "international rates," and complete exchange rate flexibility is not feasible, the only alternative is a crawling or trotting peg exchange rate subject to frequent, tiny devaluations. The other principal policy recommended to promote external stability was at least partial compensation of the effects of sector dualism, that is, the existence of an internationally competitive primary sector, together with a very uncompetitive secondary one. If relative agricultural prices are inflexible upwards for sociopolitical reasons, and relative industrial prices cannot be drastically reduced in the short or medium run, then the only alternative is to promote cost-reducing improvements in agricultural productivity and subsidize nontraditional exports. To help smooth out short-term balance of payments fluctuations, explicit agricultural price and feedgrain development policies were also recommended to dampen the cattle cycle and assure a more regular supply of foreign exchange.

With regard to inflation, it was argued that pursuit of the optimal objective of complete price stability is likely to continue to be counterproductive under conditions prevailing in Argentina. It is therefore preferable to concentrate on trying to implement a policy of neutral inflation, or the stabilization of key relative prices, so as to prevent inflationary erosion of the signals needed for improved resource allocation. Aside from the exchange rate and the beef/grain price ratio, a neutral inflation policy would have to give priority attention to maintaining a positive real interest rate to facilitate redevelopment of the domestic capital market and restoration of effective Central Bank control of the money market, and real tax rates and public utility tariffs would have to be better maintained to improve management of fiscal and monetary policies. If interest groups became convinced that they could not validate their claims for a larger share of resources through exorbitant wage and price demands, it might also be possible to reach agreement on an incomes policy that would reduce the rate of increase in prices over time.

Returning now to the question of efficiency versus feasibility, it could be argued that an incrementalist approach in pursuit of intermediate policy objectives might have the effect of locking the economy into a new set of distortions created by the half-measures themselves. Policies aimed at compensating sector dualism to promote manufactured exports could, for example, make later adoption of measures to reduce discrepancies between domestic and international relative prices more difficult. The counterargument is that a mediative policy approach should on the contrary contribute to the strengthening of political support for desirable economic policies. The acceptability of real exchange rate maintenance or improvement, which at present has a very small constituency in Argentina outside of the agricultural sector, would be broadened by turning more people into exporters through the subsidization of manufactures. Once industrial exports become important for a significant number of firms, more effective opposition is also likely to develop against indiscriminate ISI that increases domestic costs and reduces export profit margins. Insofar as more rapid export expansion furthermore permits a faster rate of overall economic growth with less cyclical instability, defensive attitudes toward protecting acquired positions against the threats of competition and mobility—attitudes that make good sense in a stagnant society in which someone's gain is almost necessarily at somebody else's expense—may also give way to a more dynamic, less protective outlook. The incrementalist approach to breaking out of a persistent foreign exchange bottleneck thus has as one of its main justifications the utilization of small first steps to condition opinion to accept more courageous future steps in the hope that the process may over time become reinforcing.

It might also be objected that nontraditional export subsidization runs the same risk as ISI tariff protection of being used excessively and indiscriminately. There is an important difference, however, between protective tariffs and export subsidies: the economic cost of tariffs is more diffuse and difficult to identify than the cost of subsidies. This does not mean that attempts will not be made to abuse them, but it should be recalled that agricultural support prices in Argentina, even under governments sympathetic to farmers, have generally been held below market prices in order to avoid the fiscal cost of acquiring and disposing of large surpluses. The danger of abuse will of course be approximately proportional to the degree of differentiation and complexity of the subsidy system, but it is also significant that the discriminatory export subsidy program initiated in the early 1960s has become more uniform under pressure from less favored exporters.

With respect to the gradualistic domestic stabilization policies recommended in this book, it has to be admitted that a completely neutral inflation is for all practical purposes unobtainable. Some prices are bound to lag in the inflationary competition regardless of government policy, and price expectations of different economic agents will inevitably diverge depending on their degree of confidence in official incomes policy. Pressure will also continue to be exerted on government to postpone inflationary adjustments in tax and public utility rates or to make exceptions in favor of certain interest groups whose political support is desired. The only answer to these arguments is that even greater relative price distortions are likely to be generated by inflation in the absence of a key price adjustment policy or as a result of attempted wage-price freezes that are only partially enforced.

Another objection to wage-price determination by means of an incomes policy is that differentials that should be allowed to manifest themselves in the market to provide incentives for desirable resource allocation will tend to be suppressed. One should have confidence, however, in the oft-proven experience that when it is in the mutual interest of both buyer and seller to get around controls, some way will usually be found to evade them. A more serious concern is that pressure from organized labor for real wage improvement will probably be translated mainly into increases in labor productivity instead of into more jobs. This is of course an almost universal experience in all countries regardless of the particular policies being followed, but policymakers in Argentina would be wise to give special attention in their programs to the promotion of labor-intensive activities such as construction. Maintenance of a healthy mortgage market and a brisk public investment program could be of great assistance in maintaining full employment, and the avoidance of recessionary balance of payments crises and tight money policies would also make an important contribution to this end.

In the final analysis all that can be said in general about the tradeoff between economic efficiency and political feasibility is that the best of both worlds could be more closely approximated if the "right" politicians allowed the "right" economists to maximize the national income first and then redistribute income as society wished by means of lump sum transfers that did not interfere with relative prices at the margin. Since this division of labor is impossible to put into effect, the best that realistically can be expected is that decision-makers will at least be concerned with the economic feasibility of what they consider politically efficient policies. In this context avoidance of stop-go economic behavior is almost unequivocally desirable from both the economic and political points of view. In cases where economic and political means and ends come into conflict, on the other hand, seldom will it be possible even to reach common accord on the nature of the tradeoffs involved. The mediative political economist will therefore find himself just as often obliged to try to design policies that satisfice political efficiency under economic feasibility constraints as he does the reverse.

Perhaps the most important conclusion of this study is that price stability and growth are complementary instead of competitive, as long as balance is maintained in external payments through healthy export expansion and appropriate domestic incomes and expenditure policies. In the absence of a satisfactory rate of economic growth—at least two or three times as high as Argentina has been able to achieve with its stop-go policies of the last generation—there is little hope that the tensions of a conflict society can be resolved while at the same time preserving a pluralistic form of government. Argentina's chances of succeeding in this difficult endeavor will depend on a wide variety of factors, one of the most important of which is whether Argentine leaders and policymakers can make up their minds how open their economy should be. Their task would be greatly facilitated if they could count on a team of pragmatic technocrats uncommitted to any ideal norm of economic behavior. Provision of this kind of analysis and advice constitutes a major challenge to the economic development profession in the years ahead, especially as more nations join the conflictive club of the semi-industrialized.

Appendixes
Notes
Bibliography
Index

Appendix A. The Demand for Money

A large number of regression experiments were carried out by the authors on the determinants of the demand for money in Argentina. One group of experiments used money supply as the dependent variable and different combinations and specifications of gross domestic product, price expectations, and time trend as explanatory or independent variables. Although time and savings deposits in banks were included in the definition of money supply in a number of tests, the best results were obtained using the more restrictive definition of currency and demand deposits (usually referred to as M_1 in the literature). The most satisfactory regression equation was the following, based on quarterly data for the period 1956I to 1967II:

$$(1) \quad \ln \frac{M}{N} = 1.045 + 1.252 \ln \frac{Y}{N} - .009 \, P^* - .305 \ln T,$$
$$\qquad\qquad\quad (3.671) \qquad (3.459) \ (17.786)$$

$$\bar{R}^2 = .883, DW = .615;$$

where:

     $\ln M/N$ = log of per capita money supply deflated by the cost of living index (currency in circulation outside of banks and demand deposits—see tables A-1 and B-1),

     $\ln Y/N$ = log of per capita GDP in prices of 1960, expressed as a three-quarter moving average (see explanation in Appendix B and table B–3),

     P^* = price expectations variable with a .7 weighting scheme (see table A-2).

     $\ln T$ = log time variable.

The $\bar{R}^2$ is adjusted for degrees of freedom, and the figures below the coefficients in parentheses are "T" statistics.

Another group of experiments was carried out with the velocity of circulation of money (the ratio of money supply to GDP) as the dependent variable, using the same independent variables employed in the previous experiments. This specification of the relationship between money and other economic variables proved superior, in the sense that not only were the $\bar{R}^2$ higher but the Durbin-Watson statistics indicated less likelihood of serial correlation of residuals. Attempts were made to include dummy variables in the equation to pick up seasonal fluctuations in the velocity of circulation, but the best result obtained was the following, based on quarterly data for the period 1956I to 1967II:

$$(2) \quad \frac{M}{Y} = 2.938 - .009P^* - .435 \ln T,$$
$$\phantom{(2) \quad \frac{M}{Y} = 2.938} (3.734) \quad (28.029)$$

$$\bar{R}^2 = .945, DW = 1.361;$$

where:

M = currency plus demand deposits,

Y = GDP in current prices,

and the other variables and figures have the same meaning as described in the preceding equation.

When the equation was tested with longer lags for the price expectations variable, results were less satisfactory. For example, with a .3 weighting scheme of distributed lags (price changes in period t-1 are given half the weight they receive in the .7 weighting scheme), the following results were obtained:

$$(3) \quad \frac{M}{Y} = 2.941 - .012P^* - .430 \ln T,$$
$$\phantom{(3) \quad \frac{M}{Y} = 2.941} (3.269) \quad (26.95)$$

$$\bar{R}^2 = .9415, DW = 1.248.$$

Another interesting finding was that the residuals of equation (2) are negatively correlated with changes in the rate of inflation, but we were unable to use these residuals to improve the explanatory power of the price determination equations reported on in Appendix B.

When equation (2) was rerun to include the period up to 1968II, the $\bar{R}^2$ declined, the statistical significance of the coefficients of the independent variables deteriorated, and the Durban-Watson statistic indicated greater likelihood of serial correlation of residuals. As was observed in Chapter 5, this result can be interpreted as evidence that the determinants of the demand for money changed after Krieger Vasena introduced his new stabilization policy in the second quarter of 1967. The results of the longer run are (for the period 1956I to 1968II):

$$(4) \quad \frac{M}{Y} = 2.904 - .012P^* - .416 \ln T,$$
$$\phantom{(4) \quad \frac{M}{Y} = 2.904} (3.236) \quad (26.136)$$

$$\bar{R}^2 = .932, DW = 1.133.$$

Table A-1   Money supply: quarterly averages. (billions of pesos)

1955	I	45.0	1962	I	207.4
	II	45.1		II	208.6
	III	45.6		III	209.9
	IV	48.5		IV	210.7
1956	I	53.2	1963	I	223.9
	II	53.1		II	234.7
	III	54.2		III	246.2
	IV	57.0		IV	266.6
1957	I	63.0	1964	I	295.1
	II	63.6		II	326.1
	III	63.4		III	343.1
	IV	64.7		IV	370.7
1958	I	70.0	1965	I	404.5
	II	71.8		II	424.9
	III	76.8		III	440.4
	IV	90.2		IV	462.6
1959	I	105.9	1966	I	504.4
	II	113.7		II	531.0
	III	120.4		III	567.5
	IV	132.2		IV	618.5
1960	I	146.6	1967	I	673.9
	II	154.3		II	725.5
	III	162.3		III	763.1
	IV	167.6		IV	803.0
1961	I	181.4	1968	I	869.2
	II	184.9		II	923.9
	III	186.1		III	982.8
	IV	193.5		IV	1,043.3

Source: The figures are from Banco Central, *Boletín Estadístico*, various numbers, and ibid., *Estadísticas monetarias y bancarias, años 1940-60*. Money supply is defined as currency in circulation outside of banks and demand deposits. Because of bank strikes it was necessary to interpolate figures for February 1958 and April and May 1959.

Table A-2 Geometric weighting schemes used in calculating P* variables.

Period $t-1$	Weighting scheme					
	.1	.2	.3	.5	.7	1.0
1	.10	.18	.26	.39	.52	.63
2	.09	.15	.19	.24	.25	.23
3	.08	.12	.14	.15	.12	.09
4	.07	.10	.11	.09	.06	
5	.07	.08	.08	.05		
6	.06	.07	.06	.03		
7	.05	.05	.05			
8	.05	.04	.04			
9	.04	.04	.03			
10	.04	.03	.02			
11	.03	.02				
12	.03	.02				
13	.03	.02				
14	.03	.01				
15	.02	.01				
16	.02	.01				
17	.02					
18	.02					
19	.02					
20	.01					
21	.01					
22	.01					
23	.01					
24	.01					
25	.01					
26	.01					
27	.01					

The above geometric weights, which were multiplied by price changes in the corresponding periods, were calculated using the formula:

$$\frac{\pi^n}{\underset{i=0}{}} \delta^1 (1 - \delta^1)^i$$

where:

$\delta^1 = \dfrac{2\delta}{2 + \delta}$ and δ is the specific weight chosen for the series. The higher the weighting scheme number, the shorter the periods of price expectation formation. The periods of course refer to quarters, so that the time periods range from six and three quarter years under weighting scheme .1 to three quarters of a year for weighting scheme 1.0.

Appendix B. Price Determination Functions

Diz: One of the earliest and most rigorous attempts to estimate price determination functions for Argentina was made by Adolfo Diz in "Money and Prices in Argentina, 1935-1962," Ph.D. dissertation submitted to the University of Chicago, June, 1966. Two groups of experiments were carried out. The first tries to explain changes in the rate of inflation solely in terms of variations in money supply with different lags. The best result, using quarterly percentage changes for subperiod 1946-1962 (the one we are concerned with in this study), was the following:

$$(1) \quad P = \underset{(.110)}{.629^* M_t} + \underset{(.103)}{.088\, M_{t-2}} - \underset{(.104)}{.455^* M_{t-4}} - \underset{(.114)}{.043\, M_{t-6}}, R^2 = .443,$$

where:

P = wholesale prices,

M = currency and demand deposits (a broader definition of money was tested but yielded less satisfactory results),

$t - i$ = lagged values with respect to the current quarter t, and the figures in parentheses are standard errors; an asterisk indicates significance at the 5 percent level (see Diz, *Money and Prices in Argentina*, table 15, p. 66).

Even aside from the problems of multicolinearity in such equations, the question of the extent to which lagged M values may serve partly as proxies for omitted variables, and the interpretation of the negative sign of some of the coefficients (which Diz has attempted to explain elsewhere), it is clear that most of the variance in the rate of inflation remains "unexplained." In a second group of experiments Diz therefore incorporated additional explanatory variables in his estimating equations, the most satisfactory of which for the period 1946-1962 was also for wholesale prices with all variables expressed in logs (except for R_E and S_t):

$$(2) \quad P = \underset{(.105)}{.462^* M_t} - \underset{(.108)}{.022\, M_{t-2}} - \underset{(.103)}{.217^* M_{t-4}} - \underset{(.092)}{.079\, M_{t-6}}$$

$$+ \underset{(1.196)}{4.536^* R_E} - \underset{(.234)}{.514^* Y} + \underset{(.024)}{.097^* X} + \underset{(.043)}{.033 W}$$

179

$$+ .006 \, S_1 + .017 \, S_2 + .045^*,$$
$$(.022) \quad (.019) \quad (.012)$$

$$R^2 = .760,$$

where:

R_E = price expectations with a weighting scheme of .1 for distributed lags of past price changes (indicating relatively long lags,
which consistently proved more significant than short lags in
all of Diz's experiments),

Y = average real national income,

X = official exchange rate,

W = nominal wages,

S_1, S_2, and S_2 = seasonal dummy variables, and the other symbols and
figures are as defined in equation (1) (see Diz, *Money and Prices in Argentina*, table 18, p. 75).

It is apparent that inclusion of the additional independent variables im-
proves the explanatory power of the equation (partly by reducing the size
and statistical significance of the M variables), and that price expectations
become the most important single determinant of the rate of inflation. This
is disconcerting for reasons mentioned in the text, particularly in view of the
fact that long lags of past price changes (averaging over five years) seem to
be more significant than short lags in influencing future price expectations.
It should also be noted that lagged values of the new independent variables
are not tested, and that the R^2 corrected for degrees of freedom would be
less than .7, implying that about a third of price variations still remains
"unexplained."

Diaz Alejandro: By introducing lagged values of independent variables
other than money supply, Diaz Alejandro was able to identify price determination functions with a higher explanatory power than those tested by
Diz. Using percentage changes in half-yearly data for the period 1950-1965,
his best equations for the cost of living and wholesale prices were:

$$(3) \quad P_{c. \text{ of } 1.} = -4.95 + 0.06 \, (X_6)_t + 0.22 \, (X_6)_{t-1}$$
$$(3.01) \quad (0.24) \quad \quad (0.23)$$

$$-0.26 \, (X_6)_{t-2} - 0.18 \, (X_8)_t + 0.17 \, (X_9)_t$$
$$(0.22) \quad \quad (0.19) \quad \quad (0.06)$$

$$+0.50 \, (X_{10})_t + 0.53 \, (X_{10})_{t-1} + 0.17 \, (X_{10})_{t-2},$$
$$(0.15) \quad \quad (0.14) \quad \quad (0.14)$$

$$R^2 = 0.81, DW = 1.66;$$

(4) $P_{wh.}$ $= -2.66 + 0.49\ (X_6)_t + 0.26\ (X_6)_{t-1}$
             (3.12) (0.25)   (0.23)

$-0.68\ (X_6)_{t-2} - 0.37\ (X_8)_t + 0.25\ (X_9)_t$
(0.23)   (0.19)   (0.06)

$+0.37\ (X_{10})_t + 0.41\ (X_{10})_{t-1} + 0.18\ (X_{10})_{t-2},$
(0.15)   (0.15)   (0.15)

$$R^2 = 0.86, DW = 1.56,$$

where:

X_6	= currency plus demand deposits,
X_8	= GDP plus imports ("real supplies"),
X_9	= average import-export exchange rate,
X_{10}	= average hourly money wage rates;

figures in parentheses are standard errors, R^2 is unadjusted for degrees of freedom, and DW is the Durban-Watson statistic. (See *Essays on the Economic History of the Argentine Republic*, table 7.9, p. 373.)

These results are in such marked contrast with those of equation (2) that they appear based on data from a different country. On closer analysis, however, serious problems can be detected in Diaz Alejandro's regressions. First, if the equations are rerun by stepping in independent variables one at a time, it is found that money supply is statistically significant until the exchange rate and especially the wage variable enter. Examination of the correlation matrix reveals that the simple R between (X_6) and (X_{10}) with the same lag is .66 or higher for the cost of living equation; indeed, the correlation between these two "independent" variables is higher than it is between each of them individually and the dependent variable (similar relationships hold for the wholesale price equation). Little faith can therefore be placed on the statistical significance of the coefficients because of multicolinearity.

Equally serious, the statistical significance of the equations appears to be very unstable over time. If the period is subdivided in two parts, 1950-1957 and 1957-1968, simplified versions of the equations (to take account of the fewer degrees of freedom) yield zero corrected R^2 for the first subperiod and strikingly different results for the second, as can be seen in the following (same definition of symbols as above, but covering the period from second half 1957 to first half 1968; the R^2 have also been corrected for degrees of freedom and the figures in parentheses refer to "T" statistics):

(5) $P_{c.\ of\ 1.}$ $= 3.97 + .36\,(X_6)_{t-1} + .003\,(X_8)_t$
$\qquad\quad\ (1.54)\ (2.17)\qquad\quad (.01)$

$\qquad\quad + \ .45\,(X_9)_t, \bar{R}^2 = .81, DW = 1.62;$
$\qquad\quad (7.54)$

(6) $P_{wh.}$ $= 2.73 + .23\,(X_6)_{t-1} - .02\,(X_8)_t$
$\qquad\quad\ (.86)\ (1.13)\qquad\quad (.06)$

$\qquad\quad + \ .61\,(X_9)_t, \bar{R}^2 = .82, DW = 1.35.$
$\qquad\quad (8.27)$

It will be noticed that in equation (5) money supply becomes statistically significant at the 5 percent level when the wage variable is left out, but the most important change is that the exchange rate becomes by far the most important determinant of the rate of inflation. The simple R between $(X_9)t$ and the dependent variable is .89 in equation (5) and .75 in equation (6), indicating that the other variables add very little explanatory power. Another disconcerting fact is that in all of Diaz Alejandro's regressions the constant term is rather large (and in some cases statistically significant at the 10 percent level), implying that some important independent variable or variables have been left out of the equations (or that they are not well specified).

Maynard-Van Rijckeghem: Working with annual percentage changes for the period 1950-1965, Maynard and Van Rijckeghem developed a model that has actually been used by government technicians in Argentina and has continued to predict price changes quite accurately several years after it was completed (see Willy Van Rijckeghem, *Stabilization Policy in an Inflationary Economy: A Post Mortem*). One of the most interesting aspects of the model is that bank credit to the private sector relative to changes in the wage rate correlates positively with variations in nonagricultural output and negatively with the rate of inflation, an aspect reported on in Chapter 6. The price equation of this model is as follows (see Gustav F. Papanek, ed., *Development Policy: Theory and Practice*, p. 214):

(7) P_r $= 7.16 + 0.70M_{-1/2} - 0.89z_r - 1.82\pi + 0.30N,$
$\qquad\quad (5.85)\ \ (.047)\qquad\ (0.57)\ \ (0.72)\ \ (0.26)$

$\qquad\quad R^2 = .86, DW = 1.85,$

where:

$\qquad P_r$ $=$ annual percentage change in wholesale prices excluding agricultural goods,

$M_{-1/2}$ = percentage change in total money supply (including time and savings deposits) lagged one half year,

z_r = percentage change in real GDP of the nonagricultural sectors,

π = dummy variable representing price controls in 1953 and 1954 and their elimination in 1959, and

N = percentage change in wage rates according to collective wage agreements.

The equivalent $\overline{R}^2$ corrected for degrees of freedom is .76, about the same as the best of our own equations reported on below, but surprisingly no coefficient is significant at the 5 percent level or better except that for the dummy variable. The constant term is, as in equations (3) through (6), also relatively large although statistically insignificant. Perhaps the most damaging criticism that can be leveled at the equation is that a model based on annual variations is of limited usefulness for policymakers concerned with short-term stabilization problems and that it throws very little light on the lag structure of independent variables in an economy wracked by very volatile rates of inflation.

Our own equations: We therefore decided to test equations similar to those of Maynard-Van Rijckeghem with quarterly data. Statistics were available for all of their variables on a quarterly basis beginning in 1957 except for GDP. This problem was solved by making our own estimates from a variety of sources (see table B-3 and explanatory notes) and then transforming them into three-quarter moving averages to remove the highly seasonal effect of agricultural production. It would have been possible to have made a more legitimate estimate of quarterly nonagricultural GDP if we had possessed proxies for the seasonal behavior of rural value added, but the only reliable information available was on delivery of products to market. It should therefore be kept in mind that the nonagricultural GDP variable in our equations represents a rough short-term time trend.

Despite repeated efforts, however, it was not possible to obtain satisfactory results with Maynard-Van Rijckeghem's independent variables: the lagged value of imports, bank credit to the private sector, or bank credit minus wages. It is nevertheless interesting to note that fluctuations in private bank credit were negatively correlated with the rate of increase in prices, thus providing some confirmation of one of their chief hypotheses. Experiments with changes in gross foreign exchange reserves at the end of the previous quarter as an explanatory variable, changes in money supply with longer than two period lags, changes in variables with respect to the same quarter of the previous year, indices instead of percentage changes in variables, alternative lag patterns of variables, and other permutations and combinations were also carried out. When seasonal dummy variables were included in the cost of living equation, that for the fourth quarter of the year was almost significant at the 10 percent level, and together with the first quarter dummy it increased the statistical significance of all other independent variables except the exchange rate.

The estimating equations that proved most satisfactory were therefore quite similar to those tested by Diaz Alejandro, with percentage changes in the exchange rate, GDP, the wage rate, and money supply (currency and demand deposits) as the most powerful explanatory variables. In the cost of living equations the elasticity of price increases with respect to GDP exceeds unity, for money supply (t-1) is about .6 (and about half as high for period t-1.5), for the exchange rate around .2, and for the wage rate about the same (although the combined elasticity with respect to wages in both t and t-1 is about .3). In the wholesale price equations the equivalent elasticities are somewhat smaller for GDP (in no equation is it greater than minus unity), about the same for the wage rate, and higher for money supply (t-1) and the exchange rate. It therefore might appear that stabilization of wholesale prices requires more restrictive policies than does the cost of living, but it should be recalled that the "best" wholesale price equations contain rather large negative (though statistically insignificant) constant terms.

When the cost of living equations were rerun with the velocity of circulation (the ratio of money supply to GDP) included as an explanatory variable, the coefficients of M/Y and of the exchange rate R were of approximately equal size but of opposite sign, and all of the other independent variables became statistically insignificant. Similar results were obtained by rerunning the wholesale price equations with the same change in specification. This result may be interpreted as further evidence that growth and stability tend to be complementary instead of competitive. The "best" equation including the M/Y variable was (for the period of 1957III to 1968II, "T" statistics in parentheses):

$$(8) \quad P_{c \text{ of } 1} = \underset{(6.74)}{.04} + \underset{(8.12)}{.38} R_t - \underset{(3.06)}{.32} (M/Y)_t, \; \bar{R}^2 = .68, \, DW = 1.49.$$

Other experiments, however, indicate that equation (8) exaggerates the importance of the exchange rate as a determinant of the increase in prices. For example, equation (4) from table 5-1 was rerun excluding the exchange rate with no effect on the $\bar{R}^2$, whereas both the size and statistical significance of the coefficients of the other variables increased markedly. Interestingly enough it was the GDP variable whose explanatory power was most enhanced (period 1957III to 1967I, "T" statistics in parentheses):

$$(9) \quad P_{c \text{ of } 1} = \underset{(0.52)}{.60} - \underset{(6.8)}{1.73} Y + \underset{(2.9)}{.27} W_t + \underset{(5.7)}{.98} M_{t-1}, \bar{R}^2 = .72, DW = 1.58.$$

The stability of our estimating equations was also tested by running the same equations for different time periods. As might have been expected, substantially different results were obtained, although the exchange rate did not emerge as the only significant explanatory variable, as when similar tests were performed with Diaz Alejandro's equations. When wholesale price equation (7) in table 5-1 was rerun for the period 1960I to 1967I, for example, the relative importance and statistical significance of the wage rate variable increased greatly, exchange rate variations in the current rather than in the previous quarter became more significant, and the money supply variable for all lags tended to wash out. The main reason for these changes was that multicolinearity between M and W decreased appreciably whereas between M and Y it increased very sharply. It thus appears that we have not captured much better in our equations the stable, underlying behavioral relationships that explain the dynamics of Argentine inflation, if such relationships do in fact exist.

Finally, we investigated the extent to which our regression equations accurately identified turning points in the rate of inflation, and we tried to find explanations for the especially large divergencies between estimated and observed changes in the price level. As can be seen in figures B-1 and B-2, our "best" cost of living and wholesale price equations missed about one third of the turning points. The equations predicted quite well the great inflationary surge of 1959 and the subsequent stabilization, and they also picked up the renewed spurt of prices in 1962, although they missed the upper turning point by a quarter. The variance between actual and estimated rates of inflation thereafter seems fairly randomly distributed until 1966-1967, when our equations began to overestimate quite consistently the rate of inflation. It will be recalled that this is the period when Ongania took power and Krieger Vasena became Economics Minister to carry out a stabilization program enforced by wage and price controls. It is therefore likely that our equations could be improved by introducing a dummy variable representing price restrictions during this period, together with a dummy of opposite sign representing the lifting of controls in 1959.

Table B-1 Quarterly cost of living index excluding rent and electricity, 1956–1968. (index 1960 = 100)

1956	I	20	1963	I	168
	II	22		II	178
	III	22		III	184
	IV	23		IV	201
1957	I	24	1964	I	213
	II	27		II	221
	III	29		III	224
	IV	30		IV	242
1958	I	30	1965	I	254
	II	34		II	273
	III	38		III	299
	IV	43		IV	330
1959	I	58	1966	I	342
	II	76		II	361
	III	87		III	374
	IV	92		IV	415
1960	I	97	1967	I	435
	II	99		II	460
	III	100		III	503
	IV	102		IV	543
1961	I	103	1968	I	554
	II	111		II	552
	III	117		III	556
	IV	122		IV	593
1962	I	126			
	II	139			
	III	156			
	IV	163			

Source: The cost of living index for Buenos Aires, published in *Boletín Estadístico* of the Dirección Nacional de Estadística y Censos, was converted from base 1943 to base 1960 for the period prior to March 1962, when the new index with base 1960 began to be published. This adjustment was accomplished by linking the two series in the overlapping period of 1962. Quarterly figures are arithmetic averages of monthly data.

To eliminate part of the downward bias caused by the rent freeze and unrealistic electricity prices, the cost of living was also adjusted to remove these items from the index by using the formula:

$$\frac{\text{Total} - (\text{rent and electricity}) \ (.167)}{.833}$$

prior to March 1962, and the formula:

$$\frac{\text{Total} - (\text{rent and electricity}) \ (.051)}{.949}$$

from March 1962 through 1968, to reflect the change in the weighting schemes.

186

Table B-2 Quarterly wholesale prices excluding agriculture, 1956–1968. (index 1960 = 100)

Year	Qtr	Value	Year	Qtr	Value
1956	I	18.9	1963	I	165.1
	II	20.4		II	171.6
	III	21.6		III	178.4
	IV	22.2		IV	189.4
1957	I	23.0	1964	I	203.0
	II	24.8		II	216.6
	III	27.8		III	225.5
	IV	28.7		IV	236.5
1958	I	28.9	1965	I	254.8
	II	31.0		II	277.9
	III	34.9		III	304.9
	IV	39.7		IV	312.1
1959	I	50.1	1966	I	321.0
	II	76.7		II	334.1
	III	94.8		III	350.3
	IV	97.6		IV	368.3
1960	I	100.0	1967	I	394.6
	II	99.8		II	425.8
	III	100.0		III	446.5
	IV	100.2		IV	461.3
1961	I	103.0	1968	I	467.3
	II	106.8		II	467.8
	III	111.5			
	IV	115.9			
1962	I	118.9			
	II	134.8			
	III	148.4			
	IV	156.2			

Source: Instituto Nacional de Estadística y Censos; figures prior to 1960, however, are from the old rather than the revised series.

Table B-3 Estimates of GDP in constant prices: quarterly and three-month moving averages, 1956–1968. (indices 1960 = 100)

Year	Quarter	Quarterly GDP	Three-month moving average GDP	Year	Quarter	Quarterly GDP	Three-month moving average GDP
1956	I	83.4	88.1	1963	I	100.2	97.2
	II	92.1	88.4		II	97.1	98.2
	III	89.7	91.4		III	97.2	98.7
	IV	92.4	92.2		IV	98.3	99.4
1957	I	94.6	94.4	1964	I	97.6	102.7
	II	96.1	94.8		II	106.0	103.8
	III	93.6	93.8		III	107.9	108.9
	IV	91.7	93.5		IV	112.8	110.9
1958	I	97.3	96.2	1965	I	112.1	114.2
	II	98.4	98.5		II	117.6	114.9
	III	99.7	99.2		III	115.0	116.3
	IV	99.4	101.1		IV	116.2	114.0
1959	I	104.2	100.1	1966	I	110.0	115.0
	II	96.6	96.6		II	119.6	116.0
	III	89.1	90.9		III	118.4	118.9
	IV	87.0	91.4		IV	118.6	117.2
1960	I	98.0	94.5	1967	I	114.6	119.9
	II	98.6	99.3		II	126.4	119.3
	III	101.4	100.7		III	116.8	119.2
	IV	102.2	103.3		IV	114.4	115.6

1961	I	106.3	106.1
	II	109.9	108.3
	III	108.6	105.9
	IV	99.3	106.4
1962	I	111.3	106.7
	II	109.6	105.8
	III	96.5	100.1
	IV	94.2	97.0
1968	I	115.7	119.1
	II	127.3	123.0
	III	125.9	124.7
	IV	120.9	–

Source: Annual GDP estimates in constant prices were apportioned on a quarterly basis according to the following indicators: For the period 1956I to 1957IV, bank check clearings published in Banco Central, *Boletín Estadístico;* 1958I to 1963IV, quarterly GDP estimates appearing in *Panorama de la economía argentina,* Buenos Aires, various numbers; 1964I to 1965IV, quarterly GDP estimates appearing in Oficina de Estudios para la Colaboración Económica Internacional, *Nivel de la economía argentina en 1965* (Buenos Aires, 1966), table 2, p. 9; and 1966I to 1968IV, quarterly estimates by the Central Bank published in Economics Ministry, *Informe económico,* various numbers.

Table B-4 Quarterly estimates of GDP in current prices. (indices 1960 = 100)

Year	Quarter	(1) Adjusted quarterly GDP deflator	(2) GDP index in current prices	Year	Quarter	(1) Adjusted quarterly GDP deflator	(2) GDP index in current prices
1956	I	23.0	19.2	1963	I	170.3	170.6
	II	24.7	22.7		II	179.9	174.7
	III	25.5	22.8		III	185.8	180.6
	IV	26.6	24.4		IV	203.6	200.1
1957	I	27.0	25.6	1964	I	220.0	214.7
	II	27.0	25.6		II	229.3	243.0
	III	32.2	30.2		III	232.4	250.8
	IV	33.6	30.9		IV	251.3	283.5
1958	I	34.0	33.2	1965	I	258.9	290.2
	II	38.3	37.7		II	277.8	326.7
	III	43.3	43.1		III	306.4	352.4
	IV	48.8	48.4		IV	337.7	392.4
1959	I	61.1	63.7	1966	I	338.2	372.0
	II	79.6	76.9		II	357.0	427.0
	III	91.1	81.2		III	370.3	438.4
	IV	96.0	83.5		IV	409.7	485.9
1960	I	97.3	95.3	1967	I	423.3	485.1
	II	99.7	98.2		II	448.3	566.6
	III	100.7	101.9		III	489.4	571.6
	IV	102.4	104.5		IV	528.6	604.7

Year		(1)	(2)	(3)
1961	I	104.9	111.5	
	II	112.6	123.8	
	III	119.0	129.3	
	IV	123.7	122.9	
1962	I	125.1	139.2	
	II	138.3	151.6	
	III	155.1	149.7	
	IV	161.8	152.4	
1968	I		539.0	623.6
	II		537.1	683.7

Source: Col. (1). The adjusted quarterly GDP deflator was estimated by apportioning the annual GDP deflator according to the quarterly cost of living index. The annual GDP deflator was taken from CONADE-ECLA, *Distribución del ingreso*, table III.50, for the period 1956–1963, and from Banco Central, *Boletín Estadístico*, various numbers, table VI.1, for the period 1964–1968. The two series were chainlinked by multiplying the Bank index by 1.04, the factor obtained from the immediately preceding overlapping years. For the source of the cost of living index see table B–1. Col. (2). The quarterly GDP index in current prices was computed by multiplying the quarterly GDP index in constant prices (see table B–3) by Col. (1).

Table B-5 Quarterly average exchange rate, 1956–1968. (pesos per U.S. dollar)

1956	I	24.0	1963	I	134.9
	II	21.7		II	137.8
	III	18.9		III	138.1
	IV	20.2		IV	142.4
1957	I	23.3	1964	I	133.4
	II	24.5		II	137.8
	III	26.7		III	141.0
	IV	23.5		IV	147.7
1958	I	24.1	1965	I	150.9
	II	26.6		II	166.5
	III	29.1		III	173.2
	IV	42.1		IV	181.9
1959	I	66.7	1966	I	188.8
	II	83.2		II	193.9
	III	84.1		III	211.1
	IV	82.8		IV	235.9
1960	I	83.0	1967	I	274.5
	II	83.2		II	350.0
	III	82.8		III	350.0
	IV	82.9		IV	350.0
1961	I	82.7	1968	I	350.0
	II	82.8		II	350.0
	III	82.8			
	IV	83.0			
1962	I	82.8			
	II	106.1			
	III	124.4			
	IV	141.4			

Source: Banco Central, *Annual Reports*, table 2. Quarterly figures are arithmetic averages of average official monthly selling rates.

Table B-6 Quarterly average industrial wage rate, 1956–1968. (index 1960 = 100)

1956	I	33.0	1963	I	181.0
	II	34.0		II	190.2
	III	34.0		III	200.0
	IV	34.0		IV	209.4
1957	I	34.0	1964	I	229.3
	II	34.0		II	245.6
	III	34.0		III	266.1
	IV	34.0		IV	273.7
1958	I	35.3	1965	I	310.0
	II	50.6		II	336.4
	III	54.3		III	367.4
	IV	59.1		IV	375.6
1959	I	71.6	1966	I	405.5
	II	85.9		II	456.3
	III	89.1		III	487.4
	IV	91.4		IV	503.8
1960	I	94.3	1967	I	526.3
	II	95.8		II	619.7
	III	100.2		III	629.7
	IV	109.1		IV	629.7
1961	I	114.6	1968	I	672.1
	II	120.3		II	672.1
	III	128.8		III	629.7
	IV	131.9		IV	629.7
1962	I	140.6			
	II	154.2			
	III	159.3			
	IV	165.4			

Source: Average contract wage rate of blue collar workers (*peones*) from Dirección Nacional de Estadística y Censos, *Boletín Estadístico*, various numbers.

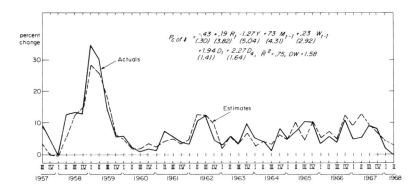

Figure B-1. Comparison of estimated with actual quarterly variations in cost of living index, 1957–1968.

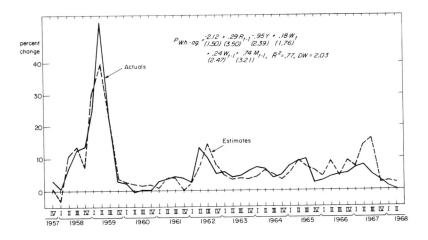

Figure B-2. Comparison of estimated with actual quarterly variations in wholesale prices excluding agriculture, 1957–1968.

Appendix C. Argentine National Accounts

The first systematic estimates of the national accounts were prepared during World War II, and beginning in 1955 annual series on the gross product and utilization of available goods and services began to be published regularly in the *Annual Reports* and monthly *Statistical Bulletin* of the Argentine Central Bank, which is the official agency primarily responsible for national accounts work. Beginning in 1966 the Bank has also prepared estimates on a quarterly basis, which appear in the *Economic Reports* of the Economics Ministry.

The first official national accounts series were published in 1946 and covered the period 1935 to 1945.[1] These estimates were based on the industrial census of 1935 and the agricultural census of 1937; at this time no population census had been carried out since 1914, and no recent information was available on the services sectors. The basic concepts utilized in these estimates are fundamentally the same as those used in later years, so that the 1946 estimates, along with the major studies of 1964, represent the main landmarks in the development of Argentine national accounting. Other revisions have reflected chiefly the appearance of new data, particularly census information which provides the benchmarks between which annual figures are interpolated. Thus, the first revision of the national accounts was based on the census of 1947, which included not only the traditional demographic information but also data on agriculture, industry, trade, finance, transport and communications, other services, and an enumeration of existing buildings, both residential and commercial. The interpolation of annual figures was also greatly assisted by the development of new statistical series on production, employment, wages and salaries paid by industrial establishments, the volume of foreign trade, retail sales, and a new cost of living index. The revised series for 1935-1954, prepared by the Secretaria de Asuntos Económicos to which the national accounts team of the Central Bank had been transferred, was published in 1955 together with detailed explanations of concepts and methodology.[2]

The revised series were thereafter continued on an annual basis by the Central Bank, although the reliability of the estimates diminished progressively over time because of the delay in developing new basic data and disagreement over the selection of a new base year. When a CONADE-ECLA research program was initiated in the early 1960s to study income distribution, it was therefore found necessary first to update the national accounts estimates on the basis of the economic census of 1953, which covered the industrial, commercial, and services sectors. The work of the CONADE-ECLA team led the Central Bank to accelerate its own revision efforts, with the result that in 1964 two new parallel series covering the years 1950 to 1963 were finished almost simultaneously.[3] Subsequent tabulation of the results of the

1963 census on industry, trade, and services enabled the Central Bank to make a new revision of the national accounts estimates which can be considered definitive for a period up to 1963; these series began to be published in 1971 and have been used in this study for analyzing the period 1960-1970. [4]

Because of the broader coverage and detail of the CONADE-ECLA estimates, they have been used as the basis for most of the national accounts series utilized in this study for the period 1950 to 1960. In addition to time series on the composition of gross product by sectors, they include data on the functional distribution of income, employment, average remunerations, and price indices for production and for the different components of expenditure. This information is contained in five volumes, organized as follows: (1) concepts, sources, and methods, (2) national accounts and complementary tables at current prices, (3) the same series at constant prices together with corresponding price indices, (4) the functional distribution of income, and (5) population, employment, and remunerations. Basic tables cover the period 1950 to 1963, but some series are carried back to 1935; detailed tables on income distribution are for the years 1953, 1959, and 1961.

The United Nations Economic Commission for Latin America also published in 1956 national accounts estimates going back to the year 1900 which include national product by sector of origin, gross investment, and the composition of imports. [5] In this same study estimates were made of the functional distribution of income, the composition of family consumption, and government income and expenditure for the period 1946 to 1955; estimates of capital stock by types and sectors according to the permanent inventory method for the period 1935 to 1955; and an input-output matrix based on the industrial census of 1950. This research, carried out in close cooperation with the statistical team of the Central Bank, is the basic source of national accounts estimates in current prices before 1950, constant price estimates prior to 1935, and of most capital stock figures in Argentina. Finally, mention should be made of the estimates of gross product by regions, provinces, and departments, and of a regional input-output matrix, prepared by the Instituto Torcuato Di Tella on the basis of the 1953 census, supplemented by estimates of the Central Bank and ECLA. [6]

Although rigorous international standards exist for estimating national accounts, as is well known it is practially impossible to follow these guidelines in detail. The practical art of national accounts making requires the imaginative use of information from a variety of sources and utilization of diverse techniques. Of the three basic methods for estimating national product—the factor income method (total income received by residents of the country), the expenditure method (final outlays by residents adjusted for the balance on current account in the balance of payments), and the production method (the value of domestic output adjusted to exclude the value of current inputs)—the latter has been most relied upon in Argentina. Long statistical series on the economic activity of principal sectors and economic censuses are in general production oriented, whereas information on income is incomplete and lacks coherence in the absence of direct measurement of investment and private consumption. Use of this method requires that information be obtained on the value of intermediate consumption, but it has the additional advantage of facilitating estimates of the functional distribution of sectoral income. Estimates of final expenditure on gross investment, inventories, government consumption, and the current account of the balance of payments are made directly, whereas private consumption is taken as the residual.

The current value of gross investment is estimated from statistics on construction plus the flow of capital goods from domestic production and imports, which are classified by end-use and adjusted to include the value of commercial markups, transportation, installation, and taxes. Inventories include agricultural products, cattle stocks, and a limited number of industrial raw materials. The value of government consumption and of the current account in the balance of payments are derived from accounting data which will be described in greater detail below.

Three types of basic data are therefore used in estimating the national accounts: periodical statistical series measuring the production of agriculture, mining, industry and foreign trade; accounting data for the expenditures of government, state enterprises, and corporations controlled by the government; and occasional and partial data for trade, road transportation, and personal services. It is clear from the above that the most reliable data are for those sectors for which current production statistics or accounting data are available. In the base year 1960 these sectors accounted for 68 percent of gross product. Intercensal interpolations for these sectors are, on the other hand, especially subject to increasing error over time because they include most of those activities which have been growing and changing most rapidly in Argentina. Each subsequent census has in fact revealed that interpolations of gross product for these sectors have had a systematic downward bias. The most dramatic example of such bias is the series on industrial GDP published prior to the revision of 1964. This series was interpolated by using the old index of industrial production constructed from the census of 1943, in which the industries that developed rapidly after World War II were very inadequately represented. When the results of the 1953 census became available, it was therefore found that the value of industrial production was 53 percent higher than national accounts estimates. This downward bias appears to have been greatly reduced in later interpolations of manufacturing GDP, the difference between the estimate for 1963 and that contained in the census for this year being about 7 percent. Differences between national accounts estimates and 1963 census data were, on the other hand, greater for the trade and services sectors, because estimates for these sectors are based on extrapolations of the work force, which during the 1950s did not adequately reflect the changes that took place in the relation between output and employment.

Differences between intercensal and revised estimates of total gross domestic product for the period 1946-1970 are summarized in table C-1. It

Table C–1 Comparison of gross product estimates for census years.

Census year	GDP estimates (billions of pesos in current prices)					Ratios between estimates			
	(1)	(2)	(3)	(4)	(5)	2/1	3/2	4/3	5/4
1946	22.4	26.2	–	26.2	–	1.17	–	–	–
1950	53.7	62.3	67.4	69.5	68.5	1.16	1.08	1.03	0.98
1953	–	111.9	129.4	130.1	131.2	–	1.15	1.01	1.01
1960	–	790.0	961.0	1,092.0	1,006.0	–	1.22	1.14	0.97
1963	–	–	1,734.1	1,939.9	1,854.9	–	–	1.12	0.96

Sources:

(1) Banco Central, *La renta nacional*, 1946, and subsequent periodical publications.
(2) Banco Central, *Producto e ingreso*, 1954, and subsequent periodical publications.
(3) Banco Central, *Origen del producto y composición del gasto nacional*, 1966.
(4) CONADE-ECLA, *Cuentas nacionales de la Argentina*, 1965.
(5) Banco Central, *Origen del producto y distribución del ingreso*, 1971.

can be seen that the reliability of intercensal estimates tends to deteriorate over time, although the CONADE-ECLA series held up remarkably well in comparison with the later revision of the Central Bank (see the last column in table C-1). The gradual improvement of national accounts estimates over time has been aided by complementary research on input-output and family and personal income and by the special characteristics of the Argentine economy. The large concentration of both population and economic activity in the national capital—34 percent of the population and 50 percent of gross domestic product in 1960—has facilitated data collection, and the almost complete absence of subsistence production and of important regional differentials in labor productivity in nonagricultural activities has simplified problems of estimation.

In view of the fact that CONADE-ECLA data serve in general as the basis for analysis of the period 1950 to 1960, whereas Central Bank series are used for later years, a brief comparison of the two will be helpful. Few differences exist between the two series in methodology or sources of information, but the new Central Bank estimates published in 1971 are based on data from the 1963 economic census which were not available when the CONADE estimates were made. Nevertheless, as can be seen in table C-2 the difference in total gross product for the common base year 1960 is only about 3 percent (actually 3.1 percent in market prices and 2.8 percent at factor cost). The difference in the 1950-1960 rate of growth of GDP between the two series is even less significant—about one tenth of 1 percent—whereas the discrepancy between average rates of increase in implicit prices for the same period is only about 1 percent (compared with an average annual increase of 26 to 27 percent).

The discrepancies between the two series are accounted for mainly by the manufacturing, trade, and other services sectors. The change in the composition of output between the censuses of 1953 and 1963 especially affected estimates of value added in industry and in those sectors greatly dependent on the flow of manufactured goods (for example, trade). For the government sector (as well as for construction) differences are explained almost entirely by utilization in the more recent Central Bank series of definitive instead of provisional figures for provincial and municipal expenditures after 1958, whereas somewhat divergent employment estimates were used for estimating income from personal services. The only other differences between the series worth mentioning are in the rate of growth of agricultural product, due mainly to more up-to-date information on the rapid expansion in forage crop production used by the Central Bank, and in the value added in mining, which in the CONADE-ECLA estimates includes a proportion of central office administrative expenditures and profits of vertically integrated oil companies.

Table C-2 Comparison of Central Bank and CONADE estimates of GDP.

	Central Bank			CONADE			Percent difference between 1960 estimates $\dfrac{(1)-(4)}{(1)} \times 100$
	GDP in 1960 (billions of pesos) (1)	Annual rate of increase in GDP, 1950–1960		GDP in 1960 (billions of pesos) (4)	Annual rate of increase in GDP, 1950–1960		
Sector		Volume index (2)	Implicit price index[a] (3)		Volume index (5)	Implicit price index[a] (6)	
Agriculture and fishing	153.7	2.1	30.0	150.9	1.8	30.0	1.8
Mining	10.3	11.0	20.0	12.3	11.0	23.0	-11.2
Manufacturing	287.8	4.1	27.0	280.6	3.9	26.0	2.5
Electricity, gas, and water	11.5	6.7	25.0	11.4	6.6	25.0	–
Construction	37.0	1.1	24.0	37.7	1.3	23.0	-1.5
Commerce, restaurants, and hotels	174.9	3.0[b]	27.0[b]	160.5	3.0[b]	27.0[b]	8.9
Transport and communications	73.0	2.3	27.0	72.6	2.5	–	–
Financial and real estate	36.6	2.8	21.0	36.6	2.8	–	–
Government	67.5	1.9	–	65.9	2.1	25.0	2.5
Other services	72.7	2.3	–	68.4	2.9	25.0	6.3
GDP at factor cost	925.0	3.0	27.0	896.7	2.9	26.0	3.1
Indirect taxes minus subsidies	81.4	–	–	81.1	–	–	–
GDP at market prices	1,006.4	3.0	27.0	977.8	2.9	26.0	2.8

Source: Banco Central, *Origen del producto y distribución del ingreso,* and CONADE, *Distribución del ingreso.*

[a]Implicit price indices not available for all sectors because of differences in sectoral classification of Central Bank and CONADE estimates.
[b]Volume and implicit price indices for commerce only, which constitutes 92 percent of sector GDP.

Table C-3   CONADE GDP estimates in constant prices, 1950–1963. (billions of 1960 pesos)

Sector	1950	1951	1952	1953	1954	1955	1956	1957	1958	1959	1960	1961	1962	1963
Agriculture	125.3	133.8	113.8	148.0	147.6	153.2	145.8	145.5	151.7	150.5	150.1	147.6	148.2	145.5
Fishing	0.5	0.7	0.7	0.7	0.7	0.7	0.7	0.7	0.7	0.8	0.8	0.8	0.9	1.1
Mining and quarrying	4.4	5.1	5.3	5.8	6.1	6.3	6.5	6.9	7.5	8.7	12.3	15.5	17.4	16.7
Manufacturing	193.9	195.6	190.5	190.5	207.9	233.1	246.3	265.4	285.1	263.7	280.6	304.4	283.9	268.2
Construction	33.0	34.6	31.3	31.0	29.8	30.6	29.6	34.9	36.9	33.8	37.7	40.6	36.8	34.7
Commerce	111.2	116.8	103.4	103.0	112.1	125.2	128.3	137.8	144.2	130.0	150.1	167.8	161.8	143.5
Transportation	49.0	51.7	49.9	50.8	53.3	57.4	57.7	60.9	62.8	59.8	63.7	66.5	63.9	59.7
Communications	8.2	8.1	7.8	7.7	8.1	8.3	8.5	8.5	9.0	8.5	9.0	9.8	9.1	8.5
Electricity, gas, and water	6.2	6.6	6.7	7.1	7.7	8.3	9.0	9.7	10.4	10.4	11.4	13.7	15.2	16.1
Financial services	13.3	13.8	14.3	14.6	15.1	15.9	16.4	16.7	17.6	18.1	18.5	19.4	20.5	20.1
Housing	14.7	15.0	15.4	15.9	16.3	16.7	17.1	17.5	17.9	18.1	18.1	18.2	18.2	18.3
Government	53.6	55.1	54.7	56.0	58.7	59.1	63.0	64.3	65.7	65.5	65.9	66.5	66.5	66.4
Other services	58.9	60.8	62.7	65.3	68.0	69.6	72.7	74.2	75.5	76.4	78.6	79.9	80.6	82.2
Total GDP at factor cost	672.1	697.6	656.6	696.4	731.5	784.4	801.7	842.5	884.9	844.3	896.7	950.7	923.0	881.0
Indirect taxes minus subsidies	60.3	63.1	59.2	63.3	66.4	71.2	72.5	76.6	80.2	76.8	81.1	85.8	83.2	79.3
Total GDP at market prices	732.4	760.7	715.8	759.8	797.9	855.6	874.2	919.2	965.1	921.1	977.8	1,036.5	1,006.2	960.2

Source: CONADE-ECLA, Distribución del ingreso, table III.15.

Table C–4 Central Bank GDP estimates in constant prices, 1950 and 1959–1969. (billions of 1960 pesos)

Sector	1950	1959	1960	1961	1962	1963	1964	1965	1966	1967	1968	1969
Agriculture and fishing	124.3	151.2	153.7	152.7	158.8	161.9	173.2	183.5	176.6	184.2	177.0	184.4
Mining and quarrying	3.8	7.5	10.3	13.4	15.1	15.1	15.3	15.9	16.8	18.8	21.2	22.2
Manufacturing	192.4	261.5	287.8	316.6	299.2	287.0	340.8	387.9	391.5	396.7	424.1	471.1
Electricity, gas, and water	6.0	10.7	11.5	13.8	15.7	16.6	18.3	21.1	22.7	24.4	26.4	29.0
Construction	33.1	31.0	37.0	39.1	35.2	33.0	35.1	35.4	38.1	42.8	50.4	54.1
Commerce, restaurants, and hotels	134.0	155.0	174.9	194.5	186.9	171.9	187.6	206.8	206.0	208.0	219.4	242.9
Transport and communications	58.3	68.8	73.0	77.8	75.0	73.1	81.0	88.5	88.5	89.3	94.1	99.5
Financial and real estate	27.9	36.0	36.6	37.8	38.8	39.4	40.0	41.5	42.7	43.9	45.8	48.1
Government and other services	108.8	135.4	140.2	145.1	149.5	153.2	158.6	165.0	171.0	175.0	179.5	184.5
Total GDP at factor cost	688.6	856.9	924.9	990.9	974.1	951.2	1,049.9	1,145.6	1,154.0	1,183.2	1,237.8	1,335.9
Indirect taxes minus subsidies	60.1	74.9	81.4	86.9	85.6	83.3	92.3	101.3	101.9	103.9	108.8	117.3
Total GDP at market prices	748.7	931.9	1,006.3	1,077.8	1,059.7	1,034.5	1,142.2	1,246.9	1,255.9	1,287.1	1,346.5	1,453.2

Source: Banco Central, *Origen del producto*, table 43.

Appendix D. Estimates of Consumption and Investment

The composition of national expenditure is estimated by the flow of goods method with private consumption taken as a residual. This latter category therefore picks up the cumulative errors made in estimates of the other components of expenditure. One important source of such errors is the difficulty of determining the end-use of certain kinds of articles that can be used either as final goods or intermediate inputs, or for both investment and consumption. Problems of aggregation in production statistics and in price indices and the paucity of information on manufacturing inventories also limit the reliability of flow of goods estimates, although input-output research has been helpful in checking the consistency of estimates. In any event, direct flow of goods calculations of private consumption contained in the CONADE-ECLA study previously cited reveal maximum deviations of only 2 percent of GDP between these calculations and residual consumption estimates.

With regard to estimates of investment, inclusion of repairs requires special comment because of unique circumstances in Argentina. In the early 1950s it was concluded that because of severe import controls an important share of capital goods not produced in the country was being used far beyond useful life as reflected in depreciation statistics; much of this equipment was apparently being virtually reconstructed in local workshops. It was therefore decided to include expenditure on prolonging the useful life of this equipment in estimates of investment, although sources of quantitative data were very poor except for the railways. Repairs represented about 8 percent of total investment up to 1950, but thereafter their relative importance declined. For the remainder of investment in machinery and equipment the flow of imported capital goods has of course played a major role. Aside from the problem of identifying imports by end-use, which was complicated by the change in the classification of import statistics in 1951 and again in 1965, the main difficulty has been the valuation of capital goods imports benefiting from selective import duty exemptions, which were widely used in the late 1950s and 1960s as an industrial promotion device.

Three basic sources of information have been used to estimate investment in construction. For the public sector accounting data from the government and public enterprises are utilized, which in addition to the difficulties mentioned in the previous section entail differentiating global expenditures that include both construction and the installation of equipment in complex public projects. Agricultural construction and improvements are estimated from agricultural census data and are interpolated on the basis of rough estimates of the flow of goods and materials used principally for agricultural purposes. Other private construction is estimated from construction permits and miscellaneous sources; their principal limitations arise from the incomplete coverage of the basic information and the general use of the cost of construction index as an indicator of changes in the value of all kinds of construction.

Constant price series for investment and consumption are estimated in a way similar to estimates of sectoral production. The current value of imported capital goods is deflated by the unit value of imports by principal categories, so that this series is subject to errors of aggregation especially with respect to short-term fluctuations. The estimates of depreciation in the national accounts are computed from corporate balance sheets according to the straight line method based on original cost of acquisition, a valuation which in an inflationary economy results in much smaller real figures than would otherwise be the case.

The main differences betwen Central Bank and CONADE series used in this study for investment in domestic equipment are that Bank estimates utilize more up-to-date information on repairs, which show a sharper decline after 1950 than CONADE figures, and that the 1963 census revealed a larger production of domestic capital equipment than the intercensal interpolation. For 1960 the Central Bank estimate is therefore about 6 percent higher than CONADE's. With regard to imported capital goods, the revised Bank estimates utilize the more disaggregated nomenclature adopted in 1965 which permits a more accurate classification of goods by end-use, especially with respect to the division of components and parts for machinery between investment and intermediate use. Bank estimates of capital good imports are somewhat lower than those of CONADE, but the trend in the two series is quite similar between 1950 and 1960. Finally, the discrepancy between the two series on inventories is chiefly attributable to the inclusion by the Bank of estimates for some new manufactured products after 1958, especially in the automotive and tractor industries.

Table D-1 CONADE estimates of real GDP by type of expenditure, 1950-1963. (billions of pesos at 1960 prices)

Expenditure	1950	1951	1952	1953	1954	1955	1956	1957	1958	1959	1960	1961	1962	1963
Government consumption	68.5	69.4	69.6	68.8	72.5	75.6	80.6	79.4	80.7	80.5	88.3	89.1	87.8	81.8
Private consumption	548.2	568.4	536.6	534.0	579.6	647.0	651.0	679.4	717.3	660.6	673.7	741.8	695.9	655.5
Gross fixed investment	131.9	148.5	132.4	131.5	132.4	146.5	154.1	173.3	175.6	159.6	220.9	250.3	234.8	199.7
Inventory changes	-15.2	6.1	1.2	7.5	9.9	8.5	-12.1	-7.6	-1.6	9.5	6.5	-3.7	-9.9	-6.4
Exports of goods and services	91.3	72.1	53.0	81.0	86.8	78.1	90.1	94.7	96.8	101.9	102.5	94.4	127.8	130.1
Imports of goods and services	92.2	103.7	77.0	63.2	83.3	100.2	89.5	99.9	103.7	91.0	114.1	135.4	130.1	100.4
Gross domestic product	732.4	760.7	715.8	759.8	797.9	855.6	874.2	919.2	965.1	921.1	977.8	1,036.5	1,006.2	960.2
Effect of international terms of trade	11.8	12.3	-2.8	7.2	2.4	5.2	-8.9	-15.4	-10.7	-6.3	—	1.3	-13.9	-4.4
Gross domestic income	744.2	773.1	713.0	766.9	800.3	860.8	865.3	903.8	954.5	914.8	977.8	1,037.8	992.2	955.8
Foreign factor payments	-0.5	-3.7	-0.9	-1.0	-1.1	-1.6	-2.5	-1.8	-3.5	-3.8	-4.7	-7.3	-5.7	-5.1
Gross national income	743.7	769.4	712.1	766.0	799.1	859.1	862.8	902.0	951.0	911.0	973.1	1,030.4	986.6	950.7

Source: CONADE-ECLA, *Distribución del ingreso*, tables III.1 and III.8.

Table D-2 Central Bank estimates of real GDP by type of expenditure, 1950 and 1959–1970. (billions of pesos at 1960 prices)

Expenditure	1950	1959	1960	1961	1962	1963	1964	1965	1966	1967	1968	1969	1970
Government consumption	73.0	80.2	89.6	91.4	90.7	87.0	89.3	91.1	96.0	97.4	98.1	99.0	99.5
Private consumption	578.1	694.5	710.7	788.7	751.7	738.4	821.7	894.8	902.0	925.0	964.2	1,034.7	1,068.2
Gross fixed investment	113.3	137.6	207.9	242.4	220.7	187.0	207.6	216.8	223.9	235.0	264.2	305.4	323.3
Inventory changes	-13.1	10.2	9.7	-3.8	-1.3	-7.1	19.1	26.4	1.8	0.9	0.7	0.4	4.5
Exports of goods and services	91.2	101.8	102.5	94.7	128.1	130.6	122.2	134.2	144.0	142.5	136.6	159.7	171.3
Imports of goods and services	93.8	92.5	114.1	135.6	130.2	101.4	117.7	116.4	111.9	113.7	117.3	146.0	143.9
Gross domestic product	748.7	931.9	1,006.3	1,077.8	1,059.7	1,034.5	1,142.2	1,246.9	1,255.9	1,287.1	1,346.5	1,453.2	1,522.9
Effect of international terms of trade	13.6	-4.8	—	1.1	-14.1	-3.7	7.0	5.4	0.9	-4.0	-8.6	-21.2	—
Gross domestic income	762.4	927.1	1,006.3	1,078.9	1,045.6	1,030.8	1,149.2	1,252.3	1,256.8	1,283.1	1,337.9	1,431.9	—
Foreign factor payments	-0.5	-3.8	-4.7	-7.6	-5.9	-5.3	-6.3	-4.9	-9.3	-9.6	-10.7	-12.0	—
Gross national income	761.9	923.3	1,001.6	1,071.4	1,039.7	1,025.5	1,142.9	1,247.4	1,247.5	1,273.4	1,327.2	1,419.9	—

Source: Banco Central, *Boletín Estadístico* (March 1971).

Appendix E. Balance of Payments Estimates

The balance of payments accounts are calculated by the Central Bank from customs data provided by the National Statistics Directorate and from information supplied by banks and other institutions authorized to operate in the exchange market. Long-term series are available from 1913,[1] and current estimates are published annually in the *Annual Report* of the Bank. Before 1958 balance of payments statistics were published in pesos rather than in dollars, but after Argentina joined the International Monetary Fund in 1956, new series were compiled according to the methodology recommended by the Fund and were carried back to 1951.[2] This methodology has in general continued in use up to the present, although in 1959 and 1966 small changes were introduced that disturb the comparability of the series, particularly on capital account.

Although the Bank has never published detailed explanations of the methodology and sources of information used in estimating external payments statistics, it is known that imports are registered at the moment they leave customs, not as usually recommended when they cross the frontier or become the property of Argentine residents. Exports, on the other hand, are registered at the moment of embarcation. In customs documents all trade is valued in pesos at the exchange rate corresponding to the currency used in the transaction, and then peso values are converted to dollars at the rate judged most appropriate; during periods when bilateral payments agreements and multiple exchange rates were in vogue, this procedure undoubtedly led to some arbitrary valuations. To solve the multiple exchange rate problems of introducing the current account of the balance of payments into the national accounts, the difference between the weighted average exchange rate used for converting dollar exports into pesos and the effective rate paid on imports is considered an indirect tax or subsidy according to its sign.

With respect to real and financial services, unilateral transfers, and capital movements, good information is available on operations carried out directly by the public sector, but private transactions are in general estimated from incomplete records on the purchase and sale of foreign exchange. The basic forms used for declaring the purpose of private exchange transactions are not sufficiently specific and are not backed up with strong enough controls to assure their accuracy.[3] Short-term capital movements, except for commercial credits, are presented only as net figures in the balance of payments and are presumably calculated as residuals.

Statistics on foreign assets and liabilities are not available in Argentina except for the public sector in recent years. Even estimates for the public sector differ widely by sources, particularly for the years before 1958. These

Table E-1   Imports of raw materials and intermediate products.

Year	(1) Imports (millions of current dollars)	(2) Price deflator	(3) Imports in 1960 dollars (1) x (2)
1953	284,086	131.82	215,510
1954	441,975	115.88	381,407
1955	536,675	117.67	456,084
1956	466,143	122.53	380,431
1957	539,696	117.65	458,730
1958	591,360	108.39	545,585
1959	489,605	98.22	498,477
1960	642,142	100.00	642,142
1961	814,049	97.21	837,412
1962	725,958	96.67	750,964
1963	511,790	94.43	541,978
1964	725,000	96.57	750,750

Source: Col. (1) is from CONADE-CEPAL, *Distribución del ingreso*, vol. III, table III–82, and includes items 2(a) and 2(b), excluding fuels and construction materials; the figure for 1964 was estimated from official statistics. Col. (2) was obtained from unpublished work sheets of CONADE.

divergencies impede reconciliation of balance of payments figures with statistics on foreign exchange reserves. The principal source of this divergence is the difference in valuation criteria for bilateral operations which were important in the postwar period, notably with respect to the agreement with Spain which was made in nonconvertible currency. This debt, which at the end of 1948 amounted to the equivalent of about 260 million dollars, remained unsettled until an agreement was finally reached between the two governments in 1958. As a result an adjustment of 229.3 million dollars was made in the Argentine balance of payments this year for revaluation of the debt at prevailing exchange rates. [4]

Appendix F. Monetary and Fiscal Statistics

(1) *Monetary statistics* are compiled by the Central Bank and published regularly in its *Statistical Bulletin* and *Annual Reports*. A full description of current monetary series, which in their present form date from 1940, has been published by the Bank.[1] All activities of banks are included except for those of mortgage departments of banks that have them, of specialized mortgage institutions, and of stock participation accounts. Transactions in bank acceptances and operations of consumer credit institutions are also excluded, as are the activites of other nonbanking financial intermediaries which, as was seen in Chapter 6, have expanded very rapidly during the period analyzed in this study.[2]

Monetary operations are valued in current pesos except for transactions in foreign exchange, which are converted to pesos at an exchange rate determined by the Central Bank. To take care of frequent changes in rates and the existence during certain periods of multiple rates, the Bank uses the following procedure: increases in exchange assets are valued at cost of acquisition, whereas reductions are valued at the weighted average rate for existing reserves; in the case of exchange liabilities, new debt contracted is valued at the existing exchange rate, whereas for amortization payments a weighted average rate is used. Discrepancies in the value of transactions arising from accounting rates used for conversion have been included in an exchange differential account (*diferencias de cambio*). The only other foreign exchange transactions which are presented separately in the monetary accounts are contributions and liabilities to international organizations.[3] It is virtually impossible to compare changes in foreign exchange reserves in monetary accounts with those in balance of payments statistics. The main problem is created by the inclusion in monetary accounts of net changes in assets of commercial banks according to definitions which leave a great deal of room for arbitrary manipulations.[4]

Of considerable importance in monetary statistics are movements in the National Government Unified Accounting Fund (Fondo Unificado de las Cuentas del Gobierno Nacional). This account, into which all government agencies except public enterprises are obliged to deposit their funds, is maintained in the Banco de la Nación Argentina and can be drawn upon by the National Treasury with certain restrictions.[5] In monetary statistics these operations are included in "Other Debt of the Central Government" along with temporary advances, the acquisition of government securities, and other transactions between the Central Bank and the treasury. National government deposits registered in the monetary accounts include government agency and treasury bank balances and government deposits in the Central Bank.

Table F-1 Sources of monetary expansion, 1948–1970. (year-end balances in billions of pesos)

Source	1948	1949	1950	1951	1952	1953	1954	1955	1956	1957	1958	1959
Net change in gold and foreign exchange reserves	2.5	2.3	3.2	2.5	0.9	3.0	2.9	2.3	4.4	4.2	-0.7	13.2
Public sector	13.6	16.6	17.5	18.2	19.4	24.7	30.1	35.9	38.4	46.8	74.6	104.7
Contributions to international organizations[a]	–	–	–	–	–	–	–	–	0.7	1.2	1.2	4.3
Exchange rate differential	–	–	–	–	–	–	–	–	–	–	–	17.3
Other national government debt	5.7	6.3	6.7	6.8	7.1	9.0	10.2	11.4	11.5	41.7	68.2	79.4
National Grain Board	–	–	–	–	–	–	–	–	–	–	–	–
Debt of rest of public sector	7.9	10.3	10.8	11.4	12.3	15.7	19.9	24.5	26.2	3.9	5.2	3.7
Private sector	12.0	14.8	19.8	27.1	33.2	37.9	45.8	55.2	68.7	81.0	106.9	129.8
Total	20.1	33.6	40.4	47.8	53.4	65.6	78.8	93.3	111.5	132.0	180.8	247.7

	1960	1961	1962	1963	1964	1965	1966	1967	1968	1969	1970
Net change in gold and foreign exchange reserves	32.5	18.4	−12.4	11.5	4.0	15.8	15.1	113.3	111.1	41.6	129.7
Public sector	121.5	132.8	162.1	225.9	346.8	455.5	591.8	728.7	797.9	873.6	988.0
Contributions to international organizations[a]	5.0	6.1	7.7	8.2	9.4	10.0	14.6	39.3	45.7	55.8	73.7
Exchange rate differential	21.9	24.7	21.6	26.7	35.1	42.4	59.9	56.5	62.5	67.4	63.5
Other national government debt	89.1	94.1	123.6	178.7	276.1	353.0	469.8	568.8	619.1	670.6	754.3
National Grain Board	—	—	—	—	11.6	31.2	11.4	22.4	29.4	29.4	29.9
Debt of rest of public sector	5.6	8.0	9.2	12.4	14.7	18.9	36.1	41.8	40.7	50.4	66.6
Private sector	177.2	232.8	254.4	287.9	375.4	469.1	626.2	817.8	1,179.5	1,488.8	1,788.6
Total	331.1	384.0	404.1	525.4	726.3	940.4	1,233.1	1,659.7	2,088.5	2,404.0	2,906.3

Source: Banco Central, *Estadísticas monetarias y cambiarias, 1940–1960*, supplement to the *Boletín Estadístico*, no. 6 (June 1962), and various later numbers.

[a]Beginning in 1970 these items are included with gold and foreign exchange reserves in "external sector" in Central Bank publications.

Table F-2 Utilization of the money supply 1948–1970. (year-end balances in billions of pesos)

Use	1948	1949	1950	1951	1952	1953	1954	1955	1956	1957	1958	1959
Means of payment	13.8	17.6	22.0	26.7	30.4	37.7	43.9	51.6	60.2	67.6	98.8	142.2
Currency in circulation	6.7	9.1	11.9	15.4	18.3	22.1	26.7	31.8	36.1	41.8	60.3	84.4
Demand deposits	7.0	8.5	10.1	11.4	12.2	15.7	17.1	19.8	24.1	25.8	38.5	57.7
Less liquid liabilities of banking system	10.6	12.6	14.7	16.5	18.4	21.8	26.0	30.0	34.6	45.5	58.3	75.0
Time and savings deposits	7.5	9.4	10.3	10.9	12.1	14.4	16.9	19.3	24.5	29.5	40.7	44.9
Sterilized funds	0.3	0.3	0.4	0.4	0.4	0.5	0.7	0.9	0.6	0.5	0.4	0.2
Net "patrimony"	2.1	2.7	3.4	4.3	5.2	6.2	7.4	8.7	9.6	11.2	12.4	16.3
Obligations to international organizations[a]	–	–	–	–	–	–	–	–	0.5	1.9	1.9	13.0
Miscellaneous accounts	0.8	0.1	0.5	0.9	0.7	0.7	0.9	1.1	-0.6	2.4	3.0	0.7
Government deposits	3.7	3.5	3.7	4.6	4.6	6.1	8.9	11.7	16.7	18.9	23.7	30.6
National government	–	–	1.0	0.9	0.8	0.7	0.9	2.1	5.6	3.7	3.6	2.6
Rest of public sector	–	–	2.7	3.6	3.9	5.4	8.0	9.6	11.0	15.2	20.0	28.0
Total	28.1	33.6	40.4	47.8	53.4	65.6	78.8	93.3	111.5	132.0	180.8	247.7

	1960	1961	1962	1963	1964	1965	1966	1967	1968	1969	1970
Means of payment	178.6	205.4	219.7	282.9	395.6	497.5	671.7	871.6	1,105.0	1,223.1	1,467.8
Currency in circulation	105.4	121.7	135.4	167.1	227.8	296.5	396.9	508.7	591.5	658.9	761.7
Demand deposits	73.3	83.8	84.3	115.8	167.8	200.9	274.8	362.9	513.5	564.2	706.1
Less liquid liabilities of banking system	108.6	137.4	149.4	196.9	260.0	336.4	430.2	551.5	702.8	863.1	1,083.0
Time and savings deposits	60.1	74.8	85.5	123.5	178.9	233.7	289.4	385.2	528.4	628.4	799.0
Sterilized funds	0.1	–	–	–	–	7.3	5.2	7.0	5.3	4.5	–
Net "patrimony"	21.1	37.0	44.4	49.9	63.7	78.5	95.2	128.6	184.2	224.7	261.5
Obligations to international organizations[a]	17.0	19.6	18.8	20.0	16.5	12.8	23.2	26.0	1.6	1.6	22.3
Miscellaneous accounts	10.3	6.0	0.7	3.5	0.9	4.0	17.2	4.7	-16.7	3.9	0.2
Government deposits	43.9	41.1	35.0	45.6	70.6	106.5	131.2	236.6	280.2	317.8	358.0
National government	4.0	3.4	4.3	6.1	7.1	11.9	15.8	16.6	20.6	29.8	29.9
Rest of public sector	39.8	37.7	30.7	39.5	63.5	94.5	115.4	220.0	259.6	288.0	328.1
Total	331.1	384.0	404.1	525.4	726.3	940.4	1,233.1	1,659.7	2,088.5	2,404.0	2,906.3

Source: See table F–1.

[a]See footnote previous table.

Table F-3 Income and expenditure of National Treasury and Social Security System, 1965–1970. (billions of pesos)

	1965	1966	1967	1968	1969	1970
National Treasury						
Income						
Tax revenue	203.0	252.9	419.0	431.3	498.2	605.9
Other current income	27.8	30.9	57.2	73.9	73.8	74.3
Income on capital account	20.7	23.5	12.9	70.6	85.8	83.8
Other nonbudgeted income	16.6	15.7	13.6	18.6	11.8	21.7
Total	268.3	323.1	502.8	594.4	669.6	785.7
Expenditures						
Current	243.3	361.0	427.9	448.3	506.0	588.3
Operations	–	–	246.6	278.3	330.3	373.4
Interest on public debt	–	–	27.6	27.4	22.1	25.8
Transfers	–	–	153.9	143.6	153.6	189.2
Capital	82.4	81.9	156.1	186.2	199.8	226.5
Financial investment	–	–	65.0	62.9	65.6	61.4
Fixed investment	–	–	20.5	33.9	43.3	54.2
Amortization of public debt	–	–	37.1	42.1	42.7	46.4
Transfers	–	–	33.7	47.2	48.2	55.0
Other nonbudgeted expenditures	14.9	17.6	18.0	9.7	11.0	30.2
Total	340.3	460.6	602.0	644.1	716.8	845.0
Surplus or Deficit	–72.1	–137.5	–99.2	–49.8	–47.2	–59.3
Social Security System						
Receipts	138.0	190.7	304.5	330.6	353.2	–
Payments	119.3	192.5	279.9	354.8	360.1	–
Surplus or deficit	18.7	–1.8	24.6	–24.2	–6.9	–

Source: Economics Ministry, *Economic Reports*, various numbers.

(2) *Fiscal Statistics*. Government income is registered in fiscal accounts when it is actually received, whereas expenditures correspond to commitments. This difference in classification, together with the omission of some government activities from budgetary control, are mainly responsible for the difficulties of interpreting Argentine fiscal statistics. It should also be noted that between 1957 and 1963 the fiscal year covered the

period from 1 December to 30 November, whereas in other years it coincided with the calendar year. It has therefore been necessary to make rather extensive adjustments in officially published statistics to construct the fiscal series presented in this study, which insofar as possible correspond to national accounts definitions of public sector activity and are comparable on a calendar year basis.

These adjustments were especially difficult to effect in the period prior to 1965, when all government accounts were classified according to the traditional principles of administrative responsibility. It has therefore been necessary to reclassify the allocation of nonearmarked treasury funds, that is, those to "special accounts" and decentralized agencies. Similarly, the unstable relationship over time between public sector commitments and payments, a phenomenon which has been referred to in the text but is not reflected in our fiscal series for lack of systematic data, makes it unwise to attribute much analytical meaning to the difference between government income and current expenditure, and impossible to identify the source of financing of the fiscal "deficit" with any precision. [6]

Notes

1. Argentine Policymaking: Background and Experience, 1948-1970

1. Consejo Económico Nacional, "Examen de la situación económica del país," January 31, 1949, private xerox copy, pp. 2-3, 5, and 7. According to this official document, at the end of 1948 IAPI had in storage linseed oil equivalent to three years of domestic output, two years' production of oats, over one year's output of fats, and almost seven million tons of wheat and corn, in addition to important quantities of other agricultural commodities.

2. Cited in Rosa Cuzminsky, "Debates contemporaneos: algunas opiniones polémicas sobre la política económica de la Argentina," *Revista de la Universidad de Buenos Aires*, 7 (January-March 1962), 135.

3. Article 5 of the proposed contract granted the company "the exclusive right during the contract period (forty years) to explore, perforate, extract and exploit" petroleum found in its area. It was therefore clearly not a service contract, which might have been more palatable to nationalists.

4. It has been alleged to the authors on very good authority that the outgoing Aramburu economic team briefed Frondizi on the tight economic situation after he was elected, and that they offered to implement unpopular measures such as another devaluation before he took office. Frondizi rejected these offers.

5. The degree to which Krieger Vasena locked himself into a rigid exchange policy is further illustrated by his decision in May 1968 to commit Argentina to abide by Article VIII of the IMF charter, a commitment that prohibits use of exchange restrictions and multiple rates and which has been accepted by only thirty-two countries in the world. Beginning in August 1968 he also obliged the Central Bank to intervene in the futures exchange market to prevent the discount rate from rising above 8 percent.

2. Agriculture and Export Expansion

1. Details on the evolution of land tenure in Argentina are not well documented because of the absence of accurate land records in the nineteenth century. For more information the reader is referred to Jacinto Oddone, *La burguesía terrateniente argentina*, 3d ed., (Buenos Aires, 1956), and Carl C. Taylor, *Rural Life in Argentina* (Baton Rouge, 1948).

2. For details on the provisions of these laws and subsequent revisions see Pan American Union, CIDA, *Tenencia de la tierra y desarrollo socio-económico del sector agricola, Argentina* (Washington, D.C., 1965, pp. 97ff, and Darrell F. Fienup and others, *The Agricultural Development of Argentina* (New York, 1969), chap. 8.

3. Fienup, *Agricultural Development*, table 72, p. 190.

4. Pan American Union, CIDA, *Tenencia de la tierra*, p. 105.

5. See United Nations, ECLA, "El desarrollo económico de la Argentina," mimeo, 1957, pt. II, table 94, p. 114.

6. Average annual imports of tractors rose from 3,137 units in 1937-1939 to 4,347 in 1949-1951 and 7,093 in 1952-1953. During the same period imports of parts for plows and agricultural machinery were running at about half the level of 1937-1939, and imports of machine harvesters averaged only a third of the prewar rate. See Central Bank *Memorias*, various numbers during that period.

7. See Lovell Stuber Jarvis, "Supply Response in the Cattle Industry—The Argentine Case: 1937/38-1966/67," Ph.D. diss. MIT, p. 506, for trends in rural wages relative to the prices of wheat and maize.

8. See Pan American Union, CIDA, *Tenencia de la tierra*, table 13, p. 32.

9. Carlos F. Diaz Alejandro, *Essays on the Economic History of the Argentine Republic* (New Haven, 1970), table 3.2, p. 144. His "total factor productivity" index is estimated by giving equal weights to land, labor, and capital inputs; the latter includes cattle stocks.

10. Another source of uncertainty over the significance of the index is the problem of aggregation. Although the value of total agricultural output per hectare rose by an estimated 25 percent between 1935-1939 and 1955-1959, output/hectare declined in both the pampas and the rest of the country taken separately. This apparent anomaly is explained by the fact that the value of output per hectare is considerably higher in the rest of the country and production grew much faster there than in the pampas during the period. It is not possible, however, to separate capital and labor inputs between the two regions. See ibid., p. 147.

11. Between the early 1950s and 1960s annual real fixed gross investment in agriculture is estimated to have more than doubled (see ibid., table 3.23, p. 196). During the period 1955-1960 this higher level of investment was calculated to have amounted to no less than 17.7 percent of gross farm income. See Aldo Ferrer and Alberto Fracchia, "La producción, ingresos y capitalización del sector agropecuario en el período 1950-1960," mimeo report prepared for CAFADE, Buenos Aires, April 1961. These estimates are, however, very rough.

12. According to the FAO *Production Yearbook*, this would have given Argentina about one tractor for every 165 hectares of "arable land and land under permanent crops" compared with 120 hectares per tractor in Australia, 76 in Canada, and 40 in the United States.

13. See Darrell F. Fienup, *The Agricultural Development of Argentina* (New York, 1969), pp. 111-112.

14. Ibid., pp. 104, 110, 108, 111, 113.

15. R. F. V. Cooper, "The Employment of Fertilizer as a Factor Limiting Agricultural Development in Argentina," Part II, *Review of the River Plate*, July 12, 1968, p. 30. Other interesting details are given in this article on fertilizer trials for wheat and corn which reveal the complexities and uncertainties of local research results.

16. For more information on agricultural input prices and levels of tariff protection in Argentina see particularly Fienup, *Agricultural Development*, table 105, pp. 322-323; Jarvis, "Supply Response," p. 457; United Nations, ECLA/FAO, "El uso de fertilizantes en América Latina," Santiago, Chile, March 1966, table 7; and Hugh H. Schwartz, "The Argentine Experience with Industrial Credit and Protection Incentives, 1943-1958," Ph.D.diss. Yale University, 1967, vol. I, p. 188ff and vol. II, Appendix P.

17. Between 1947/48-1951/52 and 1962/63-1966/67 average corn yields per hectare sown rose by almost 60 percent, about as large an improvement as experienced in the United States during the period, but the yield per hectare actually harvested increased by only half as much. This may partly be a problem of data reliability, but it would appear that like barley, rye, and oats, corn is increasingly being used as a mixed grain for harvesting or grazing depending on climatic conditions and the supply of forage.

18. Lucio G. Reca, "The Price and Production Duality Within Argentine Agriculture, 1923-1965," Ph.D. diss., University of Chicago, 1967, tables 21 and 22, pp. 72-73, and accompanying text. The large negative constant terms (intercepts) in these regressions also indicate that output growth and productivity improvements accelerated in the latter part of the period 1945-1965.

19. See Jarvis, "Supply Response," passim, for information on changes in breeds and other characteristics of cattle raising. Figures on seeded pasture, which include an estimate of the annual grain crops that are used partially for pasture or forage, are from Fienup, *Agricultural Development*, table 27, p. 72.

20. See Fienup, *Agricultural Development*, particularly table 28, p. 74, for data on pasture area. This source, however, uses unadjusted official estimates of cattle stocks.

21. The data in figure 2-3 are taken from FAO *Production Yearbook*, various numbers, except for Argentine figures, which are from official statistics. The relatively more favorable performance of the Argentine parity price index may be due in part to the decline in the relative prices of services, which in most other countries have tended to increase quite substantially during the period under analysis.

22. This is probably the main reason why trends in the agricultural terms of trade, if measured in implicit GDP instead of wholesale prices, have been more favorable (see again table 2-10). Implicit GDP price indices pick up the influence of changes in the composition of output because in effect they use current year production weights.

23. In this regard see Diaz Alejandro, *Essays*, pp. 178-181. His analysis is based on the coefficients of determination between both the levels and the yearly changes of the domestic and dollar prices of wheat, corn, linseed, wool, meat, and hides during the period 1951-1963.

24. FAO, *Agricultural Commodities—Projections for 1975 and 1985* (Rome, 1967), pp. 15, 87.

25. Diaz Alejandro, *Essays*, pp. 169-170; Reinaldo Antonio Colomé, "Funciones de oferta agropecuaria de la región pampeana en el período

1940-1960," Ph.D. diss., Facultad de Economía, Universidad Nacional de Córdoba, July 1966; Lucio G. Reca, "Determinantes de la oferta agropecuaria en la Argentina, 1934/35-1966/67," *Estudios sobre la economía argentina* (Instituto de Investigaciones Económicas y Financieras de la CGE), no. 5 (August 1969).

26. Reca, "Price and Production Duality," p. 58.

27. Reca, "Price and Production Duality," pp. 57-58. The standard Nerlovian model (Marc Nerlove, *The Dynamics of Supply* [Baltimore, Hopkins Press, 1958]) employing simple least square estimating techniques was used by Reca in his study, despite the fact that one of the independent variables is the lagged value of the dependent variable. This may have biased the results.

28. In Pan American Union, CIDA, *La tenencia de la tierra*, p. 111, it is estimated, for example, that the real average income of tenants per hectare of wheat in 1947-1958 was 20 percent higher than in 1935-1939 despite the sharp decline in the relative price of wheat.

29. Jarvis, "Supply Response," p. 130.

30. Diaz Alejandro, *Essays*, p. 175.

31. Jarvis, "Supply Response," chap. 8, especially tables 8.1 and 8.2, pp. 363-387. It should also be noted that the specification of Jarvis's price variables is different from that used by Diaz Alejandro. Jarvis employs the beef/grain price ratio rather than beef prices relative to the rural wholesale price index. For further evidence of the short-term perverse elasticity of supply of beef see R. Otrera, "Un modelo econométrico para analizar las exportaciones potenciales de carne argentina," Ph.D. diss. University of Texas, January 1966.

32. Martín Enrique Piñeiro, "Argentine Agriculture: Past and Potential Contributions to Country-Wide Economic Growth," Ph.D. diss. University of California, Davis, 1968, pp. 193-94.

33. Ibid., p. v. In a more recent study, Piñeiro has further elaborated his model to obtain additional results in Piñeiro and Alex F. McCalla, "Programming for Argentine Price Policy Analysis," *Review of Economics and Statistics,* 53 (February 1971), 59-66. In this study the model is also used to determine "optimum" prices that would maximize output. It is interesting to note, however, that this "optimum" solution implies 50 to 100 percent or more increases in most real agricultural commodity prices and a rise in land rents from 35 to 55 percent of gross agricultural income (see ibid., tables 1 and 2).

34. As an illustrative example, if it is assumed for simplicity that exports are composed entirely of agricultural goods, that the balance of payments is initially in equilibrium, and that no change occurs in net movements of foreign capital, then the necessary rate of growth of agricultural output would be equal to the following: the share of agricultural production consumed domestically multiplied by the income elasticity of consumption of these goods, plus the share of production exported multiplied by the income elasticity of demand for total imports. Thus, if three fourths of rural

production were consumed domestically and the remainder exported, and the income elasticities were .8 and 1 respectively, the necessary rate of growth of agricultural production would be: .75 (.8) + .25 (1) = .85, or 85 percent of the rate of growth in GDP.

35. Historically most countries have of course developed on the basis of a transfer of income out of agriculture to other activities, but it is conceivable that after a certain point, further transfers become inconsistent with healthy agricultural expansion when factor prices are bid up and land becomes scarce. Pablo Hary, longtime director of CREA, a private agricultural research and extension organization in Argentina, has on the other hand always insisted to one of the authors that agricultural production could be doubled while reducing unit costs of production.

36. See Fienup, *Agricultural Production*, chap. 4, for examples of deficiencies in the availability of special purpose capital equipment needed to improve efficiency in the production, handling, and processing of a broad number of agricultural commodities. See also Banco Ganadero Argentino, *Mercados y precios del ganado vacuno*, (Buenos Aires), n.d., pp. 32-34, for a description of the consequences of great instability in yearling steer prices on specialization between animal breeding and fattening zones in the pampas.

37. Our present knowledge of the exact nature and speed of response of farmers to changes in relative prices is, however, very limited; perhaps further research will reveal other problems that should be taken especially into account in official price policy.

3. Industrialization and Foreign Trade

1. See Diaz Alejandro, *Essays*, chap. 5.

2. In 1900-1904, value added in manufacturing is estimated to have represented 11 percent of GDP in 1935 prices, 14 percent in 1950 prices, and 15 percent in 1960 prices. For sources of these estimates and the other GDP and employment figures mentioned in this and the following paragraph see United Nations, ECLA, "El desarrollo económico de la Argentina," mimeo, 1957, appendix, and Diaz Alejandro, *Essays*, chap. 3.

3. Because of overvaluation of the peso in 1950, foreign trade coefficients measured in 1950 prices are underestimated, although changes between periods indicate the rough order of magnitude of the decline in the relative importance of trade.

4. See Hollis B. Chenery and Lance Taylor, "Development Patterns: Among Countries and Over Time," *Review of Economics and Statistics*, 50 (November 1968); and United Nations, Department of Economic and Social Affairs, *A Study of Industrial Growth* (New York, 1963).

5. Jorge Katz has pointed out that industrialization was also "forced" inadvertently by preferential tariff treatment granted to imports from Great Britain under the Roca-Runciman Treaty. This discriminatory policy provided an additional incentive for establishment of "tariff jumping"

foreign firms in Argentina, such as Standard Electric and Siemens (both established in the mid-1930s) which would otherwise have been cut out of the market.

6. See A. Maizels, *Industrial Growth and World Trade* (Cambridge, Eng., Cambridge University Press, 1963), tables A-14, E-2, E-6.

7. See CONADE's estimates of the composition of industrial production up to 1963 in *Plan nacional de desarrollo 1965-1969*, (Buenos Aires, 1965), tables 18 and 19, pp. 60-61; unpublished estimates by the World Bank for the period 1960-1969 also indicate relative constancy of the intermediate goods share.

8. See Diaz Alejandro, *Essays*, table 4.25, p. 257.

9. See Jorge M. Katz, *Production Functions, Foreign Investment and Growth*, (Amsterdam, North Holland Publishing Co., 1969), pp. 56-57.

10. The first source referred to in the text is Victor J. Elias, "Estimates of Valued Added, Capital and Labor in Argentine Manufacturing, 1935-1963," University of Chicago, June 1969. His capital stock figures are based on corporate records and are therefore likely to be overestimated insofar as the periodic revaluation of assets (especially the one that took place in 1960) exaggerated the increase in the value of corporate assets. It is indeed difficult to believe that the real industrial capital stock doubled in value between 1958 and 1965, whereas it took thirty-five years prior to 1958 to achieve the same proportional increase (see ibid., table 25, pp. 76-79).

The second source is Katz, *Production Functions*, who bases his capital stock figures on estimates of A. Fracchia and A. Balboa, "Fixed Reproducible Capital in Argentina 1935-1955," *Income and Wealth*, 8 (London, 1959). These figures, which show an increase of less than 10 percent in the real fixed stock of manufacturing capital during the investment boom years 1958-1961, would appear a priori to be an underestimate (see ibid., table 2.1, p. 24).

The 10 percent estimated increase in output due to larger factor inputs in 1954-1961 is based on Katz's estimate of a CES production function for the sector (see table 3.7, p. 59). He also found that the importance of the "residual factor" in the growth of manufacturing output before 1954 was negligible.

11. U.S. Department of Commerce, *U.S. Business Investment in Foreign Countries* (Washington, D.C, 1960), and *Survey of Current Business*, selected numbers. Judging by official foreign investment authorizations in Argentina between 1958 and 1964, U.S. investment accounted for about 60 percent of total private foreign investment in manufacturing.

12. See Katz, *Production Functions*, p. 95, and D. Chudnovsky and J. Katz, "Patentes e importación de tecnología," mimeo, Buenos Aires, 1970, p. 36.

13. See Banco Central de la República Argentina, *Origen del producto y distribución del ingreso 1950-1969*, supplement no. 1 to the *Boletín Estadístico*, January 1971; and Instituto Nacional de Estadística y Censos,

Censo nacional económico, industria manufacturera, Part I for the Federal Capital (conducted in 1965). Hal B. Lary, in his study, *Imports of Manufactures from Less Developed Countries* (New York, 1968), found that wages per employee correlated quite well with relative skill ratios for a broad array of three and four digit U.S. industries; but it is also possible that in a country like Argentina, where employers have been under continuous inflationary wage pressure, wage rates simply tend to be higher in less competitive, more capital intensive industries.

14. See, for example, T. Y. Shen, "Economies of Scale, Penrose Effect, Growth of Plants and Their Size Distribution," *Journal of Political Economy*, 78 (July/August 1970), 702-716, in which the industries enjoying economies of scale in the state of Massachusetts are listed in order of importance as transport equipment, nonferrous metals, rubber products, chemicals, paper, machinery, and ferrous metals.

15. In Elias, "Estimates of Value Added," table 37, pp. 109-110, evidence of somewhat doubtful statistical significance (sum of wage and capital elasticities greater than unity in CES production functions) indicates economies of scale in the vehicles and machinery, metals, and rubber products industries (see table 37 and pp. 109-110); María Esther Sanjurjo, in *Economías de escala y cambio tecnológico: Argentina, 1935-61*, Internal Working Paper No. 40 (Buenos Aires, July 1967), found that at least half the increase in gross product between 1935 and 1961 was due to economies of scale; and Katz, *Production Functions*, concluded that in contrast to the period 1946-1953, between 1954 and 1961 "the joint impact of technical change and returns to scale accounted for most of the observed changes in output and in labor productivity." At the individual industry level, evidence of diseconomies of small scale production in Argentina is given for the tractor industry in Comisión Asesora Honoraria para la Industria del Tractor, *El tractor en la Argentina* (Buenos Aires, May 1969); for the machine tool industry in United Nations Economic Commission for Latin America, *La fabricación de maquinarias y equipos industriales en América Latina: IV. Las máquinas-herramientas en la Argentina* (New York, 14 February 1966); and for the automobile industry in Jack Baranson, *Automotive Industries in Developing Countries*, World Bank Staff Occasional Papers No. 8 (Baltimore, 1969).

16. The list of forty industries benefiting from this law nevertheless included some quite sophisticated products, among which were electric batteries, antibiotics, photographic materials, explosives, and refrigeration equipment.

17. This list would be incomplete if it did not include a not-so-secret project initiated by Perón in the 1940s to develop independently Argentina's capacity to produce atomic energy. This unsuccessful venture had nothing to do, however, with the more recently established and highly respected Argentine Atomic Energy Commission.

18. See David Felix, "Some Notes on the Implementation of Argentine

Industrialization Policy," mimeo, September 5, 1966; and Richard D. Mallon, "Comment," in *Estrategias de industrialización para la Argentina* (Buenos Aires, 1970), pp. 85-86.

19. David Felix, "Mas allá de la sustitución de importaciones: un dilema latinoamericano," in *Estrategias de industrialización para la Argentina* (Buenos Aires, 1970), pp. 152, 155; a similar article, "The Dilemma of Import Substitution—Argentina," was published by the same author in Gustav F. Papanek, ed., *Development Policy—Theory and Practice* (Cambridge, Mass., 1968). Only imports of current inputs are included in the Felix study, and they are adjusted to exclude the effect of inventory variations. For a discussion of the index number and conceptual problems of Felix's estimates, and of the special circumstances surrounding the years he chose for comparison, see Daniel M. Schydlowsky, "Comment," in *Estrategias de Industrialización para la Argentina* (Buenos Aires, 1970); pp. 209-224, and Richard D. Mallon, "La industrialización y la sustitución de importaciones en la Argentina," *ibid.;* particularly pp. 380-381.

20. Otherwise the value of inputs imported to produce a good locally would have to exceed the cif. price of the imported good itself. This would be possible only when producers' equipment and materials inventories were being accumulated to initiate new production, unless differential pricing of inputs and final goods from abroad were highly discriminatory (for example, the delivered value of the knocked-down parts of an automobile were more expensive than the cif. price of the fully assembled vehicle). It is unlikely that differential pricing led to negative import substitution except in isolated cases, but input price padding may well have reduced the net foreign exchange saving of increased output from branch firms that restricted their purchase of inputs from foreign parents.

21. David Felix, "Import Substitution and Industrial Exporting: An Analysis of Recent Argentine Experience," paper presented to the 21st Annual Latin American Conference, University of Florida, February 17-20, 1971, table B-1. In this and the following analysis, nontraditional or manufactured exports include SITC sections 5-8 except division 68, unless otherwise noted.

22. Felix, "Import Substitution," p. 12. See, however, the different results obtained by eliminating the year 1955 from the regression analysis in Jonathan W. Eaton, "Effective Devaluation as an Export Incentive in Less Developed Countries," B.A. thesis, Harvard University, 1972, pp. 48ff.

23. Henry J. Bruton, *Latin American Exports and Import Substitution Policies*, Research Memo No. 32, Center for Development Economics, Williams College, November 1969, pp. 10-11.

24. David Felix's estimates of the "real" exchange rate for nontraditional exports in "Import Substitution," table B-5, show considerable fluctuations between 1962 and 1968 (extreme values $\pm$ 13 percent from the mean) around an average level substantially below that of 1956-1958.

25. See table 3-5 above and ibid., table B-4.

26. See Felix, "Import Substitution," tables 3.6 and 3.7, p. 85; and

United Nations, Economic Commission for Latin America, *A Measurement of Price Levels and the Purchasing Power of Currencies in Latin America, 1960-1962,* (Mar de la Plata, Argentina, 1963).

27. For estimates of effective protection of different manufactured products see Pedro Héctor Wainer, "La protección aduanera efectiva en la República Argentina," mimeo (Buenos Aires, 1967). It should also be mentioned that, with the exception of LAFTA trade concessions, export subsidies did not discriminate very strongly in favor of new and against "traditional" industries. See again Felix, "Import Substitution," table B-5, for differences in "real" exchange rates between "Type I" and "Type II" manufactures; and table B-4 for industrial exports by subsector to LAFTA and non-LAFTA countries.

28. See John R. Eriksson, "Wage Structures and Economic Development in Selected Latin American Countries: A Comparative Analysis," Ph.D. diss., University of California, Berkeley, 1966. The wage bill as a share of industrial value added in Argentina has been under 40 percent in recent years, considerably lower in comparison with other countries than productivity differentials would seem to justify. This difference may not of course be reflected in real wage rates insofar as relative prices of wage goods, notably foodstuffs, are lower in Argentina.

29. For the price to rise from *Pd* to *Pd'* in the domestic market, it must of course be assumed (usually quite realistically) that competitive imports would not be allowed in to undercut the new price.

30. For an example of capacity utilization survey results see Richard D. Mallon, "Exchange Policy—Argentina," in Papanek, ed., *Development Policy,* pp. 202-204; for a sample of evidence from individual industry studies see CONADE, *Plan Nacional de Desarrollo 1965-1969,* chap. 1, sec. 5, and UNCTAD Secretariat, Trade Plans Section, "Trade Projections for Argentina," mimeo, 15 June 1968, Part III.

31. Henry J. Bruton, "Productivity Growth in Latin America," *American Economic Review,* 57 (December 1967), 1101.

32. Although decreasing costs and relatively small market size should be expected to foster imperfect competition, very little quantitative research has been carried out on the price and production behavior of firms in Latin America, despite qualitative evidence that "umbrella pricing" and other practices in restraint of trade, defended by tightly knit trade associations or cartels, appear to be quite common.

33. On the role of market organization in foreign trade see Lou T. Wells, *The Product Life Cycle and International Trade* (Cambridge, Mass., 1971); and on the role of the multinational firm see Raymond Vernon, *Sovereignty at Bay* (New York, 1971).

4. Toward Sustained Growth With External Equilibrium

1. As late as 1964-1966 Argentina is estimated to have supplied 92 percent of its clients' imports of linseed oil, 32 percent of their beef imports,

and 22 percent of their wheat and corn. CONADE, *Plan Nacional de Desarrollo 1970-1974* (Buenos Aires, 1970), vol. 5, table 28, p. 79.

2. For a sample of research results on the demand for imports in Argentina see Diaz Alejandro, *Essays*, pp. 354-359; Jeffrey B. Nugent, "Country Study — Argentina," summer research project paper for the Office of Program Coordination, U.S.-AID, mimeo, 1965; and UNCTAD Secretariat, Trade Plans Section, "Trade Projections for Argentina," mimeo, 15 June 1968.

3. See especially Carlos Diaz Alejandro, *Exchange-Rate Devaluation in a Semi-Industrialized County: The Experience of Argenina, 1955-1961* (Cambridge, Mass., 1965).

4. The situation with respect to the measurement of import demand elasticities in Argentina appears quite similar to that described by Samuel Morley in "Import Demand and Import Substitution in Brazil," chap. 10 in Howard S. Ellis, ed., *The Economy of Brazil* (Berkeley, 1969).

5. Larry A. Sjaastad, "Comercio internacional de la Argentina: perspectivas para las industrias exportadoras tradicionales," in Mario Brodersohn, ed., *Estrategias de industrialización para la Argentina*, (Buenos Aires, 1970), pp. 395-421; the elasticity measured by Sjaastad is for per capita consumption of agricultural goods receiving little or no processing (mainly foodstuffs), expressed in pesos of 1960. Nugent, *Country Study Argentina*; Diaz Alejandro, *Exchange Rate Devaluation,* p. 91; Maynard and van Rijckeghem, "Stabilization Policy," p. 210; and Alain de Janvry, "Empirical Analysis of Consumer Behavior: An Application to Argentina," paper presented to an internal seminar of the Centro de Investigaciones Económicas, Instituto Torcuato Di Tella, July 20, 1969, table VIII, p. 59b.

6. See, for example, Harold B. Dunkerley, "Exchange Rate Systems in Conditions of Continuing Inflation—Lessons from Colombian Experience," in Papanek, ed., *Development Policy*, and Juergen B. Donges, "Brazil's Trotting Peg: A New Approach to Greater Exchange-Rate Flexibility in Less Developed Countries?" mimeo, 1972. It should also be recalled that Argentina's experiment with greater exchange rate flexibility between 1962 and 1967 was a period of strong export expansion and relative balance of payments stability (see Mallon, "Exchange Policy—Argentina," in Papanek, ed., *Development Policy*).

7. One of the authors was told of the interesting case of a prominent Argentine firm that was able to realize a small profit through interest and tax rate differentials with a stable exchange rate. The firm was able to earn about 12 percent on funds invested in the Eurodollar market, whereas it could borrow domestically at 15 percent and receive an income tax exemption equal to one third of the interest paid.

8. Caution must of course be used in drawing any policy conclusions from parity price comparisons. See Bela Balassa, "The Purchasing Power Parity Doctrine: A Reappraisal," *Journal of Political Economy*, 72 (December 1964), 584-596, and Edmar Bacha and Lance Taylor, "Foreign Exchange

Shadow Prices: A Critical Review of Current Theories," *Quarterly Journal of Economics*, 85 (May 1971), especially pp. 219-220.

9. In a recent study Lucio G. Reca found, for example, that the more intensive use of fertilizer was only marginally profitable at prevailing domestic prices. See his "Fertilizacion nitrogenada en maíz en la Argentina: resultados experimentales e implicaciones económicas," *Económica*, 16 (September-December 1970).

10. See FAO, *Second Special Inquiry on Beef and Poultry* (Rome, April 30, 1970), quoted in *Review of the River Plate*, December 22, 1970, p. 1052.

11. In this regard see Richard D. Mallon, *Balance of Payments Adjustment in a Semi-Industrialized, Agricultural Export Economy: The Argentine Case*, Economic Development Report No. 109, Harvard Development Advisory Service, 1968, p.6.

12. Marginal cost exporting has been criticized on the grounds that profit maximization by firms following this practice does not lead to an "optimum" distribution of their output between domestic and foreign consumers. See, for example, Giorgio Basevi, "Domestic Demand and Ability to Export," *Journal of Political Economy*, 78 (March/April 1970). Welfare implications cannot, however, be judged solely in terms of the effect of marginal cost exporting on domestic consumers of the commodities in question if the resulting increase in foreign exchange revenue provides compensating benefits for the economy by helping alleviate the balance of payments constraint and thereby generating fuller employment.

13. In addition to the price comparison references cited earlier, the reader is also referred to Mark R. Daniels, "Differences in Efficiency Among Industries in Developing Countries," *American Economic Review*, 59 (March 1969), in which the "aggregate efficiency ranking" of Argentine industry is found to be superior to that of Korea, Chile, Peru, and Paraguay but inferior to Spain and El Salvador (see p. 170). Perhaps even more relevant, the variance between activities in different countries was so great that only extreme ranking differentials (for example, between Argentina and Spain on the one extreme and with Paraguay on the other) were found statistically significant.

14. See G. C. Hufbauer, "*West Pakistan Exports: Policies and Problems*," in Walter P. Falcon and Gustav F. Papanek, eds., *Development Policy II—The Pakistan Experience* (Cambridge, Mass., 1971).

15. See Hyong Chun Kim, "Korea's Export Success, 1960-69," in International Monetary Fund and World Bank, *Finance and Development*, 8 (March 1971).

16. Daniel M. Schydlowsky, "Short-Run Policy in Semi-Industrialized Economies," *Economic Development and Cultural Change*, 19 (April 1971), table 9, p. 406.

5. Secular Inflation and Stabilization Policy

1. See Joseph O. Adekunle, "Rates of Inflation in Industrial, Other

Developed, and Less Developed Countries, 1949-65," *IMF Staff Papers*, 15 (November 1968), table 3, pp. 536-537.

2. In all fairness it should be pointed out here that some distinguished monetarists do not advocate discretionary control of the supply of money to manipulate the price level, or what has been called in the literature "fine tuning." As one well-known monetarist says, "The evidence suggests that monetary changes take a fairly long time to exert their influence and that the time taken varies considerably . . . There are serious limitations to the possibility of a discretionary monetary policy and much danger that a policy may make matters worse rather than better." Milton Friedman, "The Supply of Money and Changes in Prices and Output," in Edwin Dean, ed., *The Controversy over the Quantity Theory of Money* (Boston, 1965), reprinted from a study for the U.S. Congress Joint Economic Committee, Washington, D.C., 1958, p. 105.

3. See Milton Friedman, ed., *Studies in the Quantity Theory of Money* (Chicago, 1957). The data used in these studies, however, is from countries suffering from hyperinflation. For results of the application of this model to other countries see Joseph O. Adekunle, "The Demand for Money: Evidence from Developed and Less Developed Countries," *IMF Staff Papers*, 15 (July 1968), 220-266.

4. José Maria Dagnino Pastore *Ingreso y dinero: Argentina 1935-60*, Fundación de Investigaciones Económicas Latinoamericanas (Buenos Aires, 1966); Manuel Fernández López and Silvestre Damus, *Determinantes de la demanda de liquidez por el sector privado en la Argentina, 1959-1963*, Instituto de Investigaciones Económicas y Sociales of the University of Buenos Aires, 1964; and Adolfo Cesar Diz, "Money and Prices in Argentina 1935-1962," in David Meiselman, ed., *Varieties of Monetary Experience* (Chicago, 1970). With respect to lags in price expectation models of this kind, however, see Dean S. Dutton, "The Demand for Money and the Price Level," *Journal of Political Economy*, 79 (September/October 1971), especially p. 1168.

5. The definition of money is M_1, or primary liquidity; the ratio of total liquidity (including time and term bank deposits) to GDP also declined by almost the same proportion from .39 to .20 during the same period. According to John G. Gurley's international financial comparisons, the "normal" ratio for Argentina should have been about .25 for M_1. See his "Financial Structures in Developing Countries," in David Krivine, ed., *Fiscal and Monetary Problems in Developing States*, Proceedings of Third Rehovoth Conference (New York, 1967). The year-to-year instability of the money ratio was also extremely high, the highest in fact of any of the thirty countries studied by Yung Chul Park in 1954-1968. See his "The Variability of Velocity: An International Comparison," *IMF Staff Papers*, 17 (November 1970), table 2, p. 625.

6. Harley Hinrichs, "Tax Strategies for Financing Economic Development" (mimeo, n.a.), p. 49, and Schwartz, "The Argentine Experience," p. 111, n. 170 (Ph.D. diss.), quoted from Consejo Federal de Inversiones and

Instituto de Investigaciones Económicas y Financieras of the C.G.E., *Programa conjunto para el desarrollo agropecuario e industrial*, first report I, 265-279.

7. For a review of the wide variety of cost-push explanations of inflation see Martin Bronfenbrenner and F. D. Holzman, "Survey of Inflation Theory," *American Economic Review*, 53 (September 1963), 593-661.

8. See A. W. Phillips, "The Relation Between Unemployment and the Rate of Change in Money Wage Rates," *Economica*, 25 (November 1958, 283-299, and "Employment, Inflation, and Growth," *Economica*, 29 (February 1962), 1-16.

9. For a brief but trenchant discussion of the inflation identification problem see Paul A. Samuelson and Robert M. Solow, "Analytical Aspects of Anti-Inflation Policy," *American Economic Review*, 50 (May 1960), 182ff.

10. See, for example, David B. Humphrey, "Changes in Protection and Inflation in Argentina, 1953-1966," *Oxford Economic Papers*, 21 (July 1969), 196-219, and Julio Olivera, "Aspectos dinámicos de la inflación estructural," *Desarrollo Económico*, 7 (October-December 1967), 261-266.

11. Javier Villanueva, *The Inflationary Process in Argentina, 1943-1960*, Internal Working Paper No. 7 (Buenos Aires, 1964), and "Price Formation in the Foodstuffs Market: Wholesale and Retail Profit Margins," mimeo, Di Tella Institute, n.d.; Aldo A. Arnaudo, *Análisis espectral de los precios mayoristas en Argentina* (Cordoba, 1967), and "Un estudio sobre la velocidad de la inflación en Argentina 1958-66," paper presented to a seminar at the Centro de Investigaciones Económicas, Córdoba, December 1969; R. A. Krieger, "Inflation Propagation in Argentina: A Short-Run Analysis," Ph.D. diss., University of Wisconsin, 1965, particularly pp. 114 and 117; Mario S. Brodersohn, "Estrategias de estabilización y expansión en la Argentina: 1959-67," mimeo, Di Tella Institute, n.d., especially table 2, p. 8.

12. Diz, "Money and Prices," tables 18 and 19, pp. 75-76 (of the unpublished version). See also Arnold Harberger, "The Dynamics of Inflation in Chile," in *Measurement in Economics: Studies in Mathematical Economics in Memory of Yehuda Grunfeld* (Stanford, 1963). More details of the work of Diz and of the other econometric studies mentioned later in the text are presented in Appendix B.

13. Diaz Alejandro, *Essays*, pp. 373-374.

14. Maynard and Van Rijckeghem, "Stabilization Policy."

15. Because of the smaller number of observations in each subseries, it was necessary to simplify the estimating equations somewhat to adjust for degrees of freedom and also to try to reduce multicolinearity. See Appendix B for more details.

16. Further exploration of this line of investigation was not considered useful, however, because of the colinearity that exists between the wage, money supply, and exchange rate variables. Lagged wage variables might in effect act as a proxy for past changes in money supply or the exchange rate,

since it is impossible to include lagged values of these latter variables explicitly in the same estimating equation because of serial correlation.

17. The existence of rather large, but statistically insignificant, negative constant terms in the wholesale price equations of course makes it rather difficult to interpret the elasticity of prices with respect to the exchange rate. It should also be pointed out that because of the importance of exported foodstuffs in the cost of living index, the greater significance of instantaneous variations in the exchange rate on the behavior of consumer prices is not as improbable from a cost-push point of view as might at first be presumed.

18. Maynard and Willy Van Rijckeghem, "Stabilization Policy," p. 212. See also Willy Van Rijckeghem, *Stabilization Policy in an Inflationary Economy: A Post-Mortem* (Brussels, March 1972); and "Política de estabilización para una economía inflacionaria," *Desarrollo Económico*, 12 (July-September 1972), 245-252.

19. Emile Depres, "Stabilization and Monetary Policy in Less Developed Countries," in Jesse W. Markham and Gustav F. Papanek, eds., *Industrial Organization and Economic Development* (Boston, 1970), p. 402. For discussion of business credit as a capacity constraint in Brazil see also Samuel A. Morley, "Inflation and Stagnation in Brazil," *Economic Development and Cultural Change*, 19 (January 1971), 196-202.

20. A similar concept appears to have been first generalized by Melvin W. Reder, "The Theoretical Problems of National Wage-Price Policy," *Canadian Journal of Economics*, 14 (February 1948), and later developed by Henri Aujac, "Inflation and the Monetary Consequence of the Behavior of Social Groups: A Working Hypothesis," *International Economic Papers*, no. 4, 1954 (originally published in French in *Economie Appliquée*, 3 (April/June 1950], 280-300), Duesenberry, Holzman, and others. See Bronfenbrenner and Holzman, "Survey of Inflation Theory," p. 623.

21. A propos of the importance of irrational expectations, it has been said that the stabilization policy of Krieger Vasena was based on the assumption that inflation was really cost-push but was psychologically demand-pull because of private expectations that the rate of price increase depended on the size of the fiscal deficit. See Juan Carlos de Pablo, *Política antinflacionaria en la Argentina, 1967-1970* (Buenos Aires, 1970).

22. For a discussion of this point see Richard D. Mallon, "Planning in Crisis," *Journal of Political Economy*, 78 (July/August 1970), Part II. 959-962.

6. Inflation, the Distribution of Income, and the Financing of Growth

1. In figure 6-1 changes in relative prices between sectors are measured in terms of differences between current and 1960 implicit GDP prices. It should be noted that this measurement of the sectoral terms of trade reflects changes in the composition of output within sectors as well as changes in relative commodity prices between them. This is not a drawback, however, insofar as we are also interested in the effect of substitution on real income

transfers between sectors due to changes in relative prices. The discontinuity in 1964 is explained by the shift from CONADE to Central Bank series.

2. For data on Argentine wage shares see United Nations, Department of Economic and Social Affairs, *Economic Development and Income Distribution in Argentina*, doc. no. E/CN. 12/802 (New York, 1969), and Banco Central de la República Argentina, *Origen del producto y distribución del ingreso 1950-1969*. (Buenos Aires, January 1971).

3. See United Nations, Department of Economic and Social Affairs, *Economic Development*, table 4, p. 15, and tables 26 to 28, pp. 118-121.

4. With respect to construction, however, estimates of the wage share may be subject to significant error.

5. See United Nations, Department of Economic and Social Affairs, *Economic Development*, table 29, pp. 126-127.

6. See ibid., tables 26-28, pp. 118-121, and table 29, pp. 126-127. It should also be mentioned that changes in wage shares within sectors explain about three fourths of the change in the total wage share in Argentine income; the remainder is of course explained by intersectoral shifts in employment.

7. For further discussion of measurements of income dispersion see Richard Weisskoff, *Income Distribution and Economic Growth in Puerto Rico, Argentina, and Mexico*, Yale University Economic Growth Center Discussion Paper No. 93, August 1970.

8. Gross domestic savings are defined as the difference between gross national income and total consumption, both government and private; gross investment includes both fixed capital formation and changes in certain inventories (especially cattle stocks and off-farm storage of major agricultural crops); and available goods and services are equal to domestic output adjusted for the net balance in foreign trade (imports of goods and services less exports).

9. The behavior of relative investment goods prices in Argentina affords a dramatic example of what can happen in a semiclosed, inflationary economy. During the period under analysis the distortion in relative prices was so great that it has been estimated that Argentina's 19 percent average savings rate was equivalent to about 13 percent at relative international prices. For further discussion of this phenomenon see Rolf Hayn, "Capital Formation and Argentina's Price-Cost Structure, 1935-1958," *Review of Economics and Statistics*, 44 (August 1962), 340-343; Diaz Alejandro, *Essays*, chap. 5; and CONADE-CEPAL, *Distribución del ingreso y cuentas nacionales en la Argentina* (Buenos Aires, 1965), *Distribución del ingreso* III, tables III-75 and 76.

10. See United Nations, Department of Economic and Social Affairs, *Economic Development*, pp. 155-156.

11. The differences between the shaded area in the current and constant price series is explained not only by changes in relative domestic prices, as pointed out in the text, but also by inclusion in the constant price series of the effect of changes in the international terms of trade. The terms of trade were particularly adverse during 1956-1959 and again in 1962-1963 and

1968-1969, whereas they were especially favorable in the early 1950s and again in 1964-1965. Their effect in the former case was to increase the ratio of gross domestic savings to gross national income and thus to shrink the shaded area (or expand the barred area) in 1960 prices relative to that in current prices in the figure. In the latter case the effect was the reverse. See Banco Central de la Republica Argentina, *Boletín Estadístico,* supplement January 1971, and CONADE-CEPAL, *Distribución del ingreso y cuentas nacionales en la Argentina,* I, 185, for an explanation of the handling of the terms of trade in the national accounts.

12. See CONADE-CEPAL, *Distribución del ingreso y cuentas nacionales en la Argentina,* III, table III-10, pp. 24-25. In this source fixed investment by state enterprises is included in the public sector along with estimated fixed capital expenditures of central, provincial, and municipal governments.

13. See Antonín Basch and Milic Kybal, *Capital Markets in Latin America: A General Survey and Six Country Studies* (New York, 1970), chap. 5.

14. See Hugh Schwartz, "The Argentine Experience with Industrial Credit and Protection Incentives, 1943-1958," mimeo, 1967, especially vol. I, table 4, pp. 80-81. Reported bank loans are adjusted upwards to include loans of less than 50,000 pesos and refer to those outstanding at the end of June in both years. Excluding such loans, total bank credit to the sector amounted to 10.8 percent of manufacturing GDP in 1945 and 17.5 percent in 1948.

15. United Nations, Department of Economic and Social Affairs, *Economic Development,* table 61, p. 215.

16. Ibid., p. 139.

17. For an analysis of corporate and noncorporate balance sheets see Samuel Itzcovich and Ernesto Feldman, *Un sistema de transacciones financieras para la Argentina (1955-1965),* Internal Working Paper No. 40 (Buenos Aires, February 1969).

18. See Walter Lee Ness, Jr., "Inflation Expectations, the Interest Rate, and Financial Market Development," Ph.D. diss., M.I.T., 1969, pp. 120-121.

19. No information is available, however, on the extent to which noncorporate enterprises may have transformed themselves into corporations during this period.

21. Harley H. Hinricks, "Determinants of Government Revenue Shares in Less Developed Countries," *Economic Journal,* 75 (September 1965), 546-556, and *La estructura tributaria durante el desarrollo* (Mexico, 1967).

22. The regression results are $R = 15.33 - 0.348 P$, $\bar{R}^2 = .13$, $DW = 2.36$; (2.15) where R is the annual percentage change in real national government revenue during the period 1946-1970, P is the annual percentage change in the rate of increase in the cost of living index during the same period, and the figure in parenthesis is the *"T"* statistic. These results should, however,

be interpreted in light of the fact that price variations "explain" only 13 percent of variations in real government revenue.

23. See Ministerio de Economia y Trabajo, *Informe Económico* for the fourth quarter of 1970, Appendix tables 45 and 46, pp. 86-89. It is really quite impossible, however, to reconstruct the deficits of state enterprises from published statistics: their accounts are in a number of cases so tangled by floating debts, important omissions, and other flaws that their true financial and economic implications will probably never be known with any accuracy.

24. The regression results are $E = 16.50 - 0.461\ P,\ \bar{R}^2 = .16,\ DW =$
$$(2.33)$$
1.80; where $E =$ the annual percentage change in real national government current expenditure during the period 1946-1970, and the other figures are defined in the same way as in the government revenue regression. The relationship between changes in the rate of inflation and variations in government savings (revenue minus current expenditure) was also tested, but results were insignificant both with savings as the dependent variable and, lagged by one year, as the independent variable.

25. See CONADE, *Plan nacional de desarrollo 1965-1969*, table 96, p. 180, and table 97, p. 181; and *Plan nacional de desarrollo 1970-1974*, vol. 1, table 11, p. 116, and table 40, p. 195.

26. See Consejo Federal de Inversiones, *Política fiscal en la Argentina*, II (Buenos Aires, 1963).

7. A Mediative Approach to Macroeconomic Policymaking

1. In this analysis "middle income" countries are defined as those with roughly $200 to $600 GDP per capita, and "substantial" domestic market is defined as a total GDP in excess of $3.5 billion (to exclude entrepot economies while including at the margin such countries as Greece and Chile); both measurements were made for the year 1955.

2. See Alfred Maizels, *Industrial Growth and World Trade* (Cambridge, Eng., 1963), p. 59. It is probably fair to say that the United States surplus agricultural disposal program (P.L. 480) has also had a depressing effect on the rate of growth of commercial import demand for temperate agricultural commodities in developing countries.

3. The election of 1973 confirmed the dominant positions of the Peronist and Radical parties in Argentina, although the former alone won almost half the total popular vote. This result is widely interpreted to represent not so much the enhanced power of organized labor as it does popular repudiation of the former military regime and general dissatisfaction with the ineffectiveness of government, particularly on the part of youth. The electorate has therefore shown what is is against; it is up to the new administration to try to win the support of a viable majority of organized labor, the middle classes, and young people for a positive new program.

4. In this respect see Austin Ranney, ed., *Political Science and Public*

Policy (Chicago, 1968), and his review article in Social Science Research Council, *Items*, 22 (September 1968). The contrast between the "rational" economic and the bureaucratic approaches to decision-making is also exceedingly well analyzed in Graham Allison, *The·Essence of Decision* (Boston, 1971).

5. On this point see in particular C. E. Lindblom, "Tinbergen on Policy Making," *Journal of Political Economy*, 66 (December 1958), 531-538; H. A. Simon, "A Behavioral Model of Rational Choice," *Quarterly Journal of Economics*, 69 (February 1955), 99-118, and "Theories of Decision-Making in Economics and Behavioral Science," *American Economic Review*, 49 (June 1959), 253-283.

6. Charles E. Lindblom, *The Policy-Making Process* (Englewood Cliffs, N.J., 1968), pp. 25-26.

7. H. A. Simon, "Theories of Decision-Making," p. 255.

8. Lindblom, *The Policy-Making Process,* pp. 26-27.

9. In this regard see the interesting article by Carl Kaysen, "Model-Makers and Decision-Makers: Economists and the Policy Process," *The Public Interest*, 12 (Summer 1968), 80-95.

10. The quotations are, respectively, from Samuel P. Huntington, *Political Order in Changing Societies* (New Haven, 1968), p. 196, and Kalman H. Silvert, *The Conflict Society*, rev. ed. (New York, 1966), p. 88. See also Tomas R. Fillol, *Social Factors in Economic Development: The Argentine Case* (Cambridge, Mass., 1961), and Albert O. Hirschman, "Models of Reformmongering," *Quarterly Journal of Economics*, 77 (May 1963), especially pp. 250-257 and n. 5. The word "compromise" in fact has no exact counterpart in the Spanish language; the customary Spanish synonyms imply moral turpitude or laxity on the part of the compromiser.

Appendix C. Argentine National Accounts

1. See Banco Central de la República Argentina, *La renta nacional de la República Argentina* (Buenos Aires, 1946).

2. See Secretaría de Asuntos Económicos, *Producto e ingreso de la Republica Argentina en el período 1935-1954* (Buenos Aires, 1955).

3. CONADE-CEPAL, *Distribución del ingreso y cuentas nacionales en Argentina* (Buenos Aires, 1965), and United Nations, *Economic Development and Income Distribution in Argentina* (New York 1969); Banco Central de la República Argentina, *Producto bruto interno de la República Argentina, 1950 to 1962*, supplement to the *Boletín Estadístico*, no. 2 (February 1964), and *Origen del producto y composición del gasto nacional*, supplement to the *Boletín Estadístico*, no. 6 (June 1966).

4. See Banco Central de la República Argentina, *Origen del producto y distribución del ingreso, 1950-69*, supplement to the *Boletín Estadístico*, no. 1 (January 1971), and *Estimaciones del gasto nacional e inversión bruta interna, 1950-1970*, supplement to the *Boletín Estadístico* (March 1971), pp. 75-77.

5. United Nations, Department of Economic and Social Affairs, *El desarrollo económico de la Argentina,* Appendix, "Algunos estudios especiales y estadísticas macroeconómicas preparadas para el informe."

6. Di Tella Institute, *Relevamiento de la estructura regional de la economía argentina* (Buenos Aires, 1961).

Appendix E. Balance of Payments Estimates

1. See Banco Central de la República Argentina, *La evolución del balance de pagos de la República Argentina* (Buenos Aires, 1952).

2. See Banco Central de la República Argentina, *Balance de pagos de la República Argentina, 1951-1958,* supplement to the *Boletín Estadístico,* no. 1 (January 1960).

3. See CONADE-CEPAL, *Distribución del ingreso,* I, 175.

4. See Banco Central de la República Argentina, *Annual Reports* for 1946, 1947, 1948, and 1958, and *Balance de pagos,* 1958.

Appendix F. Monetary and Fiscal Statistics

1. Banco Central de la República Argentina, *Estadísticas monetarias y bancarias, 1940-1960,* supplement to the *Boletín Estadístico,* no. 6 (June 1962).

2. In this regard see Itzcovich and Feldman, *Un sistema de transacciones financieras para la Argentina (1955 to 1965),* and Juan Sourrouille, "Un esquema para las transacciones financieras en la Argentina," mimeo for a symposium on capital markets, Buenos Aires, 1972.

3. Up to 1970 contributions to international organizations were included with "exchange differentials" under government in the monetary accounts, whereas liabilities to these organizations were registered under "factors of absorption." Since this year the latter have been included among net foreign assets.

4. See Banco Central de la República Argentina, *Estadísticas monetarias,* p. 67.

5. See Decree no. 8586/47.

6. For further details on adjustment in the fiscal accounts contained in this study see CONADE-CEPAL, *Distribucion del ingreso,* I, 167-173.

Bibliography

Books, Documents, Journal Articles, and Reports

Adekunle, Joseph O. "The Demand for Money: Evidence from Developed and Less Developed Economies," *IMF Staff Papers*, 15 (July 1968), 220-266.
_____ "Rates of Inflation in Industrial, Other Developed, and Less Developed Countries, 1949-65," *IMF Staff Papers*, 15 (November 1968), 531-559.
Aldabe, Hernan, and Willy Van Rijckeghem. "The Use of Simulation for Forecasting Changes in the Argentine Cattle Stock," paper presented at the Bellagio Conference, Harvard Development Advisory Service, June 1966.
Aleman, Roberto T. *Como superar la crisis económica actual: Hacia una política argentina de inversiones*. Buenos Aires, Selección Contable, 1956.
Alexander, Robert J. *The Perón Era*. New York, Columbia University Press, 1951.
Allison, Graham. *The Essence of Decision*. Boston, Little, Brown, 1971.
Almada, Miguel A., and Hector L. Diéguez. *Protección efectiva y tipo de cambio*. Internal Working Paper No. 64. Buenos Aires, Instituto Torcuato Di Tella, December 1968.
Argentina 1930-1960. Anthology. Buenos Aires, Editorial Sur, 1961.
Argentine Government. Banco Central de la República Argentina. *Balance de pagos, período 1966-71*. Buenos Aires, 1972.
_____ _____ *Distribución funcional del ingreso en la República Argentina 1950-1968*. Buenos Aires, 1970.
_____ _____ *Evolución de la economía durante el año 1966*. Buenos Aires, January 16, 1967.
_____ _____ *Evolución de la economiá durante el primer trimestre de 1967*. Buenos Aires, May 12, 1967.
_____ _____ *Inversiones y fuentes de recursos, balances agregados y resultados de un conjunto de sociedades anónimas nacionales: años 1955-59*. Buenos Aires, November 1961.
_____ _____ *Origen del producto y distribución del ingreso 1950-1969. Buenos Aires, January 1971*.
_____ _____ *Reforma del sistema financiero argentino*. Buenos Aires, 1971.
_____ _____ *Régimen de financiación de exportaciones promocionadas*. September 3, 1969.
_____ _____ *Reseña de los acontecimientos monetarios, bancarios y y cambiarios en la Argentina desde 1963*. Buenos Aires, November 1966.

238   Bibliography

_____ _____ *Síntesis de las disposiciones cambiarias y de los regimenes de importación y exportación vigentes en la República Argentina.* Buenos Aires, December 31, 1962.

_____ Comisión Asesora Honoraria para la Industria del Tractor. *El tractor en la Argentina.* Buenos Aires, May 1969.

_____ Consejo Económico Nacional. "Examen de la situación económica del pais," mimeo, Buenos Aires, January 31, 1949.

_____ _____ "Plan de acción en materia económica," mimeo, Buenos Aires, June 1, 1949.

_____ _____ "Situatión de divisas al 31 de diciembre de 1949 y estimación del probable balance de pagos para 1950," mimeo, Buenos Aires, 1950.

_____ _____ "Situación económica y perspectivas—año 1950," mimeo, Buenos Aires, 1950.

_____ _____ "Situación económica actual y perspectivas para 1952," mimeo, Buenos Aires, 1951.

_____ Consejo Federal de Inversiones. *Gastos e ingresos públicos 1964-1965.* Buenos Aires, 1968.

_____ _____ *Política fiscal en la Argentina.* Buenos Aires, 1963.

_____ _____ *Programa conjunto para el desarrollo agropecuario e industrial.* Buenos Aires, November 1962.

_____ Consejo Nacional de Desarrollo (CONADE). *Análisis de la economía argentina.* Buenos Aires, May 1968.

_____ _____ and United Nations Economic Commission for Latin America (CEPAL), *Distribución del ingreso y cuentas nacionales en la Argentina.* Buenos Aires, 1965.

_____ _____ *Estimación y análisis del gasto público: período 1955-1961.* Buenos Aires, October 1963.

_____ _____ *Evolución y perspectivas de la producción de carne vacuna.* Buenos Aires, December 1965.

_____ _____ *Informe sobre las condiciones de comercialización de productos alimenticios en la Capital Federal y Gran Buenos Aires.* Buenos Aires, 1965.

_____ _____ *Ingresos y gastos corrientes del sector público nacional—series estadísticas 1955-1966.* Buenos Aires, December 1967.

_____ _____ *Plan nacional de desarrollo 1965-1969.* Buenos Aires, 1965.

_____ _____ *Plan nacional de desarrollo 1970-1974.* Buenos Aires, 1970.

_____ _____ *Plan nacional de desarrollo y seguridad 1971-1975.* Buenos Aires, 1971.

_____ _____ *Presupuesto económico nacional 1965 (informe preliminar).* Buenos Aires, June 1965.

_____ _____ *Resultados de la encuesta sobre expectativas de producción e inversión de las empresas industriales..* Buenos Aires, March 1965.

_____ _____ *Serie anual de la población de la República Argentina por sexo y grupos de edades, 1947/1970.* Buenos Aires, 1965.

_____ Direccion Nacional de Estadística y Censos, later Instituto Nacional de Estadística y Censos. *Censo nacional de población, familias y viviendas; resultados provisionales.* Buenos Aires, 1970.

——— ——— *Censo nacional económico, industria manufacturera.* Part I. Buenos Aires, 1970.

——— ——— *Costo del nivel de vida en la Capital Federal.* Buenos Aires, 1968.

——— ——— *Hechos demográficos en la República Argentina 1961-1966.* Vol. I. Buenos Aires, 1968.

——— ——— *Intercambio comercial argentino según N.A.B.—años 1967 y 1968.* Buenos Aires, 1968.

——— Junta Consultativa Nacional. *Respuesta a la consulta del gobierno de la nación.* Buenos Aires, Imprenta del Congreso de la Nación, 1956.

——— Ministerio de Asuntos Técnicos. *Anuario esadístico de la República Argentina.* Buenos Aires, 1948/1950.

——— Ministerio de Economía y Trabajo. *Política económica argentina: discursos del Ministro de Económia y Trabajo.* Buenos Aires, 1968.

——— ——— *Speeches by the Minister of Economy and Labour, Dr. Jose Maria Dagnino Pastore.* Buenos Aires, 1969.

——— Ministerio de Hacienda. *Exposiciones del Señor Ministro Dr. Alberto Krieger Vasena.* Buenos Aires, 1957.

——— Ministerio de Industria, Comercio y Minería. *Exportaciones argentinas clasificadas según grado de elaboración y tradicionalidad, años 1966/1970.* Buenos Aires, 1972.

——— Ministerio de Trabajo y Seguridad Social. *Conflictos del trabajo.* Buenos Aires, 1965.

——— ——— *Informe del gobierno argentino sobre asuntos laborales.* Buenos Aires, 1965.

——— ——— *Sueldos y jornales del trabajador agropecuario.* Buenos Aires, n.d.

——— Presidencia de la Nación. *La política económica argentina.* Buenos Aires, 1967.

——— Secretaría de Prensa. *Reseña de la obra de gobierno.* Buenos Aires, October 1963-June 1964.

Arnaudo, Aldo A. *Análisis espectral de los precios mayoristas en Argentina.* Córdoba, Universidad Nacional de Córdoba, 1967.

——— "Un estudio sobre la velocidad de la inflación en Argentina 1958-66," mimeo, Seminario Interno del Centro de Investigaciones Económicas, Universidad Nacional de Córdoba, December 1969.

Aujac, Henri. "Inflation and the Monetary Consequence of the Behavior of Social Groups: A Working Hypothesis," *International Economic Papers*, no. 4, 1954 (originally published in French in *Economie Appliquée*, 3 [April/June 1950], 280-300).

Bacha, Edmar, and Lance Taylor. "Foreign Exchange Shadow Prices: A Critical Review of Current Theories," *Quarterly Journal of Economics*, 85 (May 1971), 197-224.

Balassa, Bela. "The Purchasing Power Parity Doctrine: A Reappraisal," *Journal of Political Economy*, 72 (December 1964), 584-596.

——— "Trade Policy and Planning in Korea," *American Economic Review*, 61 (May 1971), 178-187.

Balboa, Manuel. *Comparación de la estructura intersectorial de la producción de Argentina y de Perú.* Santiago, U.N./ECLA, May 20, 1959.
Ballesteros, Mario A. "Argentine Agriculture, 1908-1954: A Study in Growth and Decline," Ph.D. diss., University of Chicago, 1958.
Banco Ganadero Argentino. *Mercados y precios del ganado vacuno.* Buenos Aires, n.d.
Baranson, Jack. *Automotive Industries in Developing Countries.* World Bank Staff Occasional Papers No. 8. Baltimore, Johns Hopkins Press, 1969.
_____ "The Heavy Mechanical Equipment Industry in Argentina," mimeo, 1965.
Barraclough, Solon L. "Agricultural Policy and Land Reform," *Journal of Political Economy,* Part II, 78 (July/August 1970), 906-947.
Basch, Antonín, and Milic Kybal. *Capital Markets in Latin America: A General Survey and Six Country Studies.* New York, Praeger, 1970.
Basevi, Giorgio. "Domestic Demand and Ability to Export," *Journal of Political Economy,* 78 (March/April 1970), 330-337.
Beker, Víctor A. "Elasticidades de oferta de la producción agropecuaria: trigo, maíz y carne," *Económica,* 15 (May-August 1969), 145-181.
Belloni, Alberto. *Del anarquismo al peronismo: historia del movimiento obrero argentino.* Buenos Aires, Peña Lillo, 1960.
Berlinski, Julio. "The Behaviour of Provincial Finances in Argentina," Ph.D. diss., Harvard University, 1969.
Blanco, Eugenio A. "Política monetaria y crediticia," mimeo, 1966.
_____ *La política presupuestaria, la deuda pública y la economía nacional.* Buenos Aires, Ministerio de Hacienda, 1956.
_____ *Realidad económica argentina.* Buenos Aires, Ministerio de Hacienda, 1956.
Blanco, General Guido. "Sin siderurgia no hay independencia," *Clarín,* September 28, 1966.
Bortnik, Rubén. *El ejército argentino y el arte de lo posible.* Buenos Aires, Ediciones Güemes, 1967.
Brodersohn, Mario S. "Estrategias de estabilización y expansión en la Argentina: 1959-67," mimeo, n.d.
_____ ed. *Estrategias de industrialización para la Argentina.* Buenos Aires, Instituto Torcuato Di Tella, 1970.
_____ "Fiscal Policy and the Composition of Government Purchases: The Case of Argentina," *Public Finance,* 19 (1964), 228-238.
_____ Regional Development and Industrial Location Policy in Argentina. Internal Working Paper No. 29. Buenos Aires, Instituto Torcuato Di Tella, July 1967.
Broner, Julio, and D. Larriqueta. *La revolución industrial argentina.* Buenos Aires, Editorial Sudamericana, 1969.
Bronfenbrenner, Martin, and F. D. Holzman. "A Survey of Inflation Theory," *American Economic Review,* 53 (September 1963), 593-661.
Bronfman, José A. "Pricing of Public Service in Argentina: The Telephone

Case," paper, Harvard University, spring 1967.

Bruton, Henry J. *Latin American Exports and Import Substitution Policies*, Research Memo No. 32, Center for Development Economics, Williams College, November 1969.

—————— "Productivity Growth in Latin America," *American Economic Review*, 57 (December 1967), 1099-1116.

CAFADE, National Institute of Agricultural Technology (INTA), National Development Council (CONADE), Secretariat of Agriculture and Livestock, National Meat Board, Banco Central, College of Economic Sciences, USAID/Argentina. *Agricultural Development and Economic Growth*, Buenos Aires, 1962.

Cafiero, Antonio F. *Cinco años después* . . . Buenos Aires, El Gráfico, 1961.

Cámara Argentina de Fabricantes de Automotores. *Significación económica de la industria automotriz*, no. 2, 1963.

Canton, Darío. *Party Alignments in Argentina Between 1912 and 1955.* Internal Working Paper No. 31. Buenos Aires, Centro de Investigaciones Sociales, Instituto Torcuato Di Tella, September 1967.

—————— *La Primera encuesta política argentina*. Internal Working Paper No. 88. Buenos Aires, Instituto Torcuato Di Tella, August, 1967.

Carranza, R. G. "Informe hecha para la CGE," mimeo, Buenos Aires, 1969.

Carri, Roberto. *Sindicatos y poder en la Argentina*. Buenos Aires, Editorial Sudestada, 1967.

Ceconi, Tulio Alberto. "El desarrollo económico argentino," paper, Rosario, August 1968.

Chenery, Hollis B., and Lance Taylor. "Development Patterns: Among Countries and Over Time," *Review of Economics and Statistics*, 50 (November 1968), 391-416.

Chiaramonte, José Carlos. *Nacionalismo y liberalismo económico en Argentina 1860-1880*. Buenos Aires, Solar/Hachette, 1971.

Chudnovsky, D., and J. Katz. "Patentes e importación de tecnología," mimeo, Buenos Aires, 1970.

Ciria, Alberto. *Partidos y poder en la Argentina moderna (1930-46)*. Buenos Aires, Jorge Alvarez, Editor. 1964.

Clague, Christopher. "The Determinants of Efficiency in Manufacturing Industries in an Underdeveloped Country," *Economic Development and Cultural Change*, 18 (January 1970), 188-205.

Cohen, Benjamin I. "Measuring the Short-Run Impact of a Country's Import Restrictions on Its Exports," *Quarterly Journal of Economics*, 80 (August 1966), 456-462.

Colomé, Reinaldo Antonio. "Funciones de oferta agropecuaria de la región pampeana en el período 1940-1960," chap. 3 of Ph.D. diss. "La oferta agropecuaria de la región pampeana," Universidad Nacional de Córdoba, July 1966.

"El comercio exterior argentino y las medidas de estímulo a las exportaciones," mimeo, 1971.

Confederación General del Trabajo. *Hacia el cambio de estructuras.* Buenos Aires, 1965.

Confederación General Económica (CGE), Instituto de Investigaciones Económicas y Financieras and Consejo Federal de Inversiones, *Programa conjunto para el desarrollo agropecuario e industrial,* Buenos Aires, series 1962-1964.

———— *Estudios sobre la económia,* series 1968-1969.

Consejo Federal de Inversiones. *Bases para el desarrollo regional argentino.* Buenos Aires, 1963.

———— *Relevamiento de la estructura regional de la economía argentina.* Buenos Aires, 1962.

Constitución de la nación argentina y estatuto de la revolución argentina. Buenos Aires, Editorial Huemul S.A., 1966.

Copper, R. F. V. "The Employment of Fertilizer as a Factor Limiting Agricultural Development in Argentina," Part II, *Review of the River Plate,* July 12, 1968,

Cornbilt, Oscar. *Inmigrantes y empresarios en la política argentina.* Internal Working Paper No. 20. Buenos Aires, Instituto Torcuato Di Tella, 1966.

Costanzo, G. A. "Economic Stabilization Programs in Latin America," series of lectures at Centro de Estudios Monetarios Latinoamericanos, Mexico, August 1960.

Cristiá, P., and others. *Argentina en la postguerra.* Buenos Aires, Editorial Rosario, 1946.

Cuneo, Dardo. *Comportamiento y crisis de la clase empresaria.* Buenos Aires, Planear, 1967.

Cuzminsky, Rosa. "Debates contemporáneos: algunas opiniones polémicas sobre la política económica de la Argentina," *Revista de la Universidad de Buenos Aires,* 7 (January-March 1962), 129-153.

Dagnino Pastore, José María. *The Economic Program for 1970.* Buenos Aires, Ministry of Economy and Labor, January 22, 1970.

———— *Ingreso y dinero: Argentina 1935-60.* Buenos Aires, Fundación de Investigaciones Económicas Latinoamericanas, 1966.

———— *Política económica argentina 1969-70.* Buenos Aires, Marcos Victor Durry, n.d.

———— *Productos exportables: resultados de encuestas.* Internal Working Paper No. 16. Buenos Aires, Instituto Torcuato Di Tella, n.d.

Daniels, Mark R. "Differences in Efficiency Among Industries in Developing Countries," *American Economic Review,* 59 (March 1969), 159-171.

Davis, O. A., and A. B. Whinston. "Piecemeal Policy in the Theory of the Second Best," *Review of Economic Studies,* 34 (July 1967), 323-331.

De Castro, C. Benítez *El desarrollo económico argentino.* Buenos Aires, Arayú, 1955.

De Imaz, José Luis. *Los que mandan.* Buenos Aires, EUDEBA, 1964.

De Janvry, Alain. "Empirical Analysis of Consumer Behavior: An Application to Argentina," mimeo, Buenos Aires, Seminario interno del Centro de Investigaciones Económicas, Instituto Torcuato Di Tella, July 1969.

Delaplaine, John. *The Structure of Economic Growth in Colombia and Argentina,* Harvard Development Advisory Service, Report No. 39, June 1966.

Del Mazo, Gabriel. *El radicalismo: el movimiento de intransigencia y renovación (1945-1957).* Buenos Aires, Ediciones Gure, 1957.

De Pablo, Juan Carlos. "El costo de producción en la industria textil," *Revista de Ciencias Económicas,* 44 (July, August, September 1965), 291-315.

———— "Desocupación, salario real y políticas de reactivación," *Desarrollo Económico,* 11 (July 1971-March 1972), 249-261.

———— "La ley 17.224 y la distribución intragremial del peso de la política antinflacionaria," mimeo, n.d.

———— *Política antinflacionaria en la Argentina, 1967-1970.* Buenos Aires, Amorrortu, 1970.

Depres, Emile. "Stabilization and Monetary Policy in Less Developed Countries," in Jesse W. Markham and Gustav F. Papanek, eds., *Industrial Organization and Economic Development.* Boston, Houghton Mifflin, 1970.

Diamand, Marcelo. "Bases para una política industrial argentina," *Cuadernos del Centro de Estudios Industriales,* 1 (1969).

———— "Los cuatro tipos de inflación argentina," mimeo, n.d.

———— "Desarrollo industrial, política autárquica y capital extranjero," *Situación actual y perspectivas de la economía argentina,* 6 (1969), 35-66.

———— "Estrategia global del desarrollo industrial," *Cuadernos del Centro de Estudios Industriales,* 1 (1968), 27-57.

———— "La estructura productiva desequilibrada argentina y el tipo de cambio," *Desarrollo Económico,* 12 (April-June 1972), 25-47.

———— *El fondo monetario internacional y los paises subdesarrollados.* Buenos Aires, Movimiento Soluciones Económicas, April 1963.

———— "La naturaleza de la crisis económica argentina," preliminary version, mimeo, n.d.

———— "El plan, los contraplanes y las medidas económicas anunciadas," *El Cronista Comercial,* Buenos Aires, December 9, 1971, p. 1.

————"Porqué una maxi-devaluación sería recesiva e inflacionaria," *El Cronista Comercial,* August 11-19, 1971.

———— "El régimen de drawback generalizado y las exportaciones industriales," *El Cronista Comercial,* September 9-10, 1968.

———— "Seis falsos dilemas en el debate económico nacional," *Cuadernos del Centro de Estudios Industriales,* no. 5, 1971.

Diaz Alejandro, Carlos F. *Essays on the Economic History of the Argentine Republic.* New Haven, Yale University Press, 1970.

_____ *Exchange-Rate Devaluation in a Semi-Industrialized Country: The Experience of Argentina, 1955-1961.* Cambridge, Mass., M.I.T. Press, 1965.

_____ "Industrialization and Labor Productivity Differentials," *Review of Economics and Statistics*, 47 (May 1965), 207-214.

Diéguez, Hector L. *Argentina y Australia: algunos aspectos de su desarrollo económico comparado.* Internal Working Paper No. 53. Buenos Aires, Centro de Investigaciones Económicas, Instituto Torcuato Di Tella, July 1968.

_____ *Money, Prices and Fiscal Lags: A Comment.* Internal Working Paper No. 56. Buenos Aires, Instituto Torcuato Di Tella, August 1968.

Di Tella, Guido. "Objectivos específicos de una política industrial," *Cuadernos del Centro de Estudios Industriales*, 1 (1968), 59-83.

_____ *Teoría de la firma y restricción financiera.* Internal Working Paper No. 6. Instituto Torcuato Di Tella, n.d.

Di Tella, Torcuato S., Gino Germani, and Jorge Graciarena. *Argentina, sociedad de masas.* Buenos Aires, EUDEBA, 1965.

_____ and T. Halperin, Eds. *Los fragmentos del poder.* Buenos Aires, Jorge Alvarez, 1969.

Diz, Adolfo César. *Determinantes de la oferta de dinero en la República Argentina (1935-1962)*, cuaderno no. 64-1, Tucumán, Universidad Nacional de Tucumán, April 1964.

_____ "Money and Prices in Argentina 1935-1962," in David Meiselman, ed., *Varieties of Monetary Experience.* Chicago, University of Chicago Press, 1970.

_____ *La oferta de dinero en la República Argentina (1935-1962)*, cuaderno no. 63-3, Tucumán, Universidad Nacional de Tucumán, July 1963.

Donges, Juergen B. "Brazil's Trotting Peg: A New Approach to Greater Exchange-Rate Flexibility in Less Developed Countries?" mimeo, 1972.

_____ and W. Kasper. "Mayor flexibilidad des los tipos de cambio y su importancia para los paises en desarrollo," *El Trimestre Económico*, 37 (1970), 823ff.

Dunkerley, Harold B. "Exchange Rate Systems in Conditions of Continuing Inflation—Lessons from Colombian Experience," in Gustav F. Papanek, ed., *Development Policy—Theory and Practice.* Cambridge, Mass., Harvard University Press, 1968.

Dutton, Dean S. "The Demand for Money and the Price Level," *Journal of Political Economy*, 79 (September/October 1971), 1161-1170.

Eaton, Jonathan W. "Effective Devaluation as an Export Incentive in Less Developed Countries," B.A. thesis, Harvard University, March 1972.

Elias, Victor Jorge. "Estimates of Value Added, Capital and Labor in Argentine Manufacturing, 1935-1963," Ph.D. diss., University of Chicago, 1969.

Eriksson, John R. "Notes on Export Promotion Policies and Experience in Argentina," mimeo, November 1966.

———— "Wage Structures and Economic Development in Selected Latin American Countries: A Comparative Analysis," Ph.D. diss., University of California, Berkeley, 1966.

Felix, David. "Economic Development: Take-Offs into Unsustained Growth," *Social Research*, 36 (Summer 1969), 267-293.

———— *Did Import Substituting Industrialization in Argentina Save Foreign Exchange in 1953-1960? A Report on Some Findings.* Internal Working Paper No. 7. Buenos Aires, Instituto Torcuato Di Tella, September 1965.

———— "The Dilemma of Import Substitution—Argentina," chap. 3 in Gustav F. Papanek, ed., *Development Policy—Theory and Practice,* Cambridge, Mass., Harvard University Press, 1968.

———— *Import Substituting Industrialization and Industrial Exporting in Argentina.* Buenos Aires, Centro de Investigaciones Económicas, Instituto Torcuato Di Tella, September 7, 1964.

———— *Import Substitution and Industrial Exporting: An Analysis of Recent Argentine Experience,* paper presented at the 21st Annual Latin American Conference, University of Florida, February 17-20, 1971.

———— "Más allá de la sustitución de importaciones: un dilema latinoamericano," in *Estrategias de industrialización para la Argentina.* Buenos Aires, Instituto Torcuato Di Tella, 1970.

———— "Some Notes on the Implementation of Argentine Industrialization Policy," mimeo, September 5, 1966.

———— *Subsidies, Depression and Non-Traditional Industrial Exporting in Argentina,* Economic Development Report No. 107, Development Advisory Service, Harvard University, September 1968.

Fernández Balmaceda, Osvaldo, Reynaldo Felix Bajraj, Guillermo A. R. Calvo, and Julio Alberto Piekarz. "Construcción de modelos de insumo-producto en la república argentina," mimeo, Consejo Nacional de Desarrollo, n.d.

Fernández López, Manuel, and Silvestre Damus. *Determinantes en la demanda de liquidez por el sector privado en la Argentina, 1959-63.* Buenos Aires, Instituto de Investigaciones Económicas y Sociales de la Universidad de Buenos Aires, 1964.

Ferrer, Aldo. *La economía argentina: las etapas de su desarrollo y problemas actuales.* Mexico, Fondo de Cultura Económica, 1963.

———— "Hacia un sistema industrial integrado y abierto," *Cuadernos del Dentro de Estudios Industrialies,* 1 (1968), 3-25.

———— "Industrias básicas, integración y corporaciones internacionales— notas para un análisis de la integración industrial de América Latina," paper presented at the Consejo Latinoamericano de Ciencias Sociales, Lima, October 1968.

———— and Alberto Fracchia. "La producción, ingresos y capitalización del sector agropecuario en el período 1950-1960," mimeo, Buenos Aires, CAFADE, April 1961.

———— and E. L. Wheelwright. *Industrialization in Argentina and*

Australia: A Comparative Study. Internal Working Paper No. 23. Buenos Aires, Instituto Torcuato Di Tella, June 1966.

FIAT, Oficina de Estudios para la Colaboración Económica Internacional. *Balance de Pagos de la Argentina.* Buenos Aires, 1963.

――――― ―――― *Importaciónes, industrialización, y desarrollo económico en la Argentina: evolución y perspectivas.* Buenos Aires, 1963.

――――― ―――― *Nivel de la economía argentina—síntesis de 1971 y perspectivas para 1972.* Buenos Aires, 1972.

Fienup, Darrell F., Russell H. Brannon, and Frank Fender. *The Agricultural Development of Argentina.* New York, Praeger, 1969.

Fillol, Tomás Roberto. *Social Factors in Economic Development: The Argentine Case.* Cambridge, Mass., MIT Press, 1961.

Fleming, J. Marcus, "Exchange Depreciation, Financial Policy, and the Domestic Price Level," *IMF Staff Papers,* 6 (April 1958), 289ff.

Fletcher, Lehman B., and William G.Merril. *Latin American Agricultural Development and Policies.* Ames, Iowa, Iowa State University, September 1968.

Fracchia, A., and A. Balboa. "Fixed Reproducible Capital in Argentina 1935-1955," *Income and Wealth,* 8 (London, 1959), 274-292.

Freire, Remy. "Price Incentives in Argentine Agriculture," paper presented at the Bellagio Conference of Harvard Development Advisory Service, June 1966.

Friedman, Milton, ed. *Studies in the Quantity Theory of Money.* Chicago, University of Chicago, 1957.

――――― "The Supply of Money and Changes in Prices and Output," in Edwin Dean, ed., *The Controversy Over the Quantity Theory of Money.* Boston, Heath and Co., 1965.

Frigerio, Rogelio. "El camino del desarrollo," *Clarín,* September 10, 1964.

――――― *Crecimiento económico y democracia.* Buenos Aires, Losada, 1963.

――――― "Integración regional, nación y monopolios," *Clarín,* February 18, 1968 and February 25, 1968.

――――― "Medidas y pautas del desarrollo," *Clarín,* July 24, 1966.

――――― *Nacionalismo, potencias industriales y subdesarrollo.* Buenos Aires, Editorial Concordia S.R.L., 1961.

――――― *Petroleo.* Buenos Aires, Editorial Desarrollo, 1964.

Frondizi, Arturo. *Estrategia y táctica del movimiento nacional.* Buenos Aires, Editorial Desarrollo, 1964.

――――― *Política económica national.* Buenos Aires, Arayu, 1963.

――――― *La política exterior argentina.* Buenos Aires, D. Francisco A. Colombo, 1962.

Fucaraccio, A. J. E. *Modelo de previsión a corto plazo.* Buenos Aires, CONADE, November 1965.

Fundación de Investigaciones Económicas Latinoamericanas (FIEL). Comparaciones de índices de costo de vida en la Argentina. *Buenos Aires, December 1966.*

――――― *Estimación del producto bruto nacional sobre la base de estadísticas monetarias,* Estudios de Coyuntura, no. 2, Buenos Aires, November 1966.

Galletti, Alfredo. *La realidad argentina en el siglo XX: I, La política y los partidos.* Mexico, Fondo de Cultura Económica, 1961.

Galvez, Manuel. *Vida de Hipólito Yrigoyen.* 5th ed. Buenos Aires, Editorial Tor, 1959.

García, Valeriano F. *Control monetario y exceso de reservas.* Buenos Aires Seminario interno del Centro de Investigaciones Económicas, Instituto Torcuato Di Tella, September 1968.

García Martinez, Carlos. *La inflación argentina.* Buenos Aires, Guillermo Kraft Ltda., 1965.

Germani, Gino. *Estructura Social de la Argentina.* Buenos Aires, Raigal.

———— *Política y sociedad en una época de transición de la sociedad tradicional a la sociedad de masas.* Buenos Aires, Editorial Paidos, 1962.

González, N., and others. *Esquema de la economía argentina.* Buenos Aires, Añeté, 1957.

Gregory, Peter. "Wage Structures in Latin America," discussion paper no. 4, Center for Economic Research, University of Minnesota, June 1971.

Grunwald, Joseph. "Invisible Hands in Inflation and Growth," mimeo, Conference on Inflation and Growth in Latin America, Rio de Janeiro, January 1963.

———— Martin Carnoy, and Miguel S. Wionczek. *Latin American Economic Integration and the United States.* Washington, D.C., Brookings Institution, January 1970.

Guadagni, Alieto A. *La elasticidad de sustitución entre los factores productivos. Cuantificación de su magnitud en la economía argentina.* Internal Working Paper No. 27. Buenos Aires, Instituto Torcuato Di Tella, October 1965.

Gugliamelli, General Juan E. "Desarrollo es sinónimo de industria pesada e infraestructura," *Clarín,* March 10, 1965.

Gurley, John G. "Financial Structures in Developing Countries," in David Krivine, ed., *Fiscal and Monetary Problems in Developing States.* Proceedings of theThird Rehovoth Conference. New York, Praeger, 1967.

Haldi, J., and D. Whitcomb. "Economies of Scale in Industrial Plants," *Journal of Political Economy,* Part I, 75 (August 1967), 373-385.

Halem, George N. *The IMF and the Flexibility of Exchange Rates,* Princeton Essays in International Finance, Princeton University Press, 1971.

Harberger, Arnold. "The Dynamics of Inflation in Chile," in *Measurement in Economics: Studies in Mathematical Economics in Memory of Yehuda Grunfeld.* Stanford, Stanford University Press, 1963.

Hart, Albert. "Indicadores económicos de corto plazo, capaces de interpolar y de extrapolar las cifras de producto bruto en forma trimestral," mimeo, Buenos Aires, August 1964.

Harvard Joint Tax Program. *Problems of Tax Administration in Latin America.* Baltimore, Johns Hopkins Press, 1965.

Hayn, Rolf. "Capital Formation and Argentina's Price-Cost Structure,

1935-1958," *Review of Economics and Statistics*, 44 (August 1962), 340-343.

Hinrichs, Harley H. "Determinants of Government Revenue Shares in Less Developed Countries," *Economic Journal*, 75 (September 1965), 546-556.

———— *La estructura tributaria durante el desarrollo.* Mexico, Centro de Estudios Monetarios Latinoamericanos, 1967.

———— "Tax Strategies for Financing Economic Development: General Theory As Applied to Afghanistan, Nigeria, and Argentina," mimeo, n.d.

Hirschman, Albert O. "Models of Reformmongering," *Quarterly Journal of Economics*, 77 (May 1963), 236-257.

Hoffman, W. G. *The Growth of Industrial Economies.* New York, Oxford University Press. 1958.

Horowitz, Morris A. *The Legacy of Juan Perón.* Boston, Bureau of Business and Economic Research, Northeastern University, 1963.

Hufbauer, G. C. "West Pakistan Exports: Policies and Problems," in Walter P. Falcon and Gustav F. Papanek, eds. *Development Policy II—The Pakistan Experience.* Cambridge, Mass., Harvard University Press, 1971.

Humphrey, David B. "Changes in Protection and Inflation in Argentina, 1953-1966," *Oxford Economic Papers*, 21 (July 1969), 196-219.

Huntington, Samuel P. *Political Order in Changing Societies.* New Haven, Yale University Press, 1968.

Illia, Arturo U. *La política económica del gobierno constitucional.* Buenos Aires, 1966.

Instituto para el Desarrollo de Ejecutivos en la Argentina. *Indice de costo de vida para ejecutivos.* Buenos Aires, March 1969.

International Development Association. *The Commodity Problem*, Staff Study of the Economic Department, International Bank for Reconstruction and Development, May 12, 1964.

International Monetary Fund. *Argentina—Use of the Fund's Resources,* Washington, D.C., January 5, 1966.

Itzcovitch, Samuel. "Análisis de la estructura financiera," mimeo, Buenos Aires, Seminario Interno del Centro de Investigaciones Económicas, Instituto Torcuato Di Tella, July 19, 1968.

———— "Análisis de la estructura financiera argentina, 1955-1965," *Desarrollo Económico*, 8 (January-March 1969), 487-509.

———— and Ernesto Feldman. *Un sistema de transacciones financieras para la Argentina (1955-1965).* Internal Working Paper No. 40. Buenos Aires, Instituto Torcuato Di Tella, February 1969.

Jarach, Dino. *Estudio sobre las finanzas argentinas 1947-1957.* Buenos Aires, Ediciones Depalma, 1959.

Jarvis, Lovell Stuber. "Supply Response in the Cattle Industry—The Argentine Case: 1937/38-1966/67," Ph.D. diss., MIT, 1969.

Joy, Leonard, and Oscar Braun. "A Model of Economic Stagnation—A Case Study of the Argentine Economy," *The Economic Journal*, 78 (December 1968), 868-887.

Katz, Jorge M. "Una interpretación de largo plazo del crecimiento industrial argentino," *Desarrollo Económico*, 8 (January-March 1969), 511-542.

_____ *Production Functions, Foreign Investment and Growth.* Amsterdam, North Holland Publishing Co., 1969.

_____ "The Sources of Manufacturing Growth in Australia and Argentina in the Period 1946-60," *Economic Record*, 44 (1968), 377-381.

Kaysen, Carl. "Model-Makers and Decision-Makers: Economists and the Policy Process," *The Public Interest*, 12 (Summer 1968), 80-95.

Kim, Hyong Chun, "Korea's Export Success, 1960-69," International Monetary Fund and World Bank, *Finance and Development*, 8 (March 1971), 14-20.

King, Timothy. "Development Strategy and Investment Criteria: Complementary or Competitive," *Quarterly Journal of Economics*, 80 (February 1966), 108-120.

Krieger, R. A. "Inflation Propagation in Argentina: A Short-Run Analysis," Ph.D. diss., University of Wisconsin, 1965.

Krieger Vasena, Adalbert. *Planificación y crecimiento económico.* Buenos Aires, Análisis, June 1964.

_____ *Política fiscal, inflación y desarrollo económico.* Buenos Aires, La Técnica Impresora S.A.C.I., June 1964.

Lary, Hal B. *Exports of Manufactures by Less Developed Countries.* New York, National Industrial Conference Board, 1966.

_____ *Imports of Manufactures from Less Developed Countries.* New York, National Bureau of Economic Research, 1968.

Laurant, Henry W. *Factors Affecting Foreign Investment in Argentina.* International Development Center, Stanford Research Institute, 1963.

Leibenstein, Harvey, "Allocative Efficiency vs. 'X-Efficiency,' " *American Economic Review*, 56 (June 1966), 392-395.

Lindblom, Charles E. *The Policy-Making Process.* Englewood Cliffs, N.J., Prentice-Hall, 1968.

_____ "Tinbergen on Policy Making," *Journal of Political Economy*, 66 (December 1958), 531-538.

Lipsey, R.S., and K. Lancaster. "The General Theory of Second Best," *Review of Economic Studies*, 24 (1956-1957).

Llorens de Azar, Carmen, and Rogelio Gende. *Precios unitarios de artículos de consumo y servicios, Capital Federal y provincias, 1901-1963.* Buenos Aires, Sección Estadística, Instituto Torcuato Di Tella, 1965.

Maizels, Alfred. *Industrial Growth and World Trade.* Cambridge, Eng., Cambridge University Press, 1963.

Mallon, Richard D. *Balance of Payments Adjustment in a Semi-Industrialized, Agricultural Export Economy: The Argentine Case,* Economic Development Report No. 109, Harvard Development Advisory Service, 1968.

_____ "Comment," in *Estrategias de industrialización para la Argentina.* Buenos Aires, Instituto Torcuato Di Tella, 1970.

_____ "Exchange Policy—Argentina," in Gustav F. Papanek, ed.,

Development Policy—Theory and Practice. Cambridge, Mass., Harvard University Press, 1968.

_____ "La industrialización y la sustitución de importaciones en la Argentina," in *Estrategias de industrialización para la Argentina.* Buenos Aires, Instituto Torcuato Di Tella, 1970.

_____ "Planning in Crisis," *Journal of Political Economy*, 78 (July/August 1970), Part II, 948-965.

Mamalakis, Markos. *The Theory of Sectoral Clashes*, reprint no. 9, The University of Wisconsin-Milwaukee Center for Latin American Studies, September 1970.

Maroni, Yves. "Argentina's Economic and Financial Record," mimeo, Board of Governors of the Federal Reserve System, September 1968.

Martínez de Hoz, José Alfredo. *La agricultura y la ganadería argentina en el período 1930-1960.* Buenos Aires, Editorial Sudamericana, 1967.

Martínez, I. Cavagua. *Sistema Bancario Argentino.* Buenos Aires, Arayú, 1954.

Masotta, Sabastián. *El movimiento sindical argentino.* Buenos Aires, Lacio, 1961.

Masson, Francis, and James Theberge. "External Capital Requirements and Economic Development: The Case of Argentina," mimeo, n.d.

_____ *Gap Evaluation: Argentina.* Washington, D.C., Agency for International Development, Department of State, n.d.

Maynard, Geoffrey, and Willy Van Rijckeghem. "Stabilization Policy in an Inflationary Economy: Argentina," in Gustav Papanek, ed., *Development Policy—Theory and Practice.* Cambridge, Mass., Harvard University Press, 1968.

_____ "Argentina 1967-70: A Stabilization Attempt That Failed," *Banca Nazionale del Lavoro Quarterly Review,* no. 103 (December 1972), 3-19.

Merkx, Gilbert. *Sectoral Clashes and Political Change: The Argentine Experience*, reprint no. 10, The University of Wisconsin-Milwaukee Center for Latin American Studies, September 1970.

Meyer, Arturo Carlos, *El comportamiento del ahorro de las empresas bajo condiciones inflacionarias.* Buenos Aires, Instituto Torcuato Di Tella, May 7, 1969.

Michalopoulos, Constantine. *Relative Prices, Capital Goods Imports and the Foreign Exchange Constraint: A Case Study of Argentina.* Discussion Paper No. 23. Washington, D.C., AID, November 1971.

Minhas, B. S. *An International Comparison of Factor Costs and Factor Use.* Amsterdam, North Holland Publishing Co., 1963.

Monti, Angel. *El acuerdo social.* Buenos Aires, Ediciones de Política Económica, 1967.

_____ *Factores del proceso inflacionario en América Latina.* Instituto Latinoamericano de Planificación Económica y Social, Economic Commission for Latin America, 1967.

Morley, Samuel A. "Import Demand and Import Substitution in Brazil," in

Howard S. Ellis, ed., *The Economy of Brazil.* Berkeley, University of California Press, 1969.

———— "Inflation and Stagnation in Brazil," *Economic Development and Cultural Change,* 19 (January 1971), 184-203.

Moyano Llerena, Carlos. "La cuestión de los salarios," *La Nación,* September 2, 1969.

Navarro Gerassi, Marysa. *Argentine Nationalism of the Right.* St. Louis, Mo., Social Science Institute, Washington University, 1965.

Nelson, Richard R. "A 'Diffusion' Model of International Productivity Differences in Manufacturing Industry," *American Economic Review,* 58 (December 1968), 1219-1248.

———— Paul T. Schultz, and Robert L. Slighton, *Structural Change in a Developing Economy.* Princeton, N.J., Princeton University Press, 1971.

———— M. J. Peck, and E. Kalachek. *Technology, Economic Growth, and Public Policy.* Washington, DC., Brookings Institution, 1967.

Ness, Walter Lee. "Inflation Expectations, the Interest Rate, and Financial Market Development," Ph.D. diss., M.I.T., 1969.

Nugent, Jeffrey B. "Country Study—Argentina," mimeo, AID Summer Research Project, 1965.

Oddone, Jacinto. *La burguesía terrateniente argentina.* 3d ed. Buenos Aires, Ediciones Libera, 1956.

Olivera, Julio. "Aspectos dinámicos de la inflación estructural," *Desarrollo Económico,* 7 (October-December 1967), 261-266.

Organization of American States/Inter-American Development Bank. *Sistemas tributarios de América Latina—Argentina.* Washington, D.C., 1966.

Orsolini, Mario Horacio. *Ejército argentino y crecimiento nacional.* Buenos Aires, Arayú, 1965.

Ortiz, Ricardo. *Historia Económica de la Argentina.* Buenos Aires, Pampa y Cielo, 1964.

Otrera, R. "Un modelo econométrico para analizar las exportaciones potenciales de carne argentina," Ph.D. diss., University of Texas, January 1966.

Pan American Union, CIDA. *Tenencia de la tierra y desarrollo socio-económico del sector agrícola, Argentina.* Washington, D.C., 1965.

Papanek, Gustav F., ed. *Development Policy—Theory and Practice.* Cambridge, Mass., Harvard University Press, 1968.

Park, Yung Chul. "The Variability of Velocity: An International Comparison," *IMF Staff Papers,* 17 (November 1970), 620-637.

Péron, Juan D. *Doctrina peronista: filosófica, política, social.* Buenos Aires, 1947.

Phillips, A. W. "Employment, Inflation, and Growth," *Economica,* 29 (February 1962), 1-16.

———— "The Relation Between Unemployment and the Rate of Change in Money Wage Rates," *Economica,* 25 (November 1958), 283-299.

Pinedo, Federico. *Siglo y medio de economía argentina*. Mexico, Centro de Estudios Monetarios Latinoamericanos, 1961.

Piñeiro, Martín Enrique. "Argentine Agriculture: Past and Potential Contributions to Country-Wide Economic Growth," Ph.D. diss., University of California, Davis, 1968.

———— and Alex F. McCalla. "Programming for Argentine Price Policy Analysis," *Review of Economics and Statistics*, 53 (February 1971), 59-66.

La política económica del gobierno constitucional. Buenos Aires, published clandestinely by members of the deposed Illia administration, 1966.

Portnoy, Leopoldo. *La realidad argentina en el siglo XX: análisis crítico de la economía*. Buenos Aires, Fondo de Cultura Económica, 1961.

Potash, Robert. *El ejército y la política en la Argentina, 1928-45*. Buenos Aires, Editorial Sudamericana, 1971.

Puiggrós, Rodolfo. *Libre empresa o nacionalización en la industria de la carne*. Buenos Aires, Editorial "Argumentos," 1957.

Ranney, Austin, ed. *Political Science and Public Policy*. Chicago, Markham Publishing Co., 1968.

———— "The Study of Policy Content: A Framework for Choice," *Items* 22 (September 1968), 25-31.

Reca, Lucio G. "El aumento de existencias de ganado vacuno en 1971," *Estudios sobre la economía argentina*, Instituto de Investigaciones Económicas y Financieras de la CGE, 11 (January 1972).

———— "Determinantes de la oferta agropecuaria en la Argentina, 1934/35-1966/67," *Estudios sobre la economía argentina*, Instituto de Investigaciones Económicas y Financieras de la CGE, no. 5 (August 1969), 57-65.

———— "Fertilización nitrogenada en maíz en la Argentina: resultados experimentales e implicaciones económicas," *Económica*, 16 (September-December 1970), 329-348.

———— "The Price and Production Duality within Argentine Agriculture, 1923-1965," Ph.D. diss., University of Chicago, December 1967.

Reder, Melvin W. "The Theoretical Problems of National Wage-Price Policy," *Canadian Journal of Economics*, 14 (February 1948), 46-61.

Risso Patrón, Roberto. *El agro y la cooperación internacional*. Buenos Aires, Arayú, 1963.

Romero, José Luis. *El desarrollo de las ideas en la sociedad argentina del siglo XX*. Mexico, Fondo de Cultura Económica, 1965.

Samuelson, Paul A., and Robert M. Solow. "Analytical Aspects of Anti-Inflation Policy," *American Economic Review*, 50 (May 1960), 177-194.

Sanjurjo, María Esther. *Economías de escala y cambio tecnológico: Argentina, 1935-61*. Internal Working Paper No. 40. Buenos Aires, Instituto Torcuato Di Tella, July 1967.

Scalabrini Ortíz, Raul. *Yrigoyen y Perón: identidad de una línea histórica de reivindicaciones populares*. Buenos Aires, Fundación Raul Scalabrini, 1961.

Schwartz, Hugh H. "The Argentine Experience with Industrial Credit and Protection Incentives, 1943-1958," *Yale Economic Essays*, 8 (fall 1968), 259-327; uncondensed version as Ph.D. diss., Yale University, 1967.

Schydlowsky, Daniel M. "Comment," in *Estrategias de industrialización para la Argentina*. Buenos Aires, Instituto Torcuato Di Tella, 1970.

———— "From Import Substitution to Export Promotion for Semi-Grown-Up Industries: A Policy Proposal," *Journal of Development Studies*, 3 (July 1967), 405-413.

———— "Short-Run Policy in Semi-Industrialized Economies," *Economic Development and Cultural Change*, 19 (April 1971), 391-413.

Shen, T. Y. "Economies of Scale, Penrose Effect, Growth of Plants and Their Size Distribution," *Journal of Political Economy*, 78 (July/August 1970), 702-716.

Sidrauski, Miguel. "Devaluation, Inflation and Unemployment," mimeo, n.d.

Sigaut, Lorenzo Juan. *Desarrollo agropecuario y proceso de industrialización en la economía argentina*. Buenos Aires, Oficina de Estudios para la Colaboración Económica Internacional, July 1964.

Silverman, Betram. *Labor Ideology and Economic Development in the Peronist Epoch*. New Brunswick, N.J., Rutgers University Press, 1970.

Silvert, Kalman H. *The Conflict Society*. Rev. ed. New York, American Universities Field Staff, Inc., 1966.

Simon, H. A. "A Behavioral Model of Rational Choice," *Quarterly Journal of Economics*, 69 (February 1955), 99-118.

———— "Theories of Decision-Making in Economics and Behavioral Science," *American Economic Review*, 49 (June 1959), 253-283.

Sjaastad, Larry A. "Argentina y el plan de desarrollo," seminar paper, Instituto Torcuato Di Tella, September 1966.

———— "Comercio internacional de la Argentina: perspectivas para las industrias exportadoras tradicionales," in Mario Brodersohn, ed., *Estrategias de industrialización para la Argentina*. Buenos Aires, Instituto Torcuato Di Tella, 1970.

Skupch, Pedro R. "Concentración industrial en la Argentina, 1956-1966," *Desarrollo Económico*, 11 (April-June 1971), 3-14.

Sourrouille, Juan V. "Aspectos regionales de la economía argentina," mimeo, 1971.

———— "El tratamiento del sector público en los sistemas de cuentas nacionales," *Desarrollo Económico*, 11 (July 1971-March 1972), 287-316.

———— "Un esquema paa las transacciones financieras en la Argentina," mimeo for symposium on capital markets, Buenos Aires, 1972.

Steed, L. Douglas. *Los impuestos y el ciclo en la Argentina, 1950-1963: Un enfoque econométrico*. Tucumán, Fundación de Investigaciones Económicas Latinoamericanas, July 1967.

Stein, Abraham. "Desarrollo industrial y el sistema cambiario," *Cuadernos del Centro de Estudios Industriales*, 1 (1968), 27-42.

Sunkel, D., G. Maynard, J. Olivera, and D. Seers. *Inflación y estructura económica*. Buenos Aires, PAIDOS, 1973.

Taylor, Carl C. *Rural Life in Argentina*. Baton Rouge, Louisiana State University Press, 1948.

United Nations. Comisión de Manufacturas, Conferencia Sobre Comercio y Desarrollo. *Medidas para el fomento, la expansión y la diversificación de las exportaciones de las manufacturas y semimanufacturas do los paises en desarrollo*. New York, April 28, 1967.

_____ Commission on Trade and Development Secretariat, Trade Plans Section. "Trade Projections for Argentina," mimeo, June 15, 1968, Part III.

_____ Department of Economic Affairs. *International Capital Movements During the Inter-War Period*. New York, United Nations, 1949.

_____ Department of Economic and Social Affairs. *Análisis y proyecciones del desarrollo económico*. Mexico, United Nations, 1959.

_____ _____ *A Study of Industrial Growth*. New York, United Nations, 1963.

_____ Economic Commission for Latin America (ECLA). *El desarrollo económico de la Argentina*. New York, United Nations, June 30, 1958.

_____ _____ "El desarrollo económico de la Argentina," unpublished Statistical Appendix, mimeo, 1957.

_____ _____ / Food and Agriculture Organization. *El uso de fertilizantes en America Latina*. Santiago, Chile, March 1966.

_____ _____ *Economic Development and Income Distribution in Argentina*. New York, United Nations, 1969.

_____ _____ *Estudio sobre la fabricación de equipos industriales de base en la Argentina*. New York, United Nations, 1962.

_____ _____ *La fabricación de maquinarias y equipos industriales en América latina: IV. Las máquinas-herramientas en la Argentina*. New York, United Nations, February 14, 1966.

_____ _____ *La industria textil en America latina*. New York, United Nations, 1965.

_____ _____ *A Measurement of Price Levels and the Purchasing Power of Currencies in Latin America, 1960-1962*. Mar de la Plata, Argentina, United Nations, 1963.

_____ _____ *Problems of the Steel Making and Transforming Industries in Latin America*. New York, United Nations, 1958.

_____ _____ "La situación argentina y la nueva política económica," *Boletín Económico de América Latina*, 1, (January 1956), 26-42.

_____ Food and Agriculture Organization. *Agricultural Commodities Projections for 1975 and 1985*. Rome, United Nations, 1967.

_____ _____ *Second Special Inquiry on Beef and Poultry*. Rome, United Nations, 1970.

United States Government. Alliance for Progress. *El esfuerzo interno y las necesidades de financiamiento externo para el desarrollo de Argentina*. Washington, D.C., 1970.

_____ Department of Agriculture. *Argentine Agriculture: Trends in Production and World Competition.* Washington, D.C., July 1968.

_____ Department of Commerce. *U.S. Business Investment in Foreign Countries.* Washington, D.C., 1960.

University of Buenos Aires. Cátedra de Política Bancaria. *Políticas del Banco Central de la República Argentina en las diferentes etapas.* Buenos Aires, 1967.

_____ _____ *La carta orgánica del Banco Central de la República Argentina: cuadro comparativo de sus textos legales a través de las sucesivas modificaciones.* Buenos Aires, 1968.

_____ Instituto de Calculo. "Un modelo económico para la República Argentina," mimeo, Buenos Aires, n.d.

Van Rijckeghem, Willy. "Política de estabilización para una economía inflacionaria," *Desarrollo Económico,* 12 (July-September 1972), 245-252.

_____ *Stabilization Policy in an Inflationary Economy: A Post-Mortem.* Centrum Voor Ekonometrie en Management Science/12, Vrije Universiteit Brussel, Brussels, March 1972.

Vendrell Alda, J. L. M. "Análisis de la tasa de interés en los últimos tres años," mimeo, Mendoza, Universidad Nacional de Córdoba, December 1965.

Vernon, Raymond. "International Investment and International Trade in the Product Cycle," *Quarterly Journal of Economics,* 80 (May 1966), 190-207.

_____ *Sovereignty at Bay.* New York, Basic Books, 1971.

Villanueva, Javier. *The Inflationary Process in Argentina, 1943-1960.* Internal Working Paper No. 7. Buenos Aires, Instituto Torcuato Di Tella, 1964.

_____ *Notas para un modelo de industrialización con dependencia externa.* Internal Working Paper. Buenos Aires, Instituto Torcuato Di Tella, 1964.

_____ "Price Formation in the Foodstuffs Market: Wholesale and Retail Profit Margins," mimeo, Buenos Aires, Instituto Torcuato Di Tella, n.d.

_____ *Trade and Industrialization.* Buenos Aires, Instituto Torcuato Di Tella, September 1966.

Wainer, Pedro Héctor. "La protección aduanera efectiva en la República Argentina," mimeo, Buenos Aires, 1970.

Weisskoff, Richard. *Income Distribution and Economic Growth in Puerto Rico, Argentina, Mexico,* Yale University Economic Growth Center, Discussion Paper No. 93, August 1970.

Wells, Lou T. *The Product Life Cycle and International Trade.* Cambridge, Mass., Harvard Business School Division of Research, 1971.

Whitaker, Arthur P., and David C. Jordan. *Nationalism in Contemporary Latin America.* New York, The Free Press, 1966.

Zuvekas, Clarence. "Argentine Economic Policy, 1958-1962: The Frondizi Government's Development Plan," *Inter-American Economic Affairs,* 22 (summer 1968), 45-75.

Periodicals

Argentine Government. Banco Central de la República Argentina. *Boletín Estadístico*, Buenos Aires.
_____ _____ *Estadísticas económico-financieras*, Buenos Aires.
_____ _____ *Informe Económico*, Buenos Aires.
_____ _____ *Memoria anual*, Buenos Aires.
_____ Dirección Nacional de Estadística y Censos, later Instituto Nacional de Estadística y Censos. *Boletín de Estadística*, Buenos Aires.
_____ _____ *Boletín mensual de estadística*, Buenos Aires.
_____ _____ *Censo nacional económico*, Buenos Aires.
_____ _____ *Comercio exterior*, Buenos Aires.
_____ _____ *Comercio interior*, Buenos Aires.
_____ _____ *Costo de la construcción*, Buenos Aires.
_____ _____ *Costo de vida*, Buenos Aires.
_____ _____ *Encuesta de empleo y desempleo*, Buenos Aires.
_____ _____ *Estadística industrial*, Buenos Aires.
_____ _____ *Indices de precios al por mayor*, Buenos Aires.
_____ Junta Nacional de Carnes. *Estadísticas basicas*, Buenos Aires.
_____ _____ *Reseña*, Buenos Aires.
_____ Ministerio de Economía y Trabajo. *Informe Económico*, Buenos Aires.
_____ Ministerio de Finanzas. *Boletín del Ministerio de Finanzas de la Nación*, Buenos Aires.
_____ Ministerio de Trabajo y Seguridad Social. *Convenios colectivos de trabajo*, Buenos Aires.
_____ Secretaría de Estado de Hacienda. *Comercio minorista, precios al por mayor*, Buenos Aires.
_____ _____ *Estadística de sociedades anónimas*, Buenos Aires.
Banco Ganadero Argentina. *La producción rural en Argentina*, Buenos Aires.
_____ *Temas de economía argentina: mercados y precios del ganado vacuno*, Buenos Aires.
Camara Argentina de Industrias Electronicas. *Boletín informativo mensual*, Buenos Aires.
Fundación de Investigaciones Económicas Latinoamericanas (FIEL). Encuesta trimestral sobre evolucion de la actividad industrial, *Buenos Aires*.
_____ *Indicadores de coyuntura*, Buenos Aires.
Instituto de Desarrollo Económico Social. *Situación actual y perspectivas de la economía argentina*, Buenos Aires.
Techint. *Boletin informativo*, Buenos Aires.
United Nations. Economic Commission for Latin America (ECLA). *Boletín estadístico de América Latina*, Santiago.
_____ Food and Agriculture Organization (FAO). *Production Yearbook*, Rome.

Index

Frigerio, Rogelio, 19
Frondizi, Arturo, 19, 25-26, 69, 80, 156, 217; developmentalist strategy, 19-21, 24, 68; policies, 19, 22, 156; attracting foreign capital, 21, 76; and exchange rate, 24, 35; and political groups, 24, 34, 217
Fruit, 37, 38
Full employment, 1, 63, 119

"Generation of the 1880s," 5
Glass, 70
Gold, 22, 23, 111, 143, 154
Gomez Morales, 11
Goods and services, 9, 11, 141
Government, 132, 143, 147, 152, 166, 197; services, 134-135, 138; expenditure, 147, 150, 171; revenue, 147, 152; savings, 150-151
Government marketing boards, 104, 152
Government securities, 131
Grain, 37, 43, 54, 57, 68; prices, 22, 101
Grain Regulating Board, 54
Great Britain, 6, 51, 81, 93
Great Depression, 7, 38, 67, 68
Gross domestic investment, 18, 141, 143
Gross domestic product (GDP), 9-10, 124-125, 131, 133, 151; per capita, 9-10, 26; prices, 13, 55, 59; growth of, 63, 124, 126, 128; industrial, 67-69, 71, 86, 133, 144, 197; and imports, 78, 86; agriculture, 133; in constant prices, 188-189; in current prices, 190-191
Gross domestic product estimates, 196, 198; Central Bank, 200, 202, 206; CONADE, 200, 201, 205
Gross domestic savings, 141, 143, 231, 232
Gross national income, 18, 141, 143, 232
Group of United Officers, 6
Growth, 68, 89, 111, 132, 141, 154; and stability, 1, 92, 100, 161, 171, 184; agricultural, 9, 92, 101; industrial, 9, 67, 127; policy, 63, 137; and foreign exchange, 105, 109
Guía de contribuyentes, 41

Hacienda system, 40
Handicrafts, 70-73

Harberger, Arnold, 120
Hegel, 4
Herbicides, 48-49
Hogs, 37
Horses, 37, 53, 60

IAME, 76
IBM, 87
Idle capacity, 84, 126
Illia, Arturo, 25-30, 34, 157
IMF, 16, 21, 24, 28, 30, 98, 154, 207
Immigration, 3, 5, 155
Import controls, 8, 43, 78, 85, 94, 142
Import demand, 63, 75, 93-96, 98, 157-159
Import duties and tariffs, 80, 88, 105-106, 110, 113, 142; increases, 6, 33; reductions, 30, 105; exemptions, 87; and industry 87, 93
Import Substituting Industrialization (ISI), 68, 75, 79, 86-90, 107, 167
Import substitution, 69, 77-78, 86, 159; and protection, 2, 120; and development, 21, 68, 157; incremental, 75; policy, 99-100; and prices, 159, 224
Import surcharges, 75-77, 92-93
Imports, 18, 67-69, 103-106, 118, 127; policy, 72, 87; quotas, 75; rationing, 78, 92, 94; prices, 92, 94, 96, 142; inventories, 94, 103; increasing, 119, 143
Imports, by product: agricultural machinery, 43, 103; automotive parts, 103; capital goods, 76, 87, 93, 95, 204; consumer goods, 69, 70, 95, 158; "essential goods," 75, 104; fuels, 94-95, 158; goods and services, 143; intermediate products, 69, 93, 95; iron and steel, 103; machinery, 68; manufactured goods, 68, 88, 95; noncapital goods, 126; raw materials, 85, 93-95, 208; textiles, 69
Improved seeds, 47-49
Incentives, 19, 92, 99
Income distribution, 36, 78, 117, 134, 139, 152, 157; sectoral, 42, 132, 134; and inflation, 118, 129, 139
Income redistribution, 9, 17-18, 89, 98, 130, 140, 161; and labor, 78, 139; and devaluation, 92, 100; and prices, 97, 142; and inflation, 113; and policymaking, 170

Income tax, 6, 21, 66, 144, 148
Incomes policy, 30, 128, 130, 162, 168-171; under Perón, 17; under Frondizi, 24; under Levingston, 33
Indians, 5, 40, 41
Industrial production, 67, 79, 96, 135; indices, 70, 71
Industrial sector, 67, 139
Industrial Union, 8
Industrialization, 68-69, 74-75, 84-85, 91, 221; and development, 20, 67, 70, 72, 155
Industry, 10, 55, 69, 72-76, 86, 109, 113, 117, 133; and capital, 22, 72, 78; labor, 72-74, 83, 89; and government policy, 77, 86, 88; local, 87, 104; prices, 109, 133; wages, 193
Inflation, 9, 11-12, 17, 30-33, 113, 126-136, 139, 144, 153, 160, 185; and Frondizi, 19, 22; and terms of trade, 54, 96, 99, 104, 112; and employment, 92; and fiscal policy, 111, 117, 146, 149; and stabilization, 113, 128-129; demand for money, 114, 115, 179; and incomes, 114, 132, 134-137, 141, 148, 161; and prices, 116-118, 120, 145, 152, 168, 180; and taxes, 117, 170; Diaz, 121; rate of, 121, 124, 130-131, 135; and credit, 127; and investment, 140, 152; and savings, 140, 141
Inflation, types of, 120; cost-push, 117-119, 124, 161, 230; demand shift, 118; sellers, 118; wage-push, 118, 119, 124; demand-pull, 119-120, 161, 230; income, 128; at international rates, 128, 167; "neutral," 128, 131, 168, 169; zero, 128
Insecticides, 48-49, 64
Institutional reform, 40
Instituto Torcuato Di Tella, 192
Insurance, 8, 144
INTA, 28, 48-49
Interest groups, 2, 4, 25, 31, 98, 111, 157, 165; and economic programs, 77, 130, 155, 162, 168, 170
Interest rates, 103, 127, 129, 131, 158; and inflation, 115, 130; ceilings, 144, 146, 153; and capital, 159, 168
International commodity prices, 12, 16, 28, 103, 110
Intransigent Radical movement, 19
Inventories, 140, 153, 217
Investment, 3, 140, 203, 231; public,

19, 151-152, 170; in agriculture, 44, 46, 218; private, 74, 143-144, 152; estimates, 197, 203, 204
Iron and steel, 68, 70-71, 76, 85
Irrigation, 37, 61
Italy, 81

Japan, 89
Jarvis, Lovell S., 53, 61-62, 220

Kaiser Motors, 13
Keynesian economics, 1, 3
Korea, 107, 113
Krieger Vasena, Adalbert, 16, 30-33; fiscal and monetary policy, 17, 30, 66, 78, 134; exchange rate policy, 32, 35, 157, 217; stabilization policies, 32-33, 133, 230; and capital, 98, 143; and demand for money, 116, 178; and inflation, 116-117; and compensated devaluation, 151; and wage and price controls, 157, 185; and Central Bank, 217; and IMF, 217

La Pampa, 37
Labor, 7, 34, 72, 76, 119, 137; courts, 7; movement, 7, 15, 72; strikes, 17; rural, 42; in industry, 67; in agriculture, 83; unskilled, 83; shortages, 85; and wages, 134-135, 170; urban, 139, 155
Labor productivity, 29, 135-136, 170
Labor unions, 24, 72, 118, 120, 130
Land, 36, 60; reform, 8, 20, 43, 66; rents, 60, 63; taxes, 65-66
Land tenure, 36, 40, 44-45, 65
Lanusse, General, 6, 34
Latifundistas, 117
Latin America, 3, 45, 73, 82, 117, 166; and Argentine exports, 79; industrialization, 84; exchange rate, 99; cost of living, 113
Latin American Free Trade Association, 81, 85
Law of Professional Associations, 8, 15
Leather, 70-71, 73, 82
Levingston, General, 6, 33
Liberalism, 5, 12, 19, 25, 155
Linseed, 3, 32, 37, 48, 225; oil, 39, 93; prices, 42, 57-58; yield, 46-50
Liquidity, 125, 228
Literacy, 3, 7
Livestock, 3, 37-38, 40-41, 62

264

Index

Steel, 68-70
Steers, 102
Stock market, 8, 144
Stone, 70
Students, 32
Subsidies, 12, 108-109, 168-169
Sugar cane, 37
Sunflower, 40, 42, 48-50
Syndicalism, 7-8
Synthetics and plastics, 71

Tariffs, 67, 75, 103, 106, 151, 156,
    169; exemptions, 87, 156; and ISI,
    88, 107
Tax system, 129, 131, 151, 153, 168
Taxes, 55, 104, 109, 145, 148; foreign
    trade, 1, 148; exemptions, 76, 151;
    revenue, 117, 146
Technological progress, 59, 77, 79, 86;
    in agriculture, 47, 54, 62; in indus-
    try, 47, 54, 62
Television, 76
Tenant farmers, 41-42, 44, 220
Textiles, 68-69, 73, 79, 82
Tobacco, 70-71, 73
"Total factor productivity" index, 47,
    218
Tractors, 47, 76, 77
Trade, 6, 17, 89, 91, 132, 159
Transportation, 68, 135, 138-139, 142,
    149
Trucks, 149
Tucumán, 27, 32

"Umbrella pricing," 85, 225
UNECLA, 15
Unemployment, 26-27, 31, 62-63, 85,
    152; under Frondizi, 24; under Lev-
    ingston, 33; urban, 74; and wage
    demands, 114; and inflation, 119
UNFAO, 57
Unions, 8, 26, 137
United States, 20, 41, 49; agriculture,
    46, 50, 53; prices, 57, 58; and
    Argentina, 73, 81, 104, 222; indus-
    try, 82, 89
United States Export-Import Bank, 13
Urbanization, 155, 157
Usury laws, 144

Van Rijckeghem, Willy, 97, 121-122,
    126-127, 130, 182
Vandor, 33
Vehicles and machinery, 70, 77
Vineyards, 37

Wage-price controls, 116, 160, 170;
    price controls, 8, 12, 21, 129, 133
Wages, 121, 124-126, 128, 137, 223;
    adjustments, 17, 21, 29, 33, 124;
    wage income, 17, 23, 139; real wage
    rates, 24, 31, 35, 63, 130, 136; pol-
    icy, 26, 135, 137; and prices, 29,
    119-121, 123, 134, 161; rural, 42-44;
    and income distribution, 63, 97,
    117; and salaries, 74, 135; and infla-
    tion, 97, 119, 135, 223; wage shares,
    137-138, 231
Watson, 122
Wheat, 37, 48, 51; exported, 32,
    39-40, 226; prices, 42, 57-58, 65;
    yield, 46, 47-51; and fertilizer, 48-49
Wholesale prices, 11, 55-56, 122-124,
    187, 194; indexes, 13, 56, 125; equa-
    tions, 184-185
Wood, 70-71, 82
Wool, 32, 38-39
Worker movement, 7. *See also* Labor
    movement
World Bank, 16, 28
World trade, 39, 93, 159-160
World War II, 68, 78, 79

Yerba mate, 37, 38
YPF, 14, 21
Yrigoyen, Hipólito, 6, 25

Publications Written under the Auspices of the Center for International Affairs, Harvard University

Created in 1958, the Center for International Affairs fosters advanced study of basic world problems by scholars from various disciplines and senior officials from many countries. The research at the Center focuses on economic, social, and political development, the management of force in the modern world, the evolving roles of Western Europe and the Communist nations, and the conditions of international order.

BOOKS

The Soviet Bloc, by Zbigniew K. Brzezinski (sponsored jointly with the Russian Research Center), 1960. Harvard University Press. Revised edition, 1967.

The Necessity for Choice, by Henry A. Kissinger, 1961. Harper & Bros.

Strategy and Arms Control, by Thomas C. Schelling and Morton H. Halperin, 1961. Twentieth Century Fund.

United States Manufacturing Investment in Brazil, by Lincoln Gordon and Engelbert L. Grommers, 1962. Harvard Business School.

The Economy of Cyprus, by A. J. Meyer, with Simos Vassiliou (sponsored jointly with the Center for Middle Eastern Studies), 1962. Harvard University Press.

Communist China 1955-1959: Policy Documents with Analysis, with a foreword by Robert R. Bowie and John K. Fairbank (sponsored jointly with the East Asian Research Center), 1962. Harvard University Press.

Somali Nationalism, by Saadia Touval, 1963. Harvard University Press.

The Dilemma of Mexico's Development, by Raymond Vernon, 1963. Harvard University Press.

Limited War in the Nuclear Age, by Morton H. Halperin, 1963. John Wiley & Sons.

The Arms Debate, by Robert A. Levine, 1963. Harvard University Press.

Africans on the Land, by Montague Yudelman, 1964. Harvard University Press.

Counterinsurgency Warfare, by David Galula, 1964. Frederick A. Praeger, Inc.

People and Policy in the Middle East, by Max Weston Thornburg, 1964. W. W. Norton & Co.

Shaping the Future, by Robert R. Bowie, 1964. Columbia University Press.

Foreign Aid and Foreign Policy, by Edward S. Mason (sponsored jointly with the Council on Foreign Relations), 1964. Harper & Row.

How Nations Negotiate, by Fred Charles Iklé, 1964. Harper & Row.

China and the Bomb, by Morton H. Halperin (sponsored jointly with the East Asian Research Center), 1965. Frederick A. Praeger, Inc.

Democracy in Germany, by Fritz Erler (Jodidi Lectures), 1965. Harvard University Press.

The Troubled Partnership, by Henry A. Kissinger (sponsored jointly with the Council on Foreign Relations), 1965. McGraw-Hill Book Co.

The Rise of Nationalism in Central Africa, by Robert I. Rotberg, 1965. Harvard University Press.

Pan-Africanism and East African Integration, by Joseph S. Nye, Jr., 1965. Harvard University Press.

Communist China and Arms Control, by Morton H. Halperin and Dwight H. Perkins (sponsored jointly with the East Asian Research Center), 1965. Frederick A. Praeger, Inc.

Problems of National Strategy, ed. Henry Kissinger, 1965. Frederick A. Praeger, Inc.

Deterrence before Hiroshima: The Airpower Background of Modern Strategy, by George H. Quester, 1966. John Wiley & Sons.

Containing the Arms Race, by Jeremy J. Stone, 1966. M.I.T. Press.

Germany and the Atlantic Alliance: The Interaction of Strategy and Politics, by James L. Richardson, 1966. Harvard University Press.

Arms and Influence, by Thomas C. Schelling, 1966. Yale University Press.

Political Change in a West African State, by Martin Kilson, 1966. Harvard University Press.

Planning without Facts: Lessons in Resource Allocation from Nigeria's Development, by Wolfgang F. Stolper, 1966. Harvard University Press.

Export Instability and Economic Development, by Alasdair I. MacBean, 1966. Harvard University Press.

Foreign Policy and Democratic Politics, by Kenneth N. Waltz (sponsored jointly with the Institute of War and Peace Studies, Columbia University), 1967. Little, Brown & Co.

Contemporary Military Strategy, by Morton H. Halperin, 1967. Little, Brown & Co.

Sino-Soviet Relations and Arms Control, ed. Morton H. Halperin (sponsored jointly with the East Asian Research Center), 1967. M.I.T. Press.

Africa and United States Policy, by Rupert Emerson, 1967. Prentice-Hall.

Elites in Latin America, edited by Seymour M. Lipset and Aldo Solari, 1967. Oxford University Press.

Europe's Postwar Growth, by Charles P. Kindleberger, 1967. Harvard University Press.

The Rise and Decline of the Cold War, by Paul Seabury, 1967. Basic Books.

Student Politics, ed. S. M. Lipset, 1967. Basic Books.

Pakistan's Development: Social Goals and Private Incentives, by Gustav F. Papanek, 1967. Harvard University Press.

Strike a Blow and Die: A Narrative of Race Relations in Colonial Africa, by George Simeon Mwase, ed. Robert I. Rotberg, 1967. Harvard University Press.

Party Systems and Voter Alignments, edited by Seymour M. Lipset and Stein Rokkan, 1967. Free Press.

Agrarian Socialism, by Seymour M. Lipset, revised edition, 1968. Doubleday Anchor.

Aid, Influence, and Foreign Policy, by Joan M. Nelson, 1968. The Macmillan Company.

International Regionalism, by Joseph S. Nye, 1968. Little, Brown & Co.

Revolution and Counterrevolution, by Seymour M. Lipset, 1968. Basic Books.

Political Order in Changing Societies, by Samuel P. Huntington, 1968. Yale University Press.

The TFX Decision: McNamara and the Military, by Robert J. Art, 1968. Little, Brown & Co.

Korea: The Politics of the Vortex, by Gregory Henderson, 1968. Harvard University Press.

Political Development in Latin America, by Martin Needler, 1968. Random House.

The Precarious Republic, by Michael Hudson, 1968. Random House.

The Brazilian Capital Goods Industry, 1929-1964 (sponsored jointly with the Center for Studies in Education and Development), by Nathaniel H. Leff, 1968. Harvard University Press.

Economic Policy-Making and Development in Brazil, 1947-1964, by Nathaniel H. Leff, 1968. John Wiley & Sons.

Turmoil and Transition: Higher Education and Student Politics in India, edited by Philip G. Altbach, 1968. Lalvani Publishing House (Bombay).

German Foreign Policy in Transition, by Karl Kaiser, 1968. Oxford University Press.

Protest and Power in Black Africa, edited by Robert I. Rotberg, 1969. Oxford University Press.

Peace in Europe, by Karl E. Birnbaum, 1969. Oxford University Press.

The Process of Modernization: An Annotated Bibliography on the Sociocultural Aspects of Development, by John Brode, 1969. Harvard University Press.

Students in Revolt, edited by Seymour M. Lipset and Philip G. Altbach, 1969. Houghton Mifflin.

Agricultural Development in India's Districts: The Intensive Agricultural Districts Programme, by Dorris D. Brown, 1970. Harvard University Press.

Authoritarian Politics in Modern Society: The Dynamics of Established One-Party Systems, edited by Samuel P. Huntington and Clement H. Moore, 1970. Basic Books.

Nuclear Diplomacy, by George H. Quester, 1970. Dunellen.

The Logic of Images in International Relations, by Robert Jervis, 1970. Princeton University Press.

Europe's Would-Be Polity, by Leon Lindberg and Stuart A. Scheingold, 1970. Prentice-Hall.

Taxation and Development: Lessons from Colombian Experience, by Richard M. Bird, 1970. Harvard University Press.

Lord and Peasant in Peru: A Paradigm of Political and Social Change, by F. LaMond Tullis, 1970, Harvard University Press.

The Kennedy Round in American Trade Policy: The Twilight of the GATT? by John W. Evans, 1971. Harvard University Press.

Korean Development: The Interplay of Politics and Economics, by David C. Cole and Princeton N. Lyman, 1971. Harvard University Press.

Development Policy II—The Pakistan Experience, edited by Walter P. Falcon and Gustav F. Papanek, 1971. Harvard University Press.

Higher Education in a Transitional Society, by Philip G. Altbach, 1971. Sindhu Publications (Bombay).

Studies in Development Planning, edited by Hollis B. Chenery, 1971. Harvard University Press.

Passion and Politics, by Seymour M. Lipset with Gerald Schaflander, 1971. Little, Brown & Co.

Political Mobilization of the Venezuelan Peasant, by John D. Powell, 1971. Harvard University Press.

Higher Education in India, edited by Amrik Singh and Philip Altbach, 1971. Oxford University Press (Delhi).

The Myth of the Guerrilla, by J. Bowyer Bell, 1971. Blond (London) and Knopf (New York).

International Norms and War between States: Three Studies in International Politics, by Kjell Goldmann, 1971. Published jointly by Läromedelsförlagen (Sweden) and the Swedish Institute of International Affairs.

Peace in Parts: Integration and Conflict in Regional Organization, by Joseph S. Nye, Jr., 1971. Little, Brown & Co.

Sovereignty at Bay: The Multinational Spread of U.S. Enterprise, by Raymond Vernon, 1971. Basic Books.

Defense Strategy for the Seventies (revision of *Contemporary Military Strategy*), by Morton H. Halperin, 1971. Little, Brown & Co.

Peasants Against Politics: Rural Organization in Brittany, 1911-1967, by Suzanne Berger, 1972. Harvard University Press.

Transnational Relations and World Politics, edited by Robert O. Keohane and Joseph S. Nye, Jr., 1972. Harvard University Press.

Latin American University Students: A Six Nation Study, by Arthur Liebman, Kenneth N. Walker, and Myron Glazer, 1972. Harvard University Press.

The Politics of Land Reform in Chile, 1950-1970: Public Policy, Political Institutions, and Social Change, by Robert R. Kaufman, 1972. Harvard University Press.

The Boundary Politics of Independent Africa, by Saadia Touval, 1972. Harvard University Press.

The Politics of Nonviolent Action, by Gene E. Sharp. 1973. Porter Sargent.

System 37 Viggen: Arms, Technology, and the Domestication of Glory, by Ingemar Dörfer, 1973. Universitetsforluget (Oslo).

University Students and African Politics, by William John Hanna, 1974. Africana Publishing Company.

Organizing the Transnational: The Experience with Transnational Enterprise in Advanced Technology, by M. S. Hochmuth, 1974. Sijthoff (Leiden).

Becoming Modern, by Alex Inkeles and David H. Smith, 1974. Harvard University Press.

Economic Nationalism and the Politics of International Dependence: The Case of Copper in Chile, 1945-1973, by Theodore Moran, 1974. Princeton University Press.

The Andean Group: A Case Study in Economic Integration among Developing Countries, by David Morawetz, 1974. M.I.T. Press.

Kenya: The Politics of Participation and Control, by Henry Bieneu, 1974. Princeton University Press.

Land Reform and Politics: A Comparative Analysis, by Hung-chao Tai, 1974. University of California Press.

Big Business and the State: Changing Relations in Western Europe, edited by Raymond Vernon, 1974. Harvard University Press.

Economic Policymaking in a Conflict Society: The Argentine Case, by Richard D. Mallon and Juan V. Sourrouille, 1975. Harvard University Press.

Harvard Studies in International Affairs*

(formerly Occasional Papers in International Affairs)

† 1. *A Plan for Planning: The Need for a Better Method of Assisting Underdeveloped Countries on Their Economic Policies*, by Gustav F. Papanek, 1961.

† 2. *The Flow of Resources from Rich to Poor*, by Alan D. Neale, 1961.

† 3. *Limited War: An Essay on the Development of the Theory and an Annotated Bibliography*, by Morton H. Halperin, 1962.

† 4. *Reflections on the Failure of the First West Indian Federation*, by Hugh W. Springer, 1962.

  5. *On the Interaction of Opposing Forces under Possible Arms Agreements*, by Glenn A. Kent, 1963. 36 pp. $1.25.

† 6. *Europe's Northern Cap and the Soviet Union*, by Nils Örvik, 1963.

  7. *Civil Administration in the Punjab: An Analysis of a State Government in India*, by E.N. Mangat Rai, 1963. 82 pp. $1.75.

  8. *On the Appropriate Size of a Development Program*, by Edward S. Mason, 1964. 24 pp. $1.00.

* Available from Harvard University Center for International Affairs, 6 Divinity Avenue, Cambridge, Massachusetts 02138

† Out of print. May be ordered from AMS Press, Inc. 56 East 13th Street, New York, N.Y. 10003

9. *Self-Determination Revisited in the Era of Decolonization*, by Rupert Emerson, 1964. 64 pp. $1.75.

10. *The Planning and Execution of Economic Development in Southeast Asia*, by Clair Wilcox, 1965. 37 pp. $1.25.

11. *Pan-Africanism in Action*, by Albert Tevoedjre, 1965. 88 pp. $2.50.

12. *Is China Turning In?* by Morton Halperin, 1965. 34 pp. $1.25.

†13. *Economic Development in India and Pakistan*, by Edward S. Mason, 1966.

14. *The Role of the Military in Recent Turkish Politics*, by Ergun Özbudun, 1966. 54 pp. $1.75.

†15. *Economic Development and Individual Change: A Social-Psychological Study of the Comilla Experiment in Pakistan*, by Howard Schuman, 1967.

16. *A Select Bibliography on Students, Politics, and Higher Education*, by Philip G. Altbach, UMHE Revised Edition, 1970. 65 pp. $2.75.

17. *Europe's Political Puzzle: A Study of the Fouchet Negotiations and the 1963 Veto*, by Alessandro Silj, 1967. 178 pp. $3.50.

18. *The Cap and the Straits: Problems of Nordic Security*, by Jan Klenberg, 1968. 19 pp. $1.25.

19. *Cyprus: The Law and Politics of Civil Strife*, by Linda B. Miller, 1968. 97 pp. $3.00.

†20. *East and West Pakistan: A Problem in the Political Economy of Regional Planning*, by Md. Anisur Rahman, 1968.

†21. *Internal War and International Systems: Perspectives on Method*, by George A. Kelley and Linda B. Miller, 1969.

†22. *Migrants, Urban Poverty, and Instability in Developing Nations*, by Joan M. Nelson, 1969. 81 pp.

23. *Growth and Development in Pakistan, 1955-1969*, by Joseph J. Stern and Walter P. Falcon, 1970. 94 pp. $3.00.

24. *Higher Education in Developing Countries: A Select Bibliography*, by Philip G. Altbach, 1970. 118 pp. $4.00.

25. *Anatomy of Political Institutionalization: The Case of Israel and Some Comparative Analyses*, by Amos Perlmutter, 1970. 60 pp. $2.50.

†26. *The German Democratic Republic from the Sixties to the Seventies*, by Peter Christian Ludz, 1970. 100 pp.

27. *The Law in Political Integration: The Evolution and Integrative Implications of Regional Legal Processes in the European Community*, by Stuart A. Scheingold, 1971. 63 pp. $2.50.

28. *Psychological Dimensions of U.S.-Japanese Relations,* by Hiroshi Kitamura, 1971. 46 pp. $2.00.
29. *Conflict Regulation in Divided Societies,* by Eric A. Nordlinger, 1972. 137 pp. $4.25.
30. *Israel's Political-Military Doctrine,* by Michael I. Handel, 1973. 101 pp. $3.25.
31. *Italy, NATO, and the European Community: The Interplay of Foreign Policy and Domestic Politics,* by Primo Vannicelli, 1974. 67 + X pp. $3.25
32. *The Choice of Technology in Developing Countries: Some Cautionary Tales*, by C. Peter Timmer, John Woodward Thomas, Louis T. Wells, Jr., and David Morawetz, 1975. Ca. 120 pp. $3.45.
33. *The International Role of the Communist Parties of Italy and France*, by Donald L. M. Blackmer and Annie Kriegel, 1975. Ca. 90 pp. $2.75.
34. *The Hazards of Peace: A European View of Détente,* by Juan Cassiers, 1975.